REFLECT [illegible] CATION

Landscapes: The Arts, Aesthetics, and Education

VOLUME 5

SCOPE

This series aims to provide conceptual and empirical research in arts education, (including music, visual arts, drama, dance, media, and poetry), in a variety of areas related to the post-modern paradigm shift. The changing cultural, historical, and political contexts of arts education are recognized to be central to learning, experience, and knowledge. The books in this series present theories and methodological approaches used in arts education research as well as related disciplines - including philosophy, sociology, anthropology and psychology of arts education.

For other titles published in this series, go to
www.springer.com/series/6199

REFLECTIVE PRACTICES IN ARTS EDUCATION

Edited by

PAMELA BURNARD
University of Cambridge, UK

SARAH HENNESSY
University of Exeter, UK

Springer

Library of Congress Control Number: 2008940151

ISBN 978-1-4020-9565-8 (PB)
ISBN 978-1-4020-4702-2 (HB)
ISBN 978-1-4020-4703-9 (ebook)

Published by Springer,
P.O. Box 17, 3300 AA Dordrecht, The Netherlands.

www.springer.com

Printed on acid-free paper

CONTENTS

SECTION 3: CASE STUDIES: REFLECTIONS IN AND ON ACTION

FOREWORD

It is an exciting time to be an artist and artist educator. Networks of schools and artists are being motivated by arts partnerships, a relatively new phenomenon in a field which whilst disparate in its character and practice, is marked by a common intention, to respond effectively and critically to politically driven agendas of accountability, school improvement and pupil attainment. More than ever artists and educators alike have begun to realise the need to develop practices which offer the development of artist educator pedagogies as agencies for change and political action. Understanding the function of reflective practice, the conditions which support it and its impact on learning, are addressed throughout this book. We hope that the book will motivate readers, with a diversity of interests and needs, to engage in reflections of their own professional practices and of the practices of the communities in which they work This book is about reflection. The thesis about the field it covers and major premise of this book is that reflection matters at every turn in arts engagement and even more so in educational settings where artist educators share a passion for facilitating and understanding the 'how' of learners engagement with particular art forms.

It aims to show ways in which reflection can inform and transform practice in terms of what, when and how reflection is embodied in arts engagement. It is about what we do every day in talking and thinking about and engaging with the arts, but trying to do it in better ways through reflective practice.

The challenge to improve arts education lies at the heart of education. It also lies at the heart of arts educators' who strive for reflective time and reflective spaces to nurture reflective cultures.

To serve these aims we invited a range of artists-teachers-scholars who were able to mesh practical expertise and interest in particular fields of art, with an extensive knowledge both of teaching and of research and development. They bring with them cultural perspectives from the UK, Canada, USA, Australia, Africa, Hong Kong and Brazil. Each is attentive to and brings into focus the significance of particular dimensions of reflective teaching in the arts. Each chapter offers insightful observations in and conceptions of reflective arts practice from a broad range of cultural and pedagogical contexts.

This book makes a contribution to the theory and practice of arts education illustrated by the experience of children of different ages, young people, artists and teachers and professional partnerships in varied formal settings including schools, universities, and less formal community settings, including galleries, recorded by artists, teachers and researchers.. The arts under consideration include visual art, and the performing arts of music, drama and dance, along with multimedia.

The book looks outwards from the work of a multidisciplinary group of experts who position reflection at the centre of educational and arts endeavour, and advocate a global concern for reviving its potential for enriching practice. It provides perspectives on *what* reflection is, *why* reflection is so important, illustrated with case studies which provide research-based forms of understanding what reflective arts practice looks like and *how* it can feed into all areas of the arts curriculum and enrich all aspects of learning. It argues how reflection provides possibilities for nurturing reflective cultures and communities.

The book is organised into three sections.

Section 1 is concerned with affirming the attention to reflection and its importance. Reflection is conceptualized through multiple lenses including the cognitive, the phenomenological, the cultural and the sociological. It provides necessary historical and theoretical background to frame issues arising from the current curriculum landscape and to offer rationale for a revival of attention to reflection in arts education.

Section 2 provides explanations and discussion of particular tools or instruments for reflecting along with ways in which reflection is central to the process of enquiry. The uses of particular strategies in facilitating reflection are mapped anew.

Section 3 presents case studies which have sought to document, describe develop, facilitate and illuminate reflective practices in arts teaching and learning.

We hope that it will stimulate personal reflection and collegial dialogue and inspire readers to practice reflective teaching of the arts. We hope it will help artists who work in schools, and arts practitioners for whom the building of reflective cultures depends upon reflexive arts curriculum and pedagogies, and researchers who are interested in introducing himself or herself to this important area of research and development.

Pamela Burnard and Sarah Hennessy
Co-editors

ENDORSEMENTS OF REFLECTIVE PRACTICES IN ARTS EDUCATION

Reflection, the arts and education go hand in hand. In *Reflective Practices in Arts Education* edited by Pamela Burnard and Sarah Hennessy, international contributors take a reflective stance upon their understandings of what it means to be a reflective arts-based educational practitioner. The volume is rich with engaging opportunities to consider reflection as a form of judgment, conversation, practice, process, and even as self-knowledge, a mode of cognition, and political action. By engaging with a wide range of perspectives, the editors have successfully portrayed the diversity of viewpoints that guide arts educators today while also addressing issues that plague classrooms, communities and teacher education programs. What constitutes reflection is multidimensional. Practitioners desiring to create communities of practice dedicated to realizing the potential of 'collective reflection' are destined to pursue educational change at a deep and mindful level. In the act of reflection, we grasp the meaning of something significant. Through gestures, sounds, images, and actions, we may gain insights that echo our literal understandings, yet, it is more likely that these sensory and expressive based reflections will compliment, extend, and perhaps even refute the engagements we have accepted through text. *Reflective Practices in Arts Education* will provoke readers to think more deeply, to engage with others more often, and to pursue educational change in ways they may not have imagined before. After all, artists thrive on transformation and educators thrive on creating meaningful environments and opportunities for learning. For those who embrace reflective practices in the arts, this volume will be necessary companion to their scholarship, practice and artistic endeavours

Rita L. Irwin
University of British Columbia, Canada

Until now, no single publication has succeeded in capturing the depth and breadth of what reflective practices can mean in arts education. Until now, critical conversations on where reflection *in, on* and *for* action can lead, have been lost in the evanescence of competing needs, space and time for many arts educators. As a result of sustained dialogue, debate and discussion, the authors take fine coloured threads of reflective theory and practice and weave a vivid tapestry, rich in meaning, and garnered through experience and wisdom. In an era of calls for increased competencies, accountability, evidence-based work and good practice in education, Burnard and Hennessy get to the heart of the matter by examining the power inherent in reflective practice and bringing the attendant imperatives to the fore. If reflection is a catalyst for change, then this reflection-on-reflection is where the transformation begins. With scholarly contributions from across art forms, artists and educators, settings and contexts, this exceptional collection of viewpoints is timely and critical, and an absolute essential for those engaging in any arts discipline at any level of education.

Regina Murphy,
St Patrick's College, Dublin City University, Ireland

ACKNOWLEDGEMENTS

We would like to thank Professor Liora Bresler, University of Illinois, Urbana-Champaign, U.S.A. for her keen interest and encouragement to produce this book.

We would also like to express our gratitude to the community of scholars who have contributed to this volume, each of whom share a passion for examining and translating what, how and why reflection is as important as it is multi-faceted, complex, dynamic and central to artistic practice.

We acknowledge also the valuable assistance of Millie Glennon who contributed significantly to the final stages of typesetting and to Bernadette Deelen-Mans of Springer for her patience and support.

ABOUT THE CONTRIBUTORS

Pamela Burnard is Senior Lecturer in Music and Arts Education at the University of Cambridge, UK, where she coordinates and teaches on the MPhil in Educational Research course, MPhil in Arts, Culture and Education, and on initial teacher education, undergraduate and postgraduate courses, supervising Mphil, MEd and PhD students. She is co-editor of the International Journal of Music Education: Practice; Associate Editor of Psychology of Music, on the editorial boards for Journal of Creativity and Thinking Skills, British Journal of Music Education, Music Education Research and the Asia-Pacific Journal for Arts Education. She publishes widely and has contributed chapters in several books on creativity and arts education. She is a Co-convener of the British Educational Reasearch Association Special Interest Group (BERA SIG), Creativity in Education.

Bruce Burton is Director of Applied Theatre Research in the Faculty of Education at Griffith University, Brisbane, Australia. Since 1996 he has been continuously involved in an international research partnership, the DRACON project (Drama and Conflict Management) researching the use of peer teaching and educational drama in conflict and bullying management in schools in Sweden, Malaysia and Australia. He has taught extensively in schools in the UK and Australia and written and directed plays in both countries. He is the author of eight books in the fields of Drama Education and Applied Theatre.

Jane Wai-Yee Cheung, GRSM, ARCM, PGCE, MA, PhD (London), taught secondary school music in the United Kingdom and Hong Kong before joining the Music Department of the Northcote College of Education as Head of Department. She was also the Head of the Creative Arts Department, the Hong Kong Institute of Education, until 2000. Dr Cheung teaches musicianship skills and music education and her research interests include computerised music instruction and IT policy, learning motivation, integrative arts education, music curriculum and instructional design. Her publications include book chapters, articles in *Psychology of Music* and *Asia-Pacific Journal for Arts Education*, CD-ROMs for teaching Chinese Instruments and Chinese Folk Songs. She is the co-editor of the journal *International Journal of Music Education* and she is currently the Deputy Head of the Creative Arts and Physical Education Department of the Hong Kong Institute of Education.

Luciana Del-Ben is a PhD and Lecturer of Music Education at the Institute of Arts, Federal University of Rio Grande do Sul, Brazil where she teaches at the undergraduate and graduate level, supervising MA and PhD students. Her publications consist of articles published national and internationally in the field of audience listening, assessment and teacher education.

Joanna Glover is Senior Research Fellow in Music Education at the University of Central England at Birmingham. She has taught music in school, community, adult and higher education settings and worked as a researcher/evaluator for Youth Music. She is co-editor of *Primary Music Today* magazine, and has written books and articles on primary music, including *Children Composing 4–14*, published by Routledge Falmer (2000)

Diana Harris BEd; MA; Ed D taught as Head of Music and Performing Arts in secondary schools for twenty years and now works for the Open University as a postgraduate lecturer and tutor on the Teacher Education and Masters in Education courses as well as supervising doctoral students. For ten years she has been involved with the Muslim community researching into aspects of music and Islam. This has taken her to many different countries both for field work and conferences. Her book *Music Education and Muslim Pupils* will be published in March 2006 by Trentham Books UK. She has also published many papers on various aspects of her work and organized conferences on behalf of the Association of Muslim Researchers and the National Association of Music Educators in UK.

Sarah Hennessy is a Senior Lecturer in music education at the School of Education and Lifelong Learning, University of Exeter. She teaches on postgraduate teacher education programmes and supervises doctoral studies. She has expertise and interests in the field of primary teaching and learning, children's music making and the work of musicians in school and community settings. She has published books, chapters and journal articles and is founding editor of the journal *Music Education Research*. She is director of the international conference for research in music education(RIME) and also chair of the National Association of Music Educators and the Orff Society.

Liane Hentschke is Professor of Music Education at the Institute of Arts, Federal University of Rio Grande do Sul, Brazil where she teaches at the undergraduate and graduate level, supervising MA and PhD students. Her publications consist of articles and book chapters published national and internationally, in the field of teacher education and formal and informal music education.

Mary Hilton is a University Lecturer in Primary Language and Literature in the Faculty of Education at Cambridge University. She originally trained and practised as an architect and taught art history before taking the PGCE in 1982. She then worked for twelve years in Primary schools, studying in detail the ways young children respond to creative tasks, particularly those in the visual and language arts. She holds an MA in Education and an MSc in Research Methods. She has published articles and chapters on children's literature, popular culture, and children's writing. Recently she has been working with the British Film Institute on the use of moving image texts in primary schools.

Janet Hoskyns is Head of the School of Secondary and Post-Compulsory Education at UCE Birmingham and has taught music in Secondary, Primary and Special Schools as well as at UCE. Her PhD thesis examined a European Dimension in Music Education and current research involves evaluating Youth Music Action Zone projects, Creative Partnerships in Birmingham and Student Perceptions of LSC funded music courses.

Dawn Joseph is a Lecturer in Music and Education Studies at Deakin University, Melbourne Campus, Australia. She lecturers in both pre-service and postgraduate courses. Her current research interests include teacher education programs, African music, cultural diversity and identity, teacher change and professional development. She is currently the Chairperson of the Australian Society for Music Education (Victorian Chapter) and is the Pan African Society for Musical Arts Education MAT Cell co-ordinator for Australia.

Jody L. Kerchner is Associate Professor and Director of Music Education at the Oberlin College Conservatory of Music (USA), where she is the secondary school music and choral music education specialist. Prior to teaching at the collegiate level, Dr. Kerchner taught K-8 general and choral music. She received degrees in music education and vocal performance from West Chester University and a PhD from Northwestern University. She has presented workshops throughout North America, Europe, and Africa. Dr. Kerchner is co-author of *Prelude to Music Education* and several chapters in edited books. She is on the editorial boards of MENC's *Music Educators Journal*, *Contributions to Research in Music Education*, and *Asia-Pacific Journal for Arts Education*. Dr. Kerchner's research interests include children's responses during music listening, choral music education, and teacher education. She has designed, implemented, and written about portfolio assessment and reflective thinking tools that pre-service music teachers experience in her music education and choral methods courses.

Eton Kung formerly taught at the Department of Creative Arts of the Hong Kong Institute of Education and specialized in teaching music education modules that focus on curriculum issues as well as the application of technology in music teaching and learning. His research interests include aesthetics and education, educational philosophy and integrative learning of the arts.

Saville Kushner has, for many years, worked in educational evaluation—and for much of those in the field of the performing arts. Throughout, he has sought to adapt the approach of Democratic Evaluation to this field, focusing on the use of case study and narrative accounting. At the time of writing he was Director of the Centre for Research in Education and Democracy at University of West England, Bristol. He currently holds a post with UNICEF as regional evaluation officer for latin America and the Caribbean.

Anna Ledgard is a teacher, facilitator and creative learning producer with 20 years experience of participatory arts practice in schools and with arts and cultural organisations. She taught at Stantonbury Campus, Milton Keynes before embarking on a freelance career in 1992. Anna is a long-term associate of LIFT (London International Festival of Theatre) and has initiated a wide-ranging programme of local, national and international collaborative performance projects. She was director of LIFT's continuing Professional Development initiative The LIFT Teacher Forum (in association with the Institute of Education, University of London) 1999–2004. She was co-ordinator of the Animarts Action Research Programme, an independent research initiative with LIFT and the Guildhall School of Music and Drama, and she co-wrote the report 'The Art of the Animateur' (June 2003) which investigated the needs of artists and teachers working in partnership. From July 2004 she led the development of TAP (Teacher Artist Partnership) a research programme investigating the shared professional development of teachers and artists in association with eight leading arts and education organisations in London. Today Anna is lead tutor on TAP and she is co-producing a two year intergenerational arts project, Boy Child, in collaboration with Dorset County Hospital, artist Mark Storor and communities in West Dorset.

Morag Morrison has been working in the Faculty of Education, University of Cambridge, in the United Kingdom since 2002. She lectures on undergraduate, graduate and postgraduate courses in Drama and Arts Education. Prior to working in the United Kingdom Morag was involved in Drama across a range of settings in Australia. She was the Head of Performing Arts in two secondary schools before she began lecturing in Drama Education and Teacher Training at tertiary level. She also performed as a member of the Red Jam collaborative theatre company and was Educational Advisor to the Australian Acting Academy. She is currently completing her PhD in drama, peer teaching and conflict resolution and has just co-authored a book on re-engagement through the arts.

John O'Toole is the new Chair of Arts Education at the University of Melbourne, Australia, following nearly twenty years as coordinator of drama and director of applied theatre research at Griffith University. He has taught and practised drama and theatre education at all ages and levels from pre-school to post-graduate and community contexts, for over thirty years, on six continents. He has written many standard text and scholarly books include Theatre in Education (1977, the first book in this field), The Process of Drama (1992), Dramawise (1987 with Brad Haseman, translated into Chinese, Italian and Danish), and Pretending to learn (with Julie Dunn, Australian Textbook of the Year 2003). In 2001 he was awarded the American Alliance for Theatre and Education Award for Lifetime Research, and in 2005 a Griffith University teaching excellence award. He is still a regular playwright and director for theatre in education and community theatre.

Charlotte Peel is a visual artist and arts educator whose practice includes delivering arts projects within gallery, school and community contexts. Currently she is Education Officer at the Sainsbury Centre for Visual Arts, University of East Anglia. This chapter builds upon the methodology of her MA research at the Institute of

Education, University of London and develops an interest in creative and experimental approaches to reflecting on practice.

Linda Rolfe is a lecturer in education at the University of Exeter, England. She is programme leader of the Masters in Education and the Creative Arts, and the Postgraduate Teacher Training course for Secondary Dance specialists. She has published books in the field of dance education and is editor of the journal, 'Research in Dance Education'. Her research interests include arts education and initial teacher training.

Rena Upitis is a former Dean of Education at Queen's University, and is currently Professor of Education and National Research Co-director of *Learning Through the Arts*, a multi-year project bringing artists to classrooms for over 100,000 students. Rena worked as a music teacher in inner-city schools in Canada and the United States and has been a studio teacher of piano and music theory for over 30 years. She frequently presents at conferences and publishes widely in academic and professional journals. Two of her books, *This Too is Music* and *Can I Play You My Song?* focus on teaching music in elementary classroom. Another co-authored book, *Creative Mathematics* explores ways of approaching mathematics through the arts. Her various research projects, funded by SSHRC and NSERC, as well as by foundations, industry, and government, have explored teacher, artist, and student transformation through the arts and the use of electronic games in mathematics and science education. Her current interest is on how school architecture both constrains and opens up possibilities for learning. Rena's research has been recognized by several awards, including the George C. Metcalf Research Award (2002) and the Canadian Association for Curriculum Studies Publicaion Award (2005).

Betty Anne Younker, PhD, is Associate Professor and Chair of Music Education at the University of Michigan. Teaching experiences over the last 20 plus years have occurred in pre-school to university settings in choral, band, general music and private studio environments. Publications have appeared as articles in major research journals of music education and chapters in a variety of books, while paper presentations have occurred at international, national, state, and provincial conferences. Dr. Younker continues to make music as a member of the Vocal Arts Ensemble in Ann Arbor, Michigan, and clinics with bands and choirs in Michigan and throughout Canada.

SECTION 1

PERSPECTIVES ON REFLECTION

PAMELA BURNARD

1. RETHINKING THE IMPERATIVES FOR REFLECTIVE PRACTICES IN ARTS EDUCATION

Professional reflection is central to the development of new awareness, knowledge and value shifts which lead to more effective practice in arts teaching (Harland et al., 2005). As individuals, and collectively, we are constrained only by our willingness to engage with and our capacity to use reflective processes effectively as a source and resource for professional agency.

In the present global context, artists and arts educators face the challenges of politically driven agendas that, most commonly, focus on accountability and pupil attainment. It is timely to open the debate about whether a focus on reflective activity should dominate our thinking about arts teaching and learning, not least in an understanding of what reflective practice discourses might mean within the context of developing arts communities.

The purpose of this chapter is twofold. First, I wish to consider what characterizes reflective practice discourses. And secondly, as an arts community, to consider collectively the impact of reflective arts practices and what we need to do to connect reflective cultures and communities of practice at the arts-education interface.

So, what is distinctive about reflection in educational discourse?

Reflective time engages us intrinsically in a sharply focused attentive mode of functioning. Artists in particular give themselves over to virtually continuous reflective time, placing reflection at the heart of the creative process.

Some authors consider that reflection is a *recollective form* constituted in a thought or action that is already passed or lived through (van Manen, 1990). Other theorists consider reflection to be constituted in action in different time frames. Such dimensions include reflection-*on*-action (Schön, 1987), reflection-*in*-action (Schön, 1983; Killian and Todnem, 1991), reflection-*in* and *on*-action (Zeichner and Liston, 1996) and reflection-*for*-action (Norlander-Case et al., 1999) with each drawing upon and utilising different time frames. These can be rapid and immediate, as automatic reflection or thoughtful reflection in the moment (called repair). Reflection can occur at a particular point in time (called review) or be more systematic over a period of time (called research). A long-term reflection can be informed by established theories (called retheorising) (Schön, 1983, 1987).

Reflections situated *in* time can be deeply concentrated; an intensified experience where one becomes totally absorbed in the consummatory moments of thought and action, with attention centered on a limited field of awareness. Reflections situated *over* time occur when actions and thoughts are recovered, reviewed, revised, re-evaluated, reordered and embodied in time's containment.

P. Burnard and S. Hennessy (eds.), *Reflective Practice in Arts Education*, 3–12.

When reflecting back in time we look critically to learn from previous work. When reflecting forward in time we anticipate—even envision—what might happen, making judgements and new connections in the framing of an arts encounter or learning experience.

Inevitably, reflection makes a major contribution to professional practice.

Reviving our concern with *reflection*—whether as artists, artist educators, arts organizations, learners researchers or parents—requires us to look back critically and constructively (*analytic self-reflection*) and draw from one's experiences (*normative reflection*[1]). This helps to build and sustain professional communities: a central aim of this book.

We do, however, engage in and learn from *reflective conversations* with self and situations differently in different circumstances. This book[2] is one such example of professional reflection.

1. A REFLECTIVE CONVERSATION WITH SELF

One example from my own experience illustrates the multidimensional nature of reflection.

> *An exemplar of the reflective self* Consider for instance, an ethnographic research project involving a lunchtime Creator's Club with a group of 12-year-old children over a period of 6 months. In the final week of the project a 'concert' was held in the school hall. The idea was to bring together the head teacher, music teachers, parents, peers of the Creators Club with compositions and improvisations performed on instruments and in settings chosen, managed and led by the children. Up to this point, in the role of researcher, I had not performed for or with the children. It was close to the end of the concert when an invitation made publicly and unexpectedly by the children came for 'Pam to make a piece on the spot for us'. I was frozen with panic and pleasure—panic at the pressure of performing without warning, and pleasure at being asked to perform. It was both politically correct and right to accept the invitation, and I would naturally be judged. At that moment I was struck by the extent of risk that participation in any spontaneous improvisatory form requires. I hadn't anticipated this. What I also felt was discomfort and stress. I needed some reflective time. The key question was 'What to do?' I was not sure which instrument to play; I had given no thought to the possibility of improvising at this concert. I asked if they had any preferences for 'which instrument? what setting?'; questions they had asked themselves over the past 6 months as part of the study. At this stage, the cameraman (a musician and friend!) volunteered to play a duo with me. A collaborative spontaneous improvisation based on a reflective conversation in musical action followed.

---

[1] Terms coined by Uljens (1997).

[2] The book comes out of a long and sustained conversation and dialogue between contributors following a symposium on 'Reflective practices in music education'. The idea was advanced as key to extending and connecting evidence-based knowledge of how reflection occurs in arts teaching *across* art forms.

> Our improvisation featured a reasonably well constructed beginning and ending with varied textures, pitch clusters, abrupt shifts of rhythmic dissonance, varied metric groupings and other impetus and decay devices featuring in between. There were sufficient continuities and regularities in events and patterns to unify the piece. Musical disruption and interruption also featured. I recall interpreting and responding to expectations implicit in musical exchanges played by my partner. I also recall critically reflecting on when and how to make the piece sound a little more agreeable. I felt an expectation to continue until we had resolved some of the musical tension. Some sounds were anticipated, others were not. There was much role shifting. We shared a fluid sense of possibility. The musical exchanges were borne out of a musical narrative lived reflectively (Burnard, 2000a/b).

This example implies a number of *reflective stances* coined by Schön (1983, 1987) as *reflection-in-action, reflection-on-action*, and *reflection-through-action*. The first is presented as it arose in uninterrupted time, immediately, instinctively lived through as a liberating conversation with self and situation during the consummatory moments prior to performing unexpectedly in concert. The second is represented as it arose in the transitions between and following this moment as one considers action from the perspectives of audience member, performer and researcher. The third is demonstrated when I rehearsed and analysed how my sharp-eyed observers, a group of 18 children whom I had been researching, might move. It was in the moments when I moved between *reflective thinking* that required continual evaluation and *reflective judgements*. This included consideration of audience expectation, the tolerance of the audience (that is, my role and how hard I could push) and an estimation of what would appeal to, and engage, my audience. Reflection mediated the risk I felt as a performer and researcher and ultimately this allowed me to look beyond the expected.

2. CHARACTERISING REFLECTION

Trying to define what reflection is—and what we can ask of it—requires a lot of ground to be covered as many scholars posit numerous characterizations of reflection. Using various psychological, philosophical and educational lenses, authors present multiple perspectives, where different shades of meaning appear in different contexts, each illuminating the multidimensionality of reflection. The most frequently and strongly identified characteristics and forms of reflection include the following:

- *Reflective thinking* as coined by Dewey (1933) who makes the distinction between on the one hand 'routine' thinking and on the other 'reflective' thinking, the later involving a process of continual evaluation of beliefs, assumptions and hypotheses. (themes elaborated by Kushner and Hilton, Kerchner and Younker).
- *Critical reflection as a form of judgement* has been identified by Gouge and Yates' (2002) taxonomy of arts reasoning and thinking skills and by King and Kitchener

(1994) who posit that knowledge moves from pre-reflective through quasi-reflective to reflective stages (similar themes elaborated by Rolfe).

- *Reflection as self-knowledge* has been identified by Jonassen et al. (1999) as one category of a taxonomy of knowledge along with *professional knowledge* and *pedagogical knowledge* (a theme elaborated by Cheung and Kung; Hentschke and Del Ben; Joseph).
- *Reflection as a form of conversation* turns experience into meaningful learning when a person is able to 'actively construct and find personal meaning within a situation' (Falk et al., 2000, p. 41). Arts making is a reflective process; descriptions of experience reflect the unique nature of arts learning and engagement (themes elaborated by Hilton, Peel, Younker, Rolfe, Hentschke, Del Ben and Joseph).
- *Reflection as an agent of change* concerns factors that trigger change and which helps change come about, (*a theme elaborated by Joseph*). Artists-practitioners beliefs have impact on pathways to change and development (Stenhouse, 1975). Changes can take their starting point in the nurturing of *cultures of reflection* with other people in and across school settings and in and across arts communities (themes elaborated by Kushner, Morrison et al., Glover and Hoskyns).
- *Reflective processes as ongoing* embody the interdependence of creative thought and action as a condition of the creative process (a theme elaborated by Hilton, Peel, Cheung and Kung).
- *Reflection as professional practice* concerns the manner in which we enter into, engage with, facilitate and handle, the challenges associated with our profession, i.e., art making, arts curriculum and pedagogies. How and when reflection occurs and what tools are used to articulate reflective processes in and between different art fields vary according to the inter-related conditions—social, technological, cultural—in which the act of reflection and creation is undertaken (a theme elaborated in all chapters).

What is shared is the imperative to reflect on our aspirations and practices in whatever art form(s) and roles played (as artist, teacher, administrator and/or researcher) with a critical eye to considering five fundamental questions:

1. Do I agree with these characterisations of reflection?
2. What are the implications of these (and other) characterisations for artists and artist-educators?
3. What educational and artistic purposes should we seek to attain in our reflective arts practices?
4. What common understanding should be developed, shared, and promoted?
5. How can reflective arts practice communities be effectively organised?

In what follows I shall argue for developing an *extended* professionalism[3] which is directed towards realising and supporting interdisciplinary understanding of reflective arts practices.

---

[3] A concept introduced by Lawrence Stenhouse (1975) which views work in the wider context of school, community and society as opposed to restricted professionalism which promotes subject-centeredness.

It is imperative that we address the disconnections in arts education, by situating our practice in a paradigm based on reflection, addressing how these multiple perspectives stand up under close scrutiny, in terms of what a reflective arts practice is and what it can aspire to in terms of transforming arts practice.

2.1 Reflection Imperative One: Building Extended Professionalism

One of the most influential and enduring dimensions of reflection in the literature concerns much of what Dewey (1933) has to say about the concept of *reflective thinking* (the focus of Kerchner's chapter). Insofar as reflective thinking rests for its legitimacy on certain forms of practice, reflection strives for open-mindedness, responsibility and wholeheartedness through the continual evaluation of beliefs and judgments. Reflective judgments are tied to our own experiences and understanding of the world and, as such, are offered as reasonable integrations or syntheses of various points of view. They involve ongoing verification and evaluation, judgments based on reflective thinking are more likely to be valid and insightful than are beliefs derived from authority, emotional commitment, or narrow reasoning. Reflective thinking and reflective judgments are central to arts processes and practice producing a unique kind of knowledge that is well documented in the creative arts literature (Ross, 1978).

Drawing on Dewey and the epistemological issues resulting from his work, King and Kitchener (1994, p. 7) propose a seven-stage model of *reflective judgment*. Their model identifies a progression of seven distinct sets of *judgments about knowledge and how knowledge is acquired*. Each set has its own logical coherence and is called a stage, with each successive staged posited to represent a more complex and effective form of justification, providing more inclusive and better integrated criteria for evaluating and defending a point of view.

On the basis of more than thirty studies, King and Kitchener (1994) claim that the model of reflective judgment is complex, inclusive and integrated, with qualitative differences that are stable across domains observable in reasoning about knowledge. The model, despite being a coherent, well-argued and extensively researched account of the development of epistemological reasoning, does not take into account *how* 'reflective thought' is evidenced in the development of epistemological reasoning in the arts.

There is evidence that assumptions about knowledge do alter according to the subject context. We know that the arts provide unique forms of knowledge and materialize in reflective processes that require accumulated observations captured across a wide range of symbolic forms, expressive languages and actions (Eisner, 2002). But as Ross (1978, p. 77) cogently argues 'The differences between the arts subjects may be as important as similarities because between them they offer a range of expressive outlets, each making demands and affording opportunities that are unique and quite specific'.

An educational imperative is to expand the borders of professionalism between teachers and artists, artists and artists, in consultation with learners and to connect the uniqueness and sameness of artistic elements in reflective discourses shared across arts communities (themes elaborated by Upitis, Rolfe and Ledgard).

Another educational imperative is that reflective conversations should occur between learners whose achievements depend on what they have access to, what they are familiar with and what they value in the arts. We need to be culturally aware and sensitive (*a theme taken up by Harris and Joseph in discussion of reflective intercultural conversations*).

In flagging up the imperative for nurturing *cultures of reflection*, several authors identify the significance of reflective thinking through the stories and accounts of learners some of whom are adolescents at the margins of schooling. Insofar as reflection rests for its legitimacy on reflective space, time and cultures, it offers learners a refuge from certain forms of authority. As Dewey (1933) posited, reflective thinking requires evaluation of beliefs and assumptions with *judgements* more likely to be valid and valued than *beliefs* derived from authority. Encouraging learners to question and challenge their own and others' values and practices is central to the development of critical reflection and to reflective practice in the arts (a theme elaborated in Kushner, Morrison et al. and Younker).

2.2 Reflection Imperative Two: Turning Experience into Meaningful Learning

Artists seek to reveal meaning. What we attach ourselves to, identify with, and become vitally interested in depends a great deal on the ways in which we reflectively construct personal meaning within a situation. The challenges for artists and artist educators come in terms of *what* they do in their studios, their classrooms and *how* they see their roles in the classroom.

So, how do we turn experience into meaningful learning?

We guide our own reflection by using different forms. These include the use of appraisals as a process of reordering, evaluating, judging or understanding experience, and the use of demonstrating, explaining, using gestures, diagrams, metaphors and progressive redrafting. In some arts contexts, to reflect means we have to step out of the present. For example, in Drama this is called METAXIS—holding two worlds at once—both engagement as fictional character and as performer: it is an intensified experience.

As with other techniques and tools described in this book, diaries and journals provide examples of tools to facilitate reflective activity. We can begin using narrative, life history or autobiography. Illuminating examples are offered of the nuggets of meaning embodied in *pedagogical reflections* as represented by stimulated recall, critical incident charting and the use of talk-and-draw techniques (Burnard, 2004).

Descriptive-interpretive studies posit that meaning is constructed through summoning memories and discovering dimensions of experience through hermeneutic phenomenological reflection[4] i.e., as something that is different from pre-reflective

[4] Hermeneutic phenomenology reflection as developed by Max van Manen (1990) is a reflective determination which is attentive to both terms of its methodology: it is a descriptive (phenomenological) methodology because it wants to be attentive to how things appear, it wants to let things speak for themselves; it is an interpretive hermeneutic methodology because it claims that there are no such things as uninterpreted phenomena.

lived understanding. This approach provides the insight that the meaning or essence of a phenomenon is multi-dimensional and multi-layered with reflection as the common form of meaning making (Burnard, 2006)[5]. Gaining a reflective grasp of the subjective experience calls upon 'a process of reflectively appropriating, of clarifying and of making explicit the structure of meaning of the lived experience' (van Manen, 1990, p. 77). Here, reflection rests its legitimacy on how it situates experience, perspectives and self in relation to others, and reveals ways of reflecting artistically. For example, if the context is musical improvisation, then communicative gesture and interaction may provide evidence of reflective thought and action (Burnard, 2002).

Whilst all research methodology subscribes to the importance of reflection, action research draws upon reflection as the agent of change in its cycle of action–breakdown–reflection–action (Kemmis, 1985). Action research provides a systematic and cyclical process for turning experience into learning and for artists and teachers working in partnership to reflect on their pedagogical practice (themes elaborated in the Upitis, Peel, Rolfe, Glover, Hoskyns and Ledgard chapters).

With the increasing political pressure to raise standards sketched against a lack of political commitment to arts education, in concert with forces of globalization, what is clear is that arts educators need to seek and connect interdisciplinary understanding of reflective practices across the arts.

2.3 Reflection Imperative Three: Rethinking the Legitamacy of Reflective Arts Practice

Reflective practice according to Shulman (1999) is what teachers do when they look back at the teaching and learning that has occurred, and reconstruct, re-enact, and/or recapture the events, the emotions, and the accomplishments. Here again, it is likely that reflection is not merely a disposition (as in, 'she's a reflective person') or a set of strategies, but also involving the use of particular kinds of analytic knowledge brought to bear on one's work.

A reflective 'practice' does not imply a precise format of instruction, but rather learning to take multiple perspectives: a mutual engagement in 'self-reflective workouts'. Correspondingly, the *reflective practitioner* is viewed as developing skills, dispositions and habits of mind in reflecting on practice (Schön, 1983, 1987; Zeichner and Liston, 1996).

For the artist, self-reflection is the means by which they simultaneously analyze situations, make judgments, and determine how successfully they handle the challenges through the transforming participation associated with art making. For the arts practitioner, educating young people in the arts involves self-reflection through which pedagogy reconciles self (the educator), the situation (art form/material/medium) and other (the child). For the *artist*, their artistic self and situation become the topic of their reflective conversations. For the *practitioner* and *artist educator*, the child's artist self and situation becomes the topic of the teachers pedagogic reflection.

[5] See Burnard (2006) for a phenomenological view of the reflective practice of musical improvisation and composition by a group of 12-year-old children.

Reflective arts practice, as with educational practice, features on-the-spot judgements, criticizing, restructuring, and testing of intuitive understanding of experienced phenomena; 'often it takes the form of a reflective conversation with the situation' (Schön, 1983, pp. 241–242). But what is different in r*eflective arts practices* is the involvement of mutuality, engagement with artistic materials, multiple perspectives, individual style, and transformative participation in artistic endeavors in which reflective processes are central. These include questioning and analysing what constitutes tacit knowledge or norms that underpin a choice, decision, or judgment; strategies and theories that support a choice, decision, or judgment; feelings in the moment that lead to a consideration, belief, value; biases that come into play as problems are identified and framed contextually and roles played out through interacting with others and creating change.

Reflective practice conversations might include questioning and formulating multiple solutions to daily challenges that arise in arts practice. Transferred to the classroom these questions might include: (1) How to recognise learners' behaviours at different stages and to develop personal relevance, instructional goals, differentiated tasks, and support; (2) What and whose are the goals and values underlying the ideas, solutions to the challenges and alternative viewpoints? (3) What might we do to build on our own and each others' ideas, to share ideas and consider alternative viewpoints? (4) What can I do to prompt and challenge my own and others thinking and reasoning? Questioning then leads reflective practitioners to plan for systematic inquiry, brainstorming ideas for solution or resolution, and planning for subsequent classroom implementation of the 'best' and most relevant solution to the questions and classroom challenges.

3. CONCLUDING THOUGHTS

An argument is emerging that arts educators need to make a commitment to more systematic forms of reflective activity and to develop reciprocal relationships (and dialogue) between the arts, education providers and the communities they serve, together with a strong framework for evaluating the pedagogical effectiveness of reflective practices.

This, then, is a call to recognise the potential of *collective reflection* as an agent of change in arts education, for *mutuality* and *support* for artists, practitioners and artist educators to go beyond the views of competing arts educators but rather to recast ourselves as an *extended professional community*, mutually informed by reflective endeavors.

Considered from the vantage point of these imperatives, we need:

- Innovation at the pedagogical level, with changes in method and ways of working with reflective arts practices that enable learning and teaching to develop and change.
- Innovation at the curriculum level, with changes in the nature of subject knowledge taught, the tone, time, space, ethos and institutional arrangements to facilitate the active sharing of reflective practices.

- Innovation at the professional development level, with changes in the ways adults (and adults and children) collaborate, cooperate, complement and connect as arts communities working together to extend professional discourse with shared agendas.

Given a commitment to such a view as the basis of betterment, we need to become more skillful at developing sophisticated models of teaching and learning in the arts that can demonstrate impact on standards. We also need to act as 'champions' among colleagues, to operationalise our own capacity for self-reflection and to nurture reflective cultures.

But the power of the individual is limited. This is why we need to organize ourselves into communities of arts practice in order to implement changes of real significance to arts curricular, involving changes in method and ways of supporting interdisciplinary understanding of reflective practices. This book represents one such attempt as authors and readers.

REFERENCES

Burnard, P. (2000a). Examining experiential differences between improvisation and composition in children's music-making. *British Journal of Music Education*, 17(3), 227–245.

Burnard, P. (2000b). How children ascribe meaning to improvisation and composition: rethinking pedagogy in music education. *Music Education Research*, 2(1), 7–23.

Burnard, P. (2002). Investigating children's meaning making and the emergence of musical interaction in group improvisation. *British Journal of Music Education*, 19(2), 157–172.

Burnard, P. (2004). Using critical incident charting for reflecting on musical learning. *The Mountain Lake Reader: Conversations on the Study and Practice of Music Teaching*. Spring, 8–21. Murfreesboro, Tennessee: Middle Tennessee State University, Music Department.

Burnard, P. (2006). Understanding children's meaning-making as composers. In I. Deliege and G. Wiggins (Eds.), *Musical Creativity: Multidisciplinary Research in Theory and Practice* (pp. 128–149). London: Psychology Press, Taylor & Francis.

Dewey, J. (1933). *How We Think*. Chicago, IL: Henry Regnery.

Eisner, E.W. (2002). What can education learn from the arts about the practice of education? *Journal of Curriculum and Supervision*, 18(1), 4–16.

Falk, J.H. and Dierking, L.D. (2000). *Learning from Museums: Visitor Experiences and the Making of Meaning*. Oxford: AltaMira Press.

Gouge, K. and Yates, C. (2002). Creating a CA programme in the arts: the Wigan LEA arts project. In M. Shayer and P. Adey (Eds.), *Learning Intelligence: Cognitive Acceleration Across the Curriculum from 5 to 15 Years* (pp. 85–102). Buckingham: Open University Press.

Harland, J., Lord, P., Stott, A., Kinder, K., Lamont, E., and Ashworth, K. (2005). *The Arts-Education Interface: A Mutual Learning Triangle?* Slough: National Foundation for Educational Research (NFER).

Jonassen, D.H., Tessmer, M., and Hannum, W.H. (1999). *Task Analysis Methods for Instructional Design*. Mahwah, NJ: Lawrence Erlbaum Associates.

Kemmis, S. (1985). Action research and the politics of reflection. In D. Boud, R. Keogh and D. Walker (Eds.), *Reflection: Turning Experience into Learning* (pp. 139–164). London: Croom Helm.

Killian, J. and Todnem, G. (1991). Reflective judgment concepts of justification and their relationship to age and education. *Journal of Applied Developmental Psychology*, 2(2), 89–116.

King, P.M. and Kitchener, K.S. (1994). *Developing Reflective Judgement: Understanding and Promoting Intellectual Growth and Critical Thinking in Adolescents and Adults*. San Francisco, CA: Jossey-Bass.

Norlander-Case, K., Reagan, T. and Case, C. (1999). *The Professional Teacher: The Preparation and Nurturance of the Reflective Practitioner*. San Francisco, CA: Jossey-Bass.

Ross, M. (1978). *The Creative Arts*. London: Heinemann.

Schön, D. (1983). *The Reflective Practitioner: How Professionals Think in Action*. New York: Basic Books.

Schön, D. (1987). *Educating the Reflective Practitioner*. San Francisco, CA: Jossey Bass.

Shulman, L.S. (1999). Knowledge and teaching: foundations of the new reform. In J. Leach and B. Moon (Eds.), *Learners and pedagogy* (pp. 61–77). London: Paul Chapman in association with The Open University.

Stenhouse, L. (1975). *An Introduction to Curriculum Research and Development*, London: Heinemann.

Uljens, M. (1997). On the philosophical foundations of phenomenography. In G. Dall'Alba and B. Hasselgren (Eds.), *Reflections on Phenomenography* (pp. 186–201). Göteborg: ACTA Universitatis Gothoburgensis.

Van Manen, M. (1990). *Researching Lived Experience: Human Science for an Action Sensitive Pedagogy*. State Canada: The Althouse Press.

Zeichner, K. and Liston, D. (1996). *Reflective Teaching: An Introduction*. Mahwah, NJ: Lawrence Erlbaum Associates, Inc.

SAVILLE KUSHNER

2. ADOLESCENTS AND CULTURES OF REFLECTION

More than Meets the Eye

. INTRODUCTION

What I want to do in this chapter is to take a critical look at reflective practice which, I will argue, is too often presented as an individual, privatised experience. I will propose the following:

- Reflective practice is based in inter-subjectivity and mutual exploration of lives, especially in collaboration with young people—but always within broader contexts of authority and politics. What we need are reflective cultures to support reflective individuals;
- Though the arts (I will often use the more inclusive term 'aesthetic') curriculum seems, under contemporary conditions, to have more success than some other disciplines in evoking life and identity (that is, educational) issues it is not privileged in carrying an obligation to do this, nor is it in any fundamental sense 'special';
- As arts experience enjoys this educational potential, it becomes enveloped by life. For the most part, we are not educating young people to become artists as much as we are employing the arts to help young people engage with life. This means that we need to reflect less on the art than on the life it evokes;
- Notwithstanding all our pressures to persuade teachers into reflective practice, they simply do not have the space to do so. Young people, on the other hand, do so vigorously. Teachers and young people are out of reflective 'synch'.

At the end, I will propose a specification for an aesthetic curriculum—what I call, simply, a 'conversational curriculum' that engages life/identity issues.

2. A CRITICAL LOOK AT REFLECTION

Cherished practices too easily become habitual: new cultural insights too readily give way to moral imperative. So it is with 'reflection'—deeply embedded in the contemporary lexicon of teaching. What was once identified by curriculum philosophers from Dewey and Schwab to Stenhouse and Elliott as a descriptor of healthy, democratic and independent intellectual communities threatens to become an instrument in the technology of school improvement. Improvement ('do what you've always done—but better') is not change ('break old habits—reconceptualise'). Reflection has a moral force behind it that is hard to deny or displace. All teachers *should* 'reflect' on their practices, through 'coaching', 'peer review', 'self study', 'collegial contracting' and, of course, what is taken to be 'action research'—the movement between experiment and

P. Burnard and S. Hennessy (eds.), *Reflective Practice in Arts Education*, 13–22.

review through which practice allegedly moves forward in relentless improvement. We have become habituated to improvement.

One of the dangers of habitualisation is that we lose a sense of purpose—that the promise of reflective practices is lost. Where reflection becomes an end in itself, rather than a means, or is reduced to a private or solitary pursuit, we lose the capacity to subject our purposes to scrutiny. Reflection is, in that sense, like a glove that needs the human hand to achieve meaning.

Long before Donald Schön (1987) published his influential book on reflective practice, Stenhouse (1975) was advocating classrooms as laboratories and as sites for knowledge experiments through teacher research. Their approaches were quite different. Schön (with his architectural design background in MIT) talked of 'personal design worlds' and of reflection as a journey of self-discovery; Stenhouse spoke of cultures of intellectuals as first envisaged by John Dewey. For Stenhouse, classroom reflection was an all-embracing ethical and cultural pursuit and his starting point was that '*curriculum research and development ought to belong to the teacher*' (1975, p. 142); for Schön reflection in (and on) action was focused on practical competence and artistry—there are no politics in his 1987 text. Stenhouse never lost sight of political authority and saw teacher reflection as a means for liberating classroom action. His focus was on curriculum—that is, the whole context within which knowledge is generated. These differences reduce to this: Schön's reflection is a private, subjective epistemological enquiry; that of Stenhouse, an inter-subjective cultural enquiry.

This chapter argues that we should take the Stenhouse route—not to dismiss Schön, but to envelope his excellent prescriptions within the broader view. In that broader view we have to take account of more than the practitioner—we have to think, in terms of what reflection can do, of the student and the knowledge-base in question and of negotiated educational purpose. I advocate reflective practice, but as a form of political action. Here, I will be mostly concerned with the student and their experience as 'reflective practitioners', but implicit throughout is the fact of curriculum as the ethical site in which they and teachers move together. What I want to show is that 'reflection' already is happening before the teacher brings their critical gaze to pedagogical interactions. It is the stuff of adolescence, in particular. Reflection involves the making transparent of otherwise concealed contingencies and determinants to collective thought and action in a context of political constraint.

3. LAZY THOUGHT IS A BARRIER TO REFLECTION

I have spent almost twenty years, on and off, evaluating performing arts projects. These have taken me across a landscape of the arts and education. I have observed music being played with pensioners, prisoners and pupils—argued over by people with terminal illness in a hospice—I have observed the arts practiced by communities and connoisseurs—ditched by the disillusioned and embraced by the hopeful. Throughout, I have kept a focus on students of the arts and on educators and on the struggles they have almost inevitably had to wage to keep their arts/education aspirations afloat. Few—even at the highest level—seem to derive enough satisfaction from art to keep going without effort. For musicians, for example, playing to and with unfamiliar audiences in situations of unfamiliar intimacy has frequently provided welcome relief, intriguing new challenges, much-valued opportunities to reflect on self and creativity. I have said and written more than once that to audiences music is a precious thing; but to its students it is a costly thing. The cost is in units of life-energy. Occasionally—but too often—it proves too high a cost to bear. So it is across the performing arts.

So I have spent a great deal of time talking to students, and to students of the arts. We could—we do—call this methodology, but that implies an end-point to the enquiry. For most of the time I was being educated by the students. I have written (Kushner, 2000) that methodology is something that we construct after the event, once we reflect on what we did and what was effective. Using hindsight we tidy up what are usually pretty messy events, but I have rarely achieved in practice the laundered crispness I strive for in my research writing—and I rarely aim for outcomes.

For example, when I first started my arts evaluation at the Guildhall School of Music and Drama—evaluating the Music Performance and Communication Skills innovation—I was told by more than one senior musician and conservatoire manager that music students are 'inarticulate'—that I wouldn't get much out of them. The reasoning was that so much of their developmental energy went into their music that they had undeveloped communications skills. This was lazy thinking, uncontaminated with curiosity, and a not untypical clue as to how what actually emerge as complex, intellectual and critical reflections of young people go unnoticed by their adult mentors. The reality is that music students and their tutors have perennial difficulty in establishing good communicative relationships. But how strange, for in fact, these students had an extraordinary capacity to reflect on self and life—something that came to underpin evaluation reports whose strength relied on the quality of student expression and analysis far more than on the expertise of the evaluator. This is a capacity that I have only been able to explain with the idea that their art required them so frequently to question self that they were well-rehearsed and ready to relieve themselves of the burden of their internal soul-searching. All art, I would contend, is self-knowledge. Would that this were made true by schools of Maths and English.

One accomplishment of that (and subsequent performing arts evaluations I conducted) was the enhanced conversation, between students and their tutors and programme managers, which was enabled once these assumptions were challenged. In fact, the world of research into the lives of young people is littered with lazy assumptions—generalisations which are based on observations of behaviour which subsequently are (a) subject to inference rather than verification (b) proliferated as unchallenged truths—like the music student's inarticulacy. Here is one especially damaging unchallenged truth—*youth is problematic*. Here's another—*adolescents are vulnerable to a range of pathological experiences such as drugs, sex, alcohol, gambling and violence*. And another—that *what you see (of adolescents) is what you get*. Each of these I, with colleagues, have found to dominate research and thinking about adolescents. They defy the more critical aspirations of 'reflective practice' which are to reveal realities of meaning and intention in such ways as to guide action with verified, authentic knowledge more than with hope, ideology or assumption.

4. RESEARCH WITH YOUNG PEOPLE

Throughout the 1980s and 1990s I worked at the Centre for Applied Research in Education at the University of East Anglia with a group of researchers who were independently-minded, methodologically creative and restless to move beyond what was already known. Many of the studies they did fell into this area of research on young people, sometimes fuelled by social concerns—occasional moral panics—at how adolescents put a drag on social statistics. There were too many teenage pregnancies, too much drug-taking, too much aggression, too much of so many things along with too little formal schooling. One of the group, John Schostak, responded to the jibe of recalcitrant children being 'maladjusted' by researching a case of a school which was failing in its community role and entitled the subsequent book, *Maladjusted Schooling* (Schostak, 1983). After this, our group mounted funded projects looking in fine-grained detail—largely by documenting lives and selves—at adolescent experience outside of the curriculum. They looked at young people in interaction with drugs, sex, alcohol, sexual and health education, gay experience, 'boy-ness' and gambling. What, broadly, did they find?

Overall they found this—that what were often thought of by adults as problems appeared in the lives of young people as solutions. There were educational issues, clearly, but these were not to do with how to avoid these activities so much as how best and safely to interact with them. Often, what were taken by adults (and research sponsors) to be pathological experiences were, rather, evidence of experimentation as young people sought among alternatives for a sense of purpose—of location. As in the case of Schostak's book title, labels and assumptions can be turned back on their users. Along the way, these icons of deviance—drugs, alcohol, gambling—provided temporary solutions to young people finding their way through the tangled undergrowth of competing pressures for conformity and autonomy, the emotional turbulence of emergent sexuality and the juggling of different adult orthodoxies.

So, in ways not that hard to relate to, lollygagging around with a reefer in one hand and a bottle of beer in the other is not so much an attempt at being that image as trying it on. Such experiences emerged from the research reports as experimental sites for identity formation—though we need a dynamic notion of identity as process rather than fact—Stanley and Billig (2004), for example, argue that identities should be considered as 'discursive constructs', and this broadly characterises what we found. Here were examples of reflection in and on action—often carried out collectively among peers, usually with a sense of emergent purpose.

Far from being problematic, then, adolescence emerges in these studies as a reflective, transformational process. As Elliott (1998, p. 47) puts it in relation to non-attendance and disruptive behaviour, adolescent practices can be '*understood as rational rather than deviant behaviours*'. Far from being vulnerable to social pathologies, adolescents need these experiences in order to conduct their identity-experiments. Far from being what they appear, adolescents are better defined by concealed qualities and complexities—i.e., behavioural observations need to be understood with data on intentionality. The problem, for there really is one, is that young people are required to engage in and reflect on these practices in subterranean ways, in ways that are not easily mediated, not made safe, not shared, too easily subsumed under implicit regimes of competitive individualism. It seems that adolescence involves a 'school within school'—albeit unnoticed.

The naturally reflective condition young people seem to find themselves in is not mirrored in the public conditions in which teachers find themselves. Notwithstanding the pressures we put on teachers to engage in reflective practice, teachers are denied reflective space. The communities of practice which were once envisioned as providing a professional resource for teachers to enquire independently into the contexts for which they are legally responsible are now effectively outlawed by government stipulation and policed by the Office for Standards in Education (Ofsted)—the national school inspection system in England. Teachers cannot question national educational goals and purposes. This is to say that the moral (reflective) trajectories of young people and their teachers are moving in different directions and at different speeds. While young people spend their lives reflecting, teachers are busy with compliance and survival. Teachers struggle to find independent, autonomous action for Stenhousian projects.

At the time of writing, England is traumatised by the sudden emergence of suicide bombing, taken aback by the apparent spontaneity of its horrible emergence. But this is, surely, evidence of the failure of curriculum. In England we have a 'transmission' curriculum that is intolerant of diverse messages; not the 'conversational' curriculum advocated by Stenhouse. Curriculum—in denial of open, critical exchange between teachers and young people—cannot host inter-subjective reflection of the kind that might well have revealed these disturbing aspects of social change and social fragmentation, so rooted in adolescent learning. Fifteen thousand hours of schooling—including arts education—may have been insufficient to protect those tragic, hapless young bombers from the ruthless terrorist recruiters. But how have we arrived at a situation in which teachers were so clearly disabled from learning about such potential? Such a burden, we might well think, falls especially heavily on teachers of the arts. We cannot argue for a privileged status for the arts (in relation to their capacity to connect with lived realities as an expressive form) without accepting the consequent obligations that creates.

5. THE ARTS AS A SITE FOR INTER-SUBJECTIVE REFLECTION

Let me come, now, to the case of the arts and to a particular example. The CEDES[1] project in Bath and North East Somerset is conceived and directed by Penny Hay.

[1] CEDES: This is a project bringing together artists, educators and young people to conduct collaborative enquiry in to the often complex realities of 'disaffection'. The project puts the term 'disaffection' under critical scrutiny, and provides a basis for subsequent arts-education interactions.

This is an action research project employing artists and teachers to work together to research pupil disaffection, and, once having understood something of the experience of young people, to design arts projects which respond to that understanding. Typically, the artists go into a school to work with the teacher and the pupils and monitor what they are doing. The results echo those findings from the CARE[2] studies. The first thing that falls away is the term 'disaffection' which achieves little purchase on the complexities of young people's experience. The next thing that happens is that artist and teacher start to look at themselves as the source of the term and the ascription. It is far less than comfortable.

The focus of the CEDES project has been a shifting target: first 'disaffection', then the artist themselves; then the nature of collaboration; occasionally, the art form. In fact, one common experience has been the value in setting the art form aside from time to time. Too often the art serves as a mediating device between adult and young person, and, though mediation is sometimes useful, at other times the urgency is for direct, unmediated interaction. (Not always—video, especially, is a powerful medium for direct exchange.)

One casualty has been the title of the project. There is the acronym—CEDES—but discovering stable words to fill it out has proved so controversial and problematic that in the end it stands alone. The mission to bring arts experience to educational issues has been the least stable of all as the project group of around 15 people has been sundered and rebuilt, lost and found members, ricocheted from one crisis to another and struggled throughout to express its key claims and aims. This is far from saying it has not been rich and productive—it has generated exciting events and videos made by young people, and generated a radical manifesto for arts education. Its strength has been withstanding the turbulence of events and the empirical 'messiness' of an action research approach. CEDES's greatest learning of all, however, has been for those engaged in it. In the end the project became a reflective practice enterprise with artists and teachers learning about each other and themselves, discovering techniques through which to forge collaborations, learning how to learn with and through young people. In one sense, a two-year project became (properly) absorbed with what projects too often dispense with in weeks—access, definition of purpose, working out what is their ethic, and working out just who they are in their CEDES guise.

One lesson I learned quickly at the Guildhall (Kushner, 1992) and carried with me to other evaluations was that music was rarely robust enough to sustain a conversation. Interviews generally started out with music, but within minutes elided into a conversation about life. Here are some brief examples:

- There was the young flautist at the conservatoire who had been told her personality stood in the way of her becoming a musician. She talked long and hard into my tape recorder—about her shyness, about her pristine appearance and living

---

[2] CARE (Centre for Applied Research in Education): This centre, based at the University of East Anglia, was part of a transatlantic collaboration throughout the 1970s and 1990s to develop case-based, action research and democratic approaches to enquiry.

quarters . . . but about the corner of her flat which was, inexplicably for her, chaotic and had to be left so. The question became one of understanding that messy corner and what it represented in her identity-struggle—music was an exemplar.

- There is a moment in a CEDES drama improvisation when young children stand in a circle facing 'in'. One stands facing 'out'—he is thought to be self-excluding. What is 'in'—the art experience—is thought to represent inclusion; what is 'out'—beyond the art moment—is thought to represent exclusion. But further research reveals a sense of alienation among young people with the 'inclusion' environment and, for many, a deep sense of relief at finding a home in (excluded) environments such as special behavioural units. The question became one of how the artists could achieve inclusion and relief from their own 'disaffection'.
- There were the young Asian primary school girls who emerged from a singing workshop chatting about religious prohibitions which persuaded them to move their lips but not to sing. One explained that when you did bad things in life your eventual grave would get narrower—but would widen with the good things you did. But she had to sing, said her teacher—it was good to sing, said the professional musician. These girls were left to juggle these competing orthodoxies.
- There was the orchestral musician whose children had left home and she missed them. She worked with deaf children, introducing them to music in a pioneering way. She talked of trying to 'prove herself' by forging a new identity, seeking new meanings in life—'an identity other than sitting at the back of the orchestra counting bars and leaping off the edge of cliffs. Simon [Rattle] says we're all neurotics in our section—we're either waiting to jump or we've jumped'.
- A CEDES artist struggles to make a connection with her collaborating teacher. They paint together and find the connection in the process. This does not transfer to the young 'disaffected' people they were to work with. The artist makes 'fuck cakes'—sponge cakes with the word 'fuck' iced on them—to show how art can extend the narrow tolerances of social conformity and institutional rules. She is in. She persuades aggressive young men to body-paint each other; they learn to touch—glimpse each other differently. The art room becomes their space—they establish rules, call those who were allowed to enter 'guests'—invert the relationship between mainstream school space and their (marginal) space such that school is marginalised and excluded.
- Then there are the children in a primary classroom with no teacher present, improvising music. The music emerges through interactions which are, in turn, aggressive, gentle, strident, cajoling—but all the time embedded in the competitive, bantering relationships enjoyed by them in their everyday school life. The music becomes a surrogate for relationship-learning among the young people.
- Finally, there is the community music project where a musician works with adults suffering from clinical depression. They make up a song-game with lyrics made up of the names of their much-loathed (because much-needed) drugs. For a moment, the art form embraces/encapsulates their dread problems. But music is, in the end, encapsulated by the struggle with depression. The musician becomes frustrated with

this, with helping people to 'find their own voice', as she puts it—yearns to return to playing challenging music that speaks to her own personal need for complexity. But she cannot let go of the urge to work with these people.

So what is the point of all of this? Well, first of all, it is clear to me that aesthetic experience is, at almost all points, contextualised by life. It is not independent of lives and nor is it enough to make up a life. This is to state the obvious, but it creates a challenge for curriculum. Reflection cannot easily be confined to the professional task as, for example, a pedagogical instrument. Rather, it will respond to those experiences, beliefs and values that make up and transform practice. Reflective practice cannot be confined to pedagogy—or to arts pedagogy. We cannot rest with being connoisseurs of curriculum—we have to become connoisseurs of life processes, for, in the end, few young people are learning 'art' so much as they are learning life.

This gives rise to the importance of shared enquiry, reflection engaged by a group, by a culture of learning. But reflection, again not as a privatised activity, nor one focused on elements of practice. Rather, reflection emerges as a form of action, and embraces contexts, purposes and alternative realities. During CEDES events the various projects were taking place, moving forward, confronting and not always solving existential dilemmas. They were becoming *bound up* in a process of development rather than merely *feeding* it. There was no separation of thought from action, as in the common diagrammatic representation of an action research process in which an essentially fragmented and linear series of events . . .

$$\text{Action}^1 \rightarrow \text{reflection} \rightarrow \text{adaptation} \rightarrow \text{action}^2$$

. . . is made cyclical by artifice. The ensuing action research cycle seems to be—often is—sealed off from daily experience, does not readily suggest a way of bringing life into the classroom, focuses too relentlessly and rationally on practice rather than experience. The CEDES experience of action research was not of a succession of positive outcomes in some sort of chronological order. There were setbacks, lurches, revelations and denials, gains and losses—mostly in unpredictable and disordered patterns. Overall the project was a substantial learning gain and there were notable and profound personal changes—the project revealed in unique ways how to manage relationships between artists and educators and between them and young people. But it was neither neat, rational nor linear.

6. MY SPECIFICATION FOR A REFLECTIVE CURRICULUM

As adult managers of young peoples' learning we are not alone. Allegedly 'disaffected' young people emerge from research as a resource—we are not alone in dealing with our or their social problems. Curriculum ought to be a site for conversation between the generations—when I say 'conversation' I imply mutual understanding, tolerance and exploration as much as conflict, tension and competition. Curriculum is not, as Stenhouse insisted, *what* we teach so much as *how* we teach—i.e., in this way he sought to shift the educational focus from aims and objectives to principles of procedure—to the conditions for mutual, shared reflection on what is educationally worthwhile.

An editorial response to a draft of this chapter asked me to make my points relevant to art forms beyond music, but this misses the point. In the end, all art forms are subservient to life and identity struggles—all curriculum is a surrogate for experience. Reflection overwhelms the substantive character of all subjects. Perhaps the reflective practice lament is that there are any discipline-based subjects at all, and that a school timetable would be better divided by lessons such as 'exploration of self', 'exploration of collectives', 'the nature of moral obligation', 'social fragmentation and social cohesion', 'rights and democracy'. These provide contexts of social meaning that give shape to the 'gloves' of the knowledge disciplines—Maths, Humanities, Arts. In this sense, we see arts teaching as an element of a reflective curriculum, rather than reflection as an element of arts practice.

We are, however, stuck with the disciplines, and so we take comfort in the relative success of aesthetic curriculum areas in, at least provoking if not responding to identity struggles. So, in conclusion—what does my ideal aesthetic curriculum look like in the light of this analysis of reflective action?

- Think in terms of lives, not stages.

Current national curriculum key stages (in England) do not map onto the stages and phases of life young people are going through. To measure the significance of knowledge against an administrative measure is to miss its significance in the development of the child.

- Think in terms of experiments, not orthodoxies.

We may be certain about the knowledge we propagate. Young people are not. For them, knowledge is experience and is provisional upon its monitored effects on their lives and interactions—their identities. Young people interact with knowledge in experimental rather than in compliant mode.

- Think in terms of event-histories, not outcomes.

A pedagogical interaction is better defined by the purposes teacher and student bring to it—and can only be understood and judged in the context of intention and experience. Outcome targets are unlikely to run in parallel to experience.

- Think in terms of judgement, not appreciation.

Art experiences—as elements of provisional knowledge—are useful as whetstones on which young people can sharpen their judgement. The question is not how a young person comes to admire Mozart or Vermeer, but how they form autonomous views about them.

- Think in terms of conversation, not demonstration.

Demonstrations of the quality of an art object will serve to present the young person with data for their deliberations, but they will not provide the feedback the teacher needs to measure the worth or significance of that data. Conversation is all.

- Think in terms of wholes, not parts.

Young people do not face fragmented challenges in life. Theirs is the task to adapt the whole of themselves to the whole of the life they encounter. It will come more naturally to a young person—more importantly, it will allow them to rehearse that challenge—to perceive the whole and deconstruct, rather than to assemble small building blocks. To encounter a painting or an opera and then to examine its constituent elements will be a more familiar task than learning appliqué and colour theory, or pitch, rhythm and sequence in the abstract.

Curriculum is a process of knowledge generation. So, at its best, is art-making—though too often art-making is the privatised activity teaching is in danger of becoming. Neither would be effective in the absence of reflection—indeed, reflection defines the nature of the practice. It is a dynamic process in which the parameters of the enquiry are themselves affected by it. Reflection, in this sense, destabilises reality—and is, in turn, destabilised by it.

To return to my opening critique of reflection, the danger, perhaps, is that we allow it to become constitutive of our shared moral endeavours rather than constituted by them. Reflection is one of the deliberative strategies we use to explore collectively what is worthwhile in knowledge.

REFERENCES

Elliott, J. (1998). *The Curriculum Experiment*. Buckingham: Open University Press.

Kushner, S. (2000). *Personalising Evaluation*. London: Sage.

Kushner, S. (1992). *The Music Case: Innovation in the Conservatoire*. Victoria (Australia): Deakin University Press.

Schön, D. (1987). *Educating the Reflective Practitioner*. San Francisco, CA: Jossey bass.

Schostak, J. (1983). *Maladjusted Schooling: Deviance Social Control and Individuality in Secondary Schooling*. London: Falmer.

Stanley, S. and Billig, M. (2004). Dilemmas of storytelling and identity. In C. Daiute and C. Lightfoot (Eds.), *Narrative Analysis: Studying the Development of Individuals in Society* (pp. 159–176). London: Sage.

Stenhouse, L. (1975). *An Introduction to Curriculum Research and Development*. London: Heinemann.

DIANA HARRIS

3. CULTURAL REFLECTIONS

Teaching Performing Arts to Muslims

1. INTRODUCTION

In this chapter my intention is to describe and discuss some of my recent research and reflections on the teaching of performing arts with Muslims in order for readers to be able to reflect on their own teaching of multi-ethnic groups. I believe that it is incumbent upon us all as arts teachers to help to dispel misunderstandings between cultures. By looking at the ideas that are germane to the teaching of the arts, in conjunction with the concept of Islam, my intention is to show how reflection on practice can result in being able to encourage participation from Muslim pupils. I do not intend to enter into the debate about entitlement, inclusion or access to arts education in the state sector, rather to promote a pro-multi ethnic stance of tolerance and sensitivity in this post 9/11 environment.

Teaching Muslims requires an holistic and ethical approach and reflection on *our* teaching and *our* values is essential to this. Of course all teaching should be holistic and ethical but this is particularly important for teaching Muslims, because in Islam there is no distinction between religious and secular life: Hussain (1999), in an interview with Harris said: 'Islam is not a private thing; it is not a personal thing; it is not a commercialised thing. Islam is in the public sphere, it is action.' This is not to say that all Muslims fulfill all the obligations of Islam, neither do all Muslims interpret these obligations in the same way, but it does mean that in introducing Muslims to an area of study that many have concerns about, it is important that we are not asking them to do anything that they feel is against their religion. In order to have an holistic approach it is necessary to understand how and why these concerns have arisen.

Day (in Loughran, 1999), named two of his six social goals as 'understanding better some client populations' and, 'understanding better some particular situations or circumstances affecting clients' (p. 217). Later in this chapter I look at what makes teaching Muslims a special case when it comes to the performing arts and what they have concerns about, but first I want to highlight the current situation.

We know that tolerance is not a sufficient response to living with other races and cultures (Harris, 2002), and that people engaged in education also need to be sensitive. Whilst tolerance does not necessarily imply any degree of understanding, to be sensitive certainly does. Renzetti and Lee (1993), quoting Seiber, wrote:

> . . . (being) culturally sensitive is learning to perceive risk factors from the perspective of the persons who will be affected . . . community-based

P. Burnard and S. Hennessy (eds.), *Reflective Practice in Arts Education*, 23–32.

> researchers must stay in touch with current opinions that are circulating in the community (p. 19).

This seems to me to be just as important for teachers as for researchers.

2. THE EFFECT OF ISLAMOPHOBIA

In the foreword to *Islamophobia: issues, challenges and action* (Commission on British Muslims and Islamophobia, 2004), Richard Stone wrote:

> Today, Britain's 1.6 million Muslims are living on a diet of death, hypocrisy and neglect that is traumatizing and radicalizing an entire generation (p. vii).

The huge increase in Islamophobia since 9/11, and the Bali, Madrid and London bombings (October '02, March '04 and July '05) are making many of the Muslims in the UK feel guilty and insecure. The war in Iraq and the ongoing atrocities in that country, whether perpetuated by the occupying forces or factions within Islam itself, are making matters worse. But Islamophobia is not new: in a report by the *European Monitoring Centre on Racism and Xenophobia* (2002), it was suggested that 9/11 provided a catalyst that reaffirmed old prejudices about Islam, as well as fuelling new fears amongst the non-Muslim world. Allen (2004), wrote:

> The distinctions between religion and ethnicity, therefore, became increasingly blurred, and the primacy of an enemy's Muslimness, whether relevant or not, was stressed in order to reinvigorate and reaffirm historical foes, albeit in a contemporary frame of reference and understanding (p. 6).

Abbas (2004), wrote: 'it is important not to treat Muslims as an undifferentiated mass, for there are many ethnic, cultural, social, economic, and political differences between individuals and groups' (p. 29). It was interesting to hear a Sikh leader talking about the play *Behzti* by Gurpreet Kaur, performed at a theatre in Birmingham in October 2004. This play was eventually abandoned because of demonstrations by Sikhs about the nature of the setting. Apart from issues of free speech, what interested me most was when the interviewee asked why the play should be thought to be acceptable to Sikhs just because it was written by someone with a Sikh name, who had grown up in a Sikh community? We would not assume that a play written by someone who had grown up in the UK, nominally Christian, would be inevitably acceptable to a Christian audience.

The most visible sign of 'Muslim-ness' is the hijab, the scarf worn by most Muslim women, or in some cases the burqa which is the garment that covers a woman from head to foot. Women across the western world have been attacked and insulted because they are seen to be Muslims. But it is not only Muslims who have been attacked. Sikhs and Hindus have also been violated because of their 'Asian-ness'. This in turn has led to the rare, and almost unbelievable, alliance between the British

National Party (a far right party), and some fringe Sikh and Hindu groups in an audio resource, '*A threat to us all*', distributed to the media (2002). At around the same time the BNP published a leaflet entitled 'I.S.L.A.M.' which stood for, 'intolerance, slaughter, looting, arson and molestation of women' (2001).

These points are important to make because of where they leave our Muslim pupils. Abbas (2004) reminds us that Muslims are already amongst the most underprivileged in our society and are also increasingly over-represented in our prisons. The isolationism that Islamophobia is establishing can only make matters worse. In 1937 Herbert Blumer introduced the idea of 'symbolic interactionism', based on the work of G. H. Mead. In this philosophy the concepts of 'self' and 'society' are not separate: the 'self' arises out of social interaction. If we were to apply this to Muslims then their self concept would be expected to be rapidly deteriorating in the face of all the criticism from society. In speaking to Muslims this is indeed what is happening; many are upset by the inability of non-Muslims to see beyond the events perpetrated by Muslim extremists.

One of the reasons why many non-Muslims are reacting in this way is not difficult to pinpoint: the media: 'Nothing in history has threatened Muslims like the western media' (Ahmed, 1994, p. 22). The populist newspapers in particular have whipped up their readership into a frenzied and illogical state of fear. Ahmed (1994), wrote in response to the fatwa declared on Salman Rushdie, author of *Satanic Verses*:

> 'average' Muslims may not agree with the Fatwa (declaration)... but they resent the cavalier way in which they are treated by association in the media ... the reality in each case is more than meets the eye ... There is no way an ordinary Muslim can make his views known in the media which floods hostile words and images over and around him ... But he is also as disgusted as he is confused with his own sense of impotence in shaping reality around him; he can no longer challenge what is real or unreal, no longer separate reality from illusion of the media (p. 17).

But the media have the power to work for good as well as evil. Madeline Bunting, writing in *The Guardian* 30 November, 2004, invited 100 young Muslims to discuss the main issues shaping their lives and their futures. The aim was 'to catch a glimpse—to eavesdrop—on how a set of issues are being debated within a new generation of British Muslims'. Her intention was to present to a non-Muslim readership rarely heard voices. By doing this she has given Muslims a voice so that their response need no longer be, 'retreat, passionate expressions of faith, anger' (Ahmed, 1994 p. 29). And this is where involvement in the performing arts could have an impact, in giving Muslims a space in which to express their personalities and culture and, as Roper and Davis (2000), wrote, allow 'the growing child to learn to deal with the world as it is rather than how it is portrayed through the media and dominant ideology'. But it is not as simple as that: the words 'performing', 'music', 'dance' and 'drama' are anathema to many Muslims and this first has to be understood.

3. MUSLIM ATTITUDES TO PERFORMING ARTS

Fundamental to the ethos of Islam are three concepts that are as relevant to music as to any other secular activity. These are the importance of *zaman* (time), *makan* (place) and *ikhwan* (associates). This means that one should not spend so much time doing the activity that it is detrimental to one's sacred duties; the place in which the activity is carried out must be acceptable, which means nowhere where any *haram* (illegal) activity takes place; and that there should be no association with anyone who is involved in *haram* activities. But what is a *haram* activity? Hussain (1999) declares that something cannot be *haram* in itself, it is the use it is put to that counts. For example you can beat a drum to accompany a belly dancer which would be *haram*, but you could beat that same drum in a holy war which would not only be *mubah* (indifferent to law), but also *halal* (your religious duty).

Although the performing arts obviously include performing, composing/creating, listening/watching and appraising, the area that causes most concern to Muslims is performing. Performing in any sense has traditionally been restricted in Muslim culture to single sex gatherings. It is immediately going to cause difficulties when we ask boys and girls, post puberty, to perform together. But even within single sex groups there are other issues pertaining to performing. One of these surrounds the value of what is being done, and any type of performing is not seen as a serious or honorable way of spending one's time. Taking this a stage further we come to the already familiar view held by many parents that there is 'no point in teaching something unless it can lead to a profession'. As teachers, therefore, we have to make explicit the reasons for engaging in the performing arts. In my experience of teaching performing arts to Muslims it has been essential to point out the educational importance of the arts from the point of view of extending the imagination and self expression, but also the links with other disciplines seen as being more academically acceptable.

It is for this reason that the admirable work done by Lucy Green and colleagues at the Institute of Education in London places teachers with Muslims in their classes with a dichotomy. Green (2001) looks at how popular musicians learn in the hope that this can be extended to music in the classroom. She points out that the world listens to pop, rock and dance music and so it needs a place in the curriculum. But it is just this type of music that presents Muslims with concerns. From their knowledge of the western pop/rock scene they have decided that if that is what school music consists of then it is not for them. Everything about the pop scene from its lyrics to its use of alcohol and drugs, and sexual presentation, alienates the majority of Muslim parents in the UK. In asking 'What is it to be musically educated?' (ibid.) Green is looking specifically at the values of western young people. It is important therefore that we reflect what is taught (curriculum) as well as the way it is taught (pedagogy).

In his chapter *Researching teaching through reflective practice*, Day writes:

> To practice effectively means engaging routinely in conscious, systematic collection and evaluation of information about these areas and the relationships between them, which affect and result from practice (in Loughran, 1999, p. 216).

It is not particularly difficult, though it is time consuming, to engage in conscious and systematic collection of information, but the difficult part is the evaluation of the information. In a chapter of this length, or indeed an entire book, it is impossible to do much more than present 'sound-bites'. Much of my research has left me far from clear about what the consensus view on music actually is. A further complication is that when people mention music they could be talking either about singing or musical instruments. Since in many Muslim cultures musical instruments are banned entirely, except for a small drum, music often just refers to singing. Let me for a moment present some of the contradictory material that I have accumulated. In interviews with Muslim women performers, it emerged that even singing is not considered *halal* (lawful) by some women. The following conversation comes from an interview I (DH), conducted in 1999 between a mother (Mrs. A), and her daughter (NA) who sings professionally. They were responding to my question about whether the Qur'an says that singing is acceptable:

Mrs. A: No, no the music is actually forbidden in Islam. It is really true, especially for girls.

NA: What it says is that the voice of a woman should not be heard outside the four walls of her home. But she can sing and welcome. Our Prophet, peace be upon him, as he entered Mecca they were singing and clapping and playing the *duff* (hand drum). They were singing then and in that procession there must have been loads of men and women. It's very confusing at times and my mother has a point.

NA: Well, I don't think there is anything bad because I think I am also giving people a lot of pleasure. God has given me a gift and the gift is my voice. If I can use my voice to give people pleasure, as well as God . . .

Mrs. A: That is the thing. Giving pleasure and earning the money giving pleasure it is *haram* (illegal).

NA: How can men and women do the *Adzan* [call to prayer] if women's voices cannot be heard outside their four walls?

Mrs. A: Adzan is always given by men

NA: But I was in Bosnia last year and I heard a woman doing it, and it's recorded and it was beautiful.

DH: So it's OK for men but not for women?

Mrs. A: That's it.

DH: singing is OK for Men?

Mrs. A: Yes

NA: I don't know.

Mrs A: When N was saying that they were singing together when the Prophet, peace be upon him, came to Medina or Mecca I don't know what they are saying, is that music alright but not the other? I don't know.

NA: But that's how it is interpreted. The general consensus is that men can sing but women can't. But I haven't read that in the Qur'an.

Confusion was also clearly to be seen in my interview with the Palestinian singer Reem Kilani (personal communication, 17 July 2000). She said that it was perfectly acceptable for her to sing in aid of the Palestinian cause during the 'intifada', but at the time I interviewed her Palestine was going through a more peaceful time and she was again being denied the right to sing because it was felt to be unacceptable for women to sing in public. Reflective conversations with Muslim pupils show just as much confusion. In Egypt I spent some time with a Muslim family who had two children at secondary school. The daughter told me that music is compulsory until the age of 14, when there is a choice between art and music and sometimes computers. At her school there is only a choice between art and music, 80% choosing the latter. It is almost unheard of for a pupil to opt out, although occasionally a girl will say that she is not allowed to sing. She told me that although they all know that music is not allowed in Islam it doesn't make any difference to their lifestyle. The son said that in his school, although music is compulsory, the boys do not take it seriously because they are not tested in it. In an inner city comprehensive school in the UK, some girls told me that at junior school they had performed in a mixed steel pans group but they said that their fathers would not let them do this now they were at secondary school. They believed it was definitely the playing with boys that was a problem although some of them felt that their fathers would not allow them to continue on any terms:

Sadia: It's not good [music]. My Dad said he wouldn't want music 'cos there's Muslims in the house and if people heard us it's not good. He doesn't like us having music but my sister's got cassettes.
Tasleem: My father doesn't like music because it's not using your time for something serious and you could be doing something for your religion.
Riffat: I'd like to play the flute and my parents would let me. My grandfather loved music but I really only got to see him 5 times. There is a limit to dancing though.
DH: What do you mean by a limit?
Riffat: Well now I'm always dancing but when I grow older they won't want me to dance as much as I do now.

Where the playing of musical instruments is concerned the picture is also far from unanimous. When Yusef Islam (Cat Stevens), embraced Islam he gave up all music. As an important role model for Muslims in this country, and the Chair of Governors at Islamia Primary School, the first Islamic school to become state funded, this meant that all music became problematic for a large number of Muslims. Since then he has gradually become active in music again. This first took the form of singing unaccompanied, then accompanied by an instrument playing the same tune, and finally with a harmonic instrumental background. This process is now almost complete with the re-release of some of his old Cat Stevens recordings. However, he, and the other trustees at Islamia, is, at the time of writing, still not ready to include musical instruments in music lessons at the school because a significant number of the parents would be unhappy. In contrast to this, a few Islamic schools are prepared to introduce keyboards and a limited number of tuned percussion instruments. These variations in practice further emphasize the differences between Muslims. In the instances where music has been accepted it is invariably because of a supportive head-teacher. In state schools with a high proportion of Muslims it is often the degree of understanding shown by the staff to the Muslims community, and a readiness to engage in meaningful discussion, which paves the way for the acceptance of performing arts in the school curriculum.

4. REFLECTING ON ASPECTS OF MUSIC

Within the Muslim community the question of music is hotly debated. At the conference *Music Education for Muslims*, Dr Tariq Ramadan (2002), a well known Swiss born Muslim who has written widely about the need for Muslims to engage in the culture of the western society in which they have chosen to live, presented a paper looking at the three different views held by Muslims about music. For some all music is *haram* (unlawful), for others singing and un-tuned percussion instruments are acceptable, and for a third group all music which follows the three laws about time, place and associates is acceptable. He said:

> The third view allows music because there is nothing in the Islamic texts which is plainly or directly clear about music; there is nothing that can sustain the opinion that it is forbidden. There are *fiqh* opinions [opinions about law] saying that there is space not only for percussion instruments but also for all instruments within the framework of Islam. But you will never find one scholar who says that all music is *halal*, there are always conditions. For example, the content of the singing, or the type of music being played must remain in agreement with Islamic ethics and not bring about an attitude which contradicts Islam.

Ramadan leaves it up to the individual to decide as to his conscience whether a particular type of music is acceptable or not. But what he does say is important is that Islamic schools should be educating their children to take a greater role in the society in which they live, and that by teaching music it is possible to advance this:

> If you want to build a selective approach, or a critical mind, it is through education, it is not through ignorance. This is why music education is very important because it builds a mindset, an attitude towards music which is not 'everything is bad', which is not 'everything is right', but is a selective approach which is needed today in the West. Music education is very important and we have to think about it within all these parameters and respect different opinions. We need to learn about it and we need to teach about it. We need to teach about music in order to build a critical, selective and creative mind.

5. REFLECTING ON ASPECTS OF DRAMA

Drama has its own particular set of issues with the representation of other people often seen as unacceptable. Muslim film stars have been known to take Hindu names in order to disguise their Muslimness. al-Faruqi (1989), wrote: 'Following Islam, figural representation was regarded by Muslims as something unbecoming and undesirable, indeed prohibited.' Along with representing figures in pictures he was also talking about representing other people in drama. The reasoning behind this is often ascribed to the belief that to represent people is to try to copy what God has made. From my point of view, and indeed that of many Muslims, that view fails to see the role of God in giving us creative minds that can engage in imagination.

Zuhra (1996), talking about drama education in Malaysia, gave three reasons why drama education is as essential to Muslims as to any other culture, first:

> Muslim students, like others, need symbolic play in their lives, to aesthetically express the 'inexpressible' as well as the intellectually comprehensible. They need an *active* means of critically, constructively and imaginatively engaging with their environment (p. 14).

The second point she makes is that since 'the world exists to be known' (p. 14), it is better, from an Islamic point of view, if drama can take place in an intercultural and international setting so that different cultures can work together. This is something that in our schools we are able to supply. But how many of us make the most of this situation? Her third point is that we need not only to encourage drama in the classroom setting but also as it evolves amongst the students in extra curricular activities and in drama outside of school altogether. Further, she writes:

> In addition we also need to see that drama education reaches those students who would neglect, shun or obstruct the arts through their own misunderstandings and misperceptions . . . we need to find ways of exposing all students to the inherent value of art, as well as to provide them with socially-acceptable means of critiquing specific artistic productions. In this way we can help them become tolerant and responsible members of their societies (p. 14).

One of the ways that she suggests that Muslim students could be more involved in drama is by using ideas from Islamic cultural traditions. Here we could run into difficulties in schools if we do not select our materials carefully. Many of the practices that appear in Muslim societies would not be acceptable to the more orthodox Muslims. For example, many Muslims watch Hindi musicals but expecting all Muslim girls to be happy to replicate this style with its sexually explicit movements would cause offence, especially in school. Similarly I have observed a teacher using a version of *Ali Baba and the Forty Thieves* where the comic characters were represented by women in burqas. Taking aspects of Muslim costume and ridiculing it is not going to lead to greater harmony. An example of Muslim drama that would be more readily acceptable is the type presented by the Khayaal Theatre Company. Khayaal, meaning 'imagination' in Arabic and Persian, presents 'wisdom-oriented entertainment' (2004). Their presentations take the form of short dramas that are similar to fables in that they have a moral. Another form of drama that has a long tradition in the Islamic world is that of story-telling, which is now becoming increasingly popular in the UK as well. This could easily be incorporated into drama lessons. The storyteller tells his story in order to elicit participation from the audience, and it is this sense of participation that is also different from how much of western performance practice is experienced.

But what of the majority of schools in the UK that have no Muslim pupils? Reflection on the teaching of performing arts in order to try to encourage better understanding of all world cultures is just as important. An initiative in Canada called 'Towards Understanding: Moving beyond Racism and Islamophobia' developed by MENTORS (*Muslim Educational Network, Training and Outreach Service*), funded by the Ministry of Canadian Heritage Multicultural Program, is using drama to challenge stereotypes. For example, students are shown an image of a young woman wearing hijab with a caption that reads: 'If you were a movie producer, how would you cast her in a role?' Responses from children as young as 8 years old invariably cast her as a 'terrorist', 'foreigner', or someone 'escaping from her husband'. She is acknowledged as a marginal player, not someone featured in a dominant or starring role. She is in fact the captain of a Muslim women's soccer team in the UK (Zine, 2004, p. 117).

6. REFLECTION IN PRACTICE

Many of the ideas that I have developed during my years of researching and reflecting on the teaching of music to Muslims have been included in an article I wrote for the National Association of Music Educators (Harris, 2000), but how can we go about reflecting in a way that will improve our understanding of Islam, particularly in relation to the arts? First of all we must look to ourselves. What are we teaching? How are we teaching it? And what are our underlying ideologies? Secondly, we must look to the pupils we are teaching; they are the ones who are living in a society that most of them feel is against them. Thirdly, we must gain as much understanding as possible about Islam from as many different sources as possible. A useful question to ask is 'Am I dealing with all my pupils as sensitively as I can?' Reflective practice 'demands a considerable investment over the course of a career both of individuals and their employers' (Day, 1999, p. 217).

> Some modes of reflection . . . may pose challenges to the efficacy of closely held beliefs, values or practices, and teachers may not always wish to confront these, or lack the practical and appropriate moral support to begin the process of change (ibid., p. 227).

This implies that if reflection is to be truly holistic it may be necessary to engage with mentors or managers who also have a role in facilitating the reflecting process. It is not just teachers who engage in the act of reflection; in our interdependent community Muslims too realize that they need to reflect on their lifestyle. Badawi (1996) wrote:

> It is imperative to formulate regulations that help Muslims live in accordance with the *sharia* (Islamic law) within a non-Islamic society, while

at the same time being citizens of that country . . . there is absolutely no need to place those Muslims who are learning music . . . outside the pale (pp. 18 and 24).

REFERENCES

Abbas, T. (2004). After 9/11: British South Asian Muslims, Islamophobia, multiculturalism, and the State. *American Journal of Islamic Social Studies*, 21(3), 26–38.

Ahmed, A.S. (1994). Muslim education and the impact of the Western mass media. *Muslim Education Quarterly*, 11(3), 16–33.

al Faruqi, I.R. (1989). Figurative representation and drama: their prohibition and transfiguration in Islamic art. *Islamic Art: Common Principles and Themes*, Damascus (following on from the International Symposium of this name in Istanbul 1983).

Allen, C. (2004). Justifying Islamophobia: a post-9/11 consideration of the European Union and British contexts. *American Journal of Islamic Social Studies*, 21(3), 1–25.

Badawi, Z. (1996). Notes of contention and jurisprudence in the nature of music. *'Much Ado About Music' Proceedings of the Conference on Islam and Music*. Association of Muslim Researchers.

British National Party. (2001). *The Truth about I.S.L.A.M.* Retrieved 1 January 2002, from http://www.bup.org.uk.

British National Party. (2002). *A Threat to Us All* (distributed to media).

Bunting, M. (2004, November 30). Young, Muslim and British. *The Guardian*.

Day, C. (1999). Researching teaching through reflective practice. In J. Loughran (Ed.), *Researching Teaching* (pp. 215–232). UK: Falmer Press.

European Monitoring Centre on Racism and Xenophobia. (2002). *Summary Report on Islamophobia in the EU after 11th September 2001*. Vienna: European Monitoring Centre on Racism and Xenophobia.

Green, L. (2001). *How Popular Musicians Learn: A Way Ahead for Music Education*. Burlington, VT: Ashgate, Aldershot Hants.

Harris, D. (2000). Some practical considerations for teaching music to Muslims. *National Association of Music Educators Journal*, 5(1), 27–31.

Harris, D. (2002). Tolerance is no longer enough. *Finnish Journal of Music Education*, 6(2), 9–21.

Hussain (1999). Interview with Dr. D. Harris 17th November.

Ramadan, T. (2002). The importance of culture and context in the question of music and Islam. *Music Education for Muslims Conference*, School of Oriental and African Arts, London University.

Renzetti, C.M. and Lee, R.M. (eds) (1993). *Researching Sensitive Topics*. UK: Sage.

Renzetti, C.M. and Lee, R.M. (2000). *Researching Sensitive Topics*. UK: Sage.

Roper, B. and Davis, D. (2000). Howard Gardner: knowledge, learning and development in drama and arts education. *Research in Drama Education*, 5(2), 217–234.

Rushdie, S. (1998). *The Satanic Verses*. London: Vintage.

Stone, R. (2004). *Islamophobia: Issues, Challenges and Action: A Report by the Commission on British Muslims and Islamophobia*. UK: Trentham Books.

Zine, J. (2004). Anti-Islamophobia education as transformative pedagogy: reflections from the educational frontlines. *American Journal of Islamic Social Studies*, 21(3), 110–119.

Zuhra, N. (1996). Drama education in an international Islamic setting. *Muslim Education Quarterly*, 13(3), 4–18.

MARY HILTON

4. REFLECTIVE CREATIVITY

Reforming the Arts Curriculum for the Information Age

Almost more than acts of creativity in education the act of reflection holds within itself seeds of change and transformation. As Donald Schön (1991) has pointed out, by exploring the patterns of spontaneous activity that make up practice, and believing there is an underlying sense to be discovered, teachers are led to reflect on their own understandings and the theoretical bases of their actions. Reflective practice in school or workplace that starts with the smallest activity, simply a teacher or student turning back to themselves to ask 'why did I do that?' is a moment that can grow, generating inquiry that spreads wider than the individual and further than the classroom or school. Perhaps most importantly however, the act of reflection frames and rehearses a habit of mind, a recurring practice which can then be modelled and shared with pupils through conversation, giving young people the intellectual structure to think and speak reflexively about their lives and their learning.

In this chapter I have chosen to focus on this seminal aspect of reflective practice. I hope to promote the idea of emancipatory and creative reflection through conversation by revisiting and re inscribing its necessary place in a reformed arts curriculum. My argument is that reflective conversation, here understood as questioning discourse energised by shared experience between teachers and pupils, should not be simply added to processes of assessment but should be reinstated as part of a cycle of creativity and reflection necessary in arts education, for, in a fundamental sense, reflective conversation is what artists practise everyday. By its very nature artistic production in all media questions and discusses the world. Work in the arts forms and is informed by these cerebral conversations, by the dialogues with the self and others that inhere within the creative process itself. Art *requires* reflective discussion to create and shape meaning. Interrogating the experiential base of an individual or group artistic creation, discussing as equal partners in a creative enterprise the ideas and systems of meaning that have been used or transformed, thinking together about the ways that creativity works to enrich experience, relationships, and knowledge within school are the deepest and surely the most transformative aspects of reflection. Yet how much space and opportunity for this deeper reflection on meaning making is currently available within the confines of school curricula? Through examining the large picture of the arts curriculum as it is presently constructed in England and observing some of its overarching constraints, I suggest ways of opening up possibilities for deeper engagement through reflective conversation within the active processes of creativity. In this I centre my argument for the reform of the curriculum on the kind of reflective exchange that I believe must happen between teachers and young artists to achieve depth and meaning in teaching and learning in the arts, particularly

P. Burnard and S. Hennessy (eds.), *Reflective Practice in Arts Education,* 33–44.

with the extraordinary possibilities and challenges opened up by the technologies of the new information age.

1. THE BIG PICTURE: PRESSURES FROM WITHOUT

The increasing forces of globalisation which promote the power of trans-national companies at the expense of nation states not only relate to the level of world trade and the 'virtual economy' or electronic flow of capital, but also to labour and production, information, ecology, legal and administrative systems, culture and civil society (Osler and Vincent, 2002). What is clear is that globalisation has ushered in an 'information age', a phenomenon that has replaced the 'industrial age'. Now manual work is done by computerised machines and routine clerical work is shrunk by information technology. These changes from an industrial to an informational mode of development have created new demands on the workforce and hence on education. Indeed the world-wide web, digital technology, and the growth of moving image as a major communicative form, have transformed the individual's relationship to information, and, as I will argue here, to creativity and the use of the imagination.

In fact globalisation in the information age has left educators with a number of problems and paradoxes. Although there are common factors at work in many countries, change still takes place within the traditional political and cultural framework of the different nation states, which has meant a relentless growth of centralised state power over education in America, Australia and most European countries. Despite a new language of 'choice' the drive to harness schooling to the needs of their economies has led to a fresh drive by national governments across the Western world to control education through the introduction of performance indicators, accountability and measurement. It has also meant a renewed impetus towards framing and fixing 'national' values through the arts and humanities; a narrowing of curriculum focus on specific works of art and stories delivered through chosen literature, history texts, and arts practices. Yet, paradoxically, although set curricula and assessment have increased the mechanical and functional demands of teachers' work, there is an increased understanding of the importance of their own creative pedagogies in the mediation of change in response to the demands of the information-based economy (Skilton-Sylvester, 2003). Also a newly perceived need has arisen from a range of ideological quarters for creativity and flexibility in schools to mirror those needed at all levels in the new economic structures. While on the one hand progressively minded teachers have always valued creativity, on the other hand the essential flexibility towards lifestyle that structures capitalism's 'planned obsolescence', where people are continuously tempted to make and to buy the new, has led to a fresh demand for imaginative ideas in both the production and consumption of goods from the world's most conservative capitalists. Politicians from across the whole ideological spectrum now believe that creativity must be engendered in all the young. Certainly in Britain 'creativity' is being sought after in a number of new curriculum initiatives (NACCCE, 1999; Bayliss et al., 2001, 2003; QCA, 2002), all underpinned by a complex mix of contradictory economic and democratic ideals.

Thus in the twenty-first century paradoxical forces now shape new, internationally shared, imperatives for educators to reform the school curriculum, particularly in the arts. Here in important ways they are building on a long tradition of imaginative protest. In Britain the arts curriculum in state schools, often reduced to mechanical exercises in drawing or instrument learning, has been a focus of dispute since the Second World War. Voices such as Herbert Read's have insisted that 'the secret of our collective ills is to be traced to the suppression of spontaneous creative ability in the individual' (Read, 1958, p. 201). Throughout the second half of the twentieth century many art educators strove to restructure the curriculum to allow work by pupils in the arts to enrich the narrow functionalism of purely academic criteria. As the report by the Gulbenkian Foundation argued in 1986, 'our concern is broader—with the development of those basic human qualities and capabilities—including the power of creative insight and activity and a concern with relationships and questions of value, which give rise to the arts in the first place' (Robinson, 1986, p. 24). Arguments over the school curriculum, particularly those pertaining to the primary years, have long focused on the need to allow space and scope for the development of individual creativity, and of mediating critical reflection on that process shared with teachers. In the twenty-first century, in the new climate of accountability and learning objectives, of targets and rising disciplinary and voluntary exclusion, these battles for the imaginative spirits of pupils, for space and respect for creative learning and reflective discussion now need to be fought over again, but in a new, very different, context.

2. THE CURRENT SCENE

Practicing teachers will surely remember this first decade of the new millennium as the time when the new technologies began to bite in the world of education. Although digital technology has been quietly shifting the nature of teaching and learning for some time, it is now that we can step back from everyday life in classrooms across the western world and see a large scale shift taking place in the ways that human beings communicate, create, and collide—in other words in the arts. This has already resulted in an extraordinary mixing of forms. Older hierarchies and formalities in the arts are giving way to new post-modern heterogeneity and re-conceptualisation. As global corporate culture strives to establish a product-driven 'culture of the new' where nuance, pastiche, changes in product design, or textual inflection are fundamental to the perpetual construction of audiences and markets, imaginative and affective uses of the new technologies support a mixing and blurring of cultural forms. As one scholar observes:

> It is increasingly hard to tell the difference between grunge and folk, between funk and rap. The airwaves are filled with hybrid cultural forms: from infotainment to docudramas, from "hard copy" to the written soundbites of *USA Today*, from Aboriginal Reggae to Californian Ice Hockey (Luke, 1994, p. viii).

Yet this dynamic, creative, and corrosive phenomenon, everywhere apparent, makes a spectacular contrast to national curricula of very literal, mono-cultural, and subject-specific design. Currently in England, in the effort to control education through targets and accountability, the National Curriculum Orders (DfEE, 2000) provides the most detailed, instrumental, and narrowly-defined list of subjects and skills perhaps ever conceived, all of which enclose and formalise 'school learning' even for the youngest children. For many years infant education in Britain has been conceived as holistic, focused on children's direct experience of the material world. Nevertheless from 1988, as volumes of curriculum documentation arrived in British primary schools and teacher accountability became ever more detailed and assessment-led, the arts went into an eclipse. The time and space needed to create works of art, and most importantly to reflect in all the arts, has diminished and become undervalued. Emphasis on subject boundaries, skills, and assessment have meant that drawing, painting, dancing, performing, and playing music, instead of flowing across the time and spaces of the school day are now prescriptively subordinated to a traditional subject taxonomy. At the same time the new technologies, while given a new and important status in *functional* terms, have been completely ignored in *aesthetic* fields. Children's media experience, for example, is invisible in the English national curriculum. There is almost no recognition that their lives are given aesthetic depth and richness through television, video, computer games, art programs, through home-based performance and music from electronic sources, and through multimedia texts and authoring now available to play with. Nor is there any sense that these experiences need to be reflected upon, interrogated, or used as the basis for new forms of expression.

Yet this situation has given rise to a fascinating culture of independence amongst even the youngest children. New technologies allow an extraordinary freedom to achieve, to mix, overlap and subvert cultural forms. The human instincts to create, and to play, runs through our society at all levels, even at the most prestigious where the processes of textual hybridisation are accelerating under fast capitalism and a globalised economy. With children and their teachers there is now evidence that, while the arts no longer hold their rightful place at the heart of the curriculum, around the edges of children's learning there is a new kind of play that has been allowed and validated by their extraordinary creative competence with multi-media technologies (Buckingham, 1993; Pompe, 1996; Kress, 1997). Here teachers need time and space to reflect. If our young pupils are even more technically competent than we are, moving across the world of visual representation, performance, moving image, and musical composition in ways that almost beggar belief then can we, as Gunther Kress observes, continue to present them with a curriculum that is an insult to their creative imaginations? As he argues:

> Current notions of literacy are so ungenerous, so unreflecting about the real needs of young people in the societies of the next decades that it is essential to advance alternative conceptions, even if they find no official favour (Kress, 1997, p. xx).

How then do we re-conceptualise the curriculum in ways that allow us to understand and respond to the real needs of young people? I am proposing a new cycle of creativity and reflection, one where arts work is stimulated by and grounded in experience, with space and time structured in to the curriculum for reflective conversation. In this way pupils and teachers would develop the habit of questioning the processes by which any art form comes into being through discussing the cultural assumptions and judgements made about its value. Research on the development of 'higher-order' thinking has shown that to achieve rich and thoughtful responses from pupils the focus of discussion must be on ideas and meanings rather than on surface features (Ross, 1986; Raney and Hollands, 2000; Urquhart, 2002). Only with this deeper, shared form of reflective engagement can the cycle of creativity and reflection help to resist new insidious forms of social exclusion engendered by relentless assessment procedures and the narrowing focus of national curricula around separate subjects and measurable skills. How, then, do we go about integrating the arts in both their traditional and their new digital manifestations in ways that promote the impulse to engage in reflective conversation around the production of meaning?

3. EXPERIENCE, DIRECT AND VIRTUAL

In spite of curriculum taxonomies and subject differentiation there is still a powerful tradition in early years education in Britain that the curriculum should be built around the child's direct experience of the material world. Countless teachers and research studies have pointed to the value of immediate sensual experience when generating creative work by young children. Actually collecting, smelling, feeling and observing autumn leaves before writing autumn poetry, for example, enriches the spirit, supports the engagement with meaning in language, and thus elevates the quality of the children's writing. From my own experience when we took the whole primary school of 300 children to the seaside the quality of visual artwork produced across the school in the next few days silenced our potentially critical school governors who had been worried about the educative value of the day out. The imaginative creativity stimulated by the sheer joy of the experience, reflected in the splashings of paint, the use of washes of brilliant colour, the intricate drawings of tiny figures beside the largeness of seascapes was breathtaking. The children of all ages cast aside their inhibitions and joyfully represented their experience of that happy day with a kind of fine carelessness as to artistic rules. Although it appears that they created art through a holistic, cerebral, yet apparently lawless *reprise* of direct experience—only possible in an arts curriculum which valued the nurturing of sensual experience—there was in fact a deep process of reflection taking place. Through sustained mutual respect and shared recollections teachers and children entered into a powerful if understated dialogue about feelings, seeing, recording, patterns and techniques that enabled our young artist pupils to enter into meaning.

In fact as children grow and develop within their culture they become increasingly aware that their knowledge of the world is communicated not only through direct experience, but also through complicated systems of signs and representations. They gather, and are shaped by, experiences that are in themselves representations. In other words alongside their *real* and sensual experiences of the world run complex versions of *virtual* experience. Stories and pictures, for example, provide the growing child with alternative worlds that depend for their verisimilitude and their emotional impact on semiotic conventions, systems of symbol, gesture, and sound. In reading a picture book or watching a film the learner has to have mastered, not simply a series of decoding skills, but an understanding of the symbolic nature of different systems of meaning, and in order to make sense of, and to communicate with, different systems of meaning learners must use the symbolic materials to construct ideas for themselves. It is here that in England the current national curriculum for the arts is too subject bound and skills based. While *direct* experience of the material world can be creatively recapitulated and reflected upon through formally categorised lists of materials, skills and techniques, *virtual* experience cannot be satisfactorily described. For example the descriptions of reading matter, an attempt to list important virtual experiences through literature, is both too prescriptive and yet too expansive, to be of much relevance in a multi-modal world. Many of the 'classic' books that teachers of literature and curriculum architects would see as essential print texts are now widely encountered, and far more popular, as moving image texts. Other rich and meaningful stories that pupils enjoy are entirely pictorial, thus disqualified from the literature curriculum altogether. Popular culture narratives created and represented in animation and live action, moving image, and comic book formats, are also absent, leaving pupils' media engagement to one side (Pompe, 1996). How can pupils and teachers engage in vital reflective conversation when they don't share the same experiences? What we need is an arts curriculum that provides not only a grounding of creativity and reflection in *real* experience but also a new categorisation of *virtual* experience. We need arts categories which span semiotic systems in the multiple ways that communicative technologies now function in our culture, and which would allow, indeed necessitate, processes of shared reflection to take place.

4. VIRTUAL EXPERIENCE AND GENRE THEORY

I believe that a good place to begin to reflect on the ways the arts curriculum could be reformed to lead to deeper processes of engagement and reflection, is to examine once again the much-maligned notion of 'genre'. Recent research work on genre has reshaped the rather mechanical texture of Australian 'genre pedagogy' which assumed that genre is merely a set of rules or conventions evident only at the level of the text. The belief was that these rules could be extracted, described, and taught as formal regularities of 'text types' such as the poem, the essay, or the advertisement and so on. Hence there has been an acceptance in curricula terms that genre 'rules' need to be taught, but not reflected upon, or transformed. It is not surprising that educators have turned away from genre theory. In its old rule-bound form, as Myra Barrs has declared, genre leads to the authoritarian and arid teaching of textual conventions (Barrs, 1994).

However a significant group of new rhetoricians argue persuasively that genre should be re-conceptualised as a set of textual features that can only be understood in terms of specific sets of social communicative practices. It is only in examining, and in the case of teachers and pupils in school, *re-enacting* these practices that it is possible to discover and transform the organising principles through which a text—by this I mean a work of art, whether it be print, music, performance, visual image, moving image or multi modal, 'speaks' to its audience (Freedman and Medway, 1994). In other words when we reflect on a revitalised significance of the arts in school and the capacity they offer for deep reflection on the self and on the world, we need to consider the arts curriculum in terms of shared enactments of genre. For if the arts depend for their meaning on different sets of social and communicative practices then it is those practices which the curriculum should aim to explore, and creatively to transform. This is not to say that there are no longer 'pure' disciplines such as history, mathematics, or science, but that they too, to a large extent, are dependent on the enactment of special kinds of communicative practices for their transmission. History, for example, depends on the telling of stories and personal accounts, on the persuasive presentation of argument and evidence, science depends on laboratories and all the social and rhetorical practices associated with experimentation. Children playing at being scientists are deeply aware from watching film and television of the self-fashioning apparatus of laboratory scientists, including their gestures, clothing, and speech forms. With the arts in their current state of flux in and out of school and their now powerful relation to new technology, 'genre' in its new active configuration provides an overarching organising principle that inherently offers opportunity for creative transformation through enactment, production, and most importantly through processes of shared reflection.

Thus, the vital aspect of a new social and active conceptualisation of genre is the facility it provides for getting to the heart of a communicative form, for examining in depth and playing with the origins of its formal conventions and rules. Genre allows an active participation in the shared communicative practices that create and sustain its meaning and existence. Take, for example, a powerful social communicative form in our society, the genre of 'news'. News is a cultural artefact that uses a variety of communicative conventions which help us to recognise it immediately, and most importantly one that moves elegantly and coherently across semiotic systems. We recognise news information in a wide variety of media, print, sound and moving image, without any great trouble in transposing the ways that meaning is created. This is because recognition, and understanding, depends on a set of familiar and coherent cultural and communicative practices. Clearly 'news' has recognizable textual rules of production, but they are symbiotically related to and dependent upon these conventional practices. For example someone authoritatively 'reports' the news. This reporter is outside the factual basis of the report creating a 'reality effect' which frames its truth status. In television broadcasting, in a further elaboration of this embodied objectivity, a news-reader turns to an 'on the spot' reporter for the creation of similitude. However, a news broadcast always takes up a set amount of allotted time, so that different items are not naturally played out in time but are prioritised according to the overarching aesthetic of the broadcasting agency or publisher. Thus despite the apparently spontaneously generated verisimilitude of news, the social practices of its production and broadcasting form a highly-constructed cultural artefact. Most teachers appreciate that if they wish young pupils to get to the heart of the ways meanings are created in this genre then it is necessary for them to enact the cultural and representational practices involved for themselves. To teach 'news' genre involves the recreation of the practices involved: the setting up of newsrooms, the collecting, editing and representing of reported news in ways which creatively rehearse the real. Most importantly, through working actively within a genre form, teachers and students can become partners in a shared reflection on experience.

Here we can see that there are significant communicative and representational practices currently absent from the school curriculum that could become new points of integration and active reflection in a reformed arts curriculum. The incorporation of virtual experience through a focus on the communicative practices that create and sustain genre, could be a basis for a revitalised arts curriculum that naturally opens itself to reflective conversation, and therefore to transformation, by pupils and their teachers. To offer another example, the construction of reality effects across semiotic systems—or 'social realism' to give it a genre title—could provide another integrating series of enactments. Children in schools across the world go home to watch one or more daily soap operas, a virtual experience of social realism that carries aesthetic, moral and representational learning, and ambiguities, yet is completely invisible as such in the English national curriculum. The way a local community is constructed and represented symbolically with all the moral dilemmas and conflicts between classes, groups and ages is of enormous relevance and interest to young people in a global world. Representations of the 'real' such as families, streets, the workaday world of the local and familiar, cluster around the key social and communicative practices of the genre of social realism. Here, the active production of a realist text, such as a soap opera or local chronicle, would not only allow creative engagement with a major strand of popular culture, but would open up a variety of art forms, including photography, literature, film, music, and performance, to a new synthesis. In the active participation that genre enactment demands, teachers can become emancipated from their roles as authority figures, engaging in creativity and reflection as knowledgeable participants.

To take another example, at the other end of this particular spectrum of virtual experiences lie the fantasy genres. The multiple layers of fantasy production, which again run across technologies and domains, are rich with potential for integration of the arts. Fantasy can be induced and embodied, carried in the head and imaginatively drawn out in music, dance, poetry, puppetry, imagery and moving image. Pupils of all ages can create fantasy inside a curriculum that allows space, time and respect. Here again the teaching of 'genre' is not a question of technical text description with associated rules, but a more generous entering into of the possibilities allowed and sustained by the key social and communicative practices of fantasy production. This means play, resources, and above all time, for young producers of texts and artefacts.

5. EXPERIENCE AND REFLECTION

There are many more genres to be explored in their social, performative, and creative richness through practice and transformation. Is this concentration on genre as an organising principle in danger of subordinating the arts curriculum to language, or more intensely to isolating individual work at the computer? Certainly direct experience, alongside virtual experience, must remain as vital stimulus of creative expression in all pupils and a central set of themes and categories in the arts curriculum. Hearing the music, seeing the sea, tasting the air, feeling the sun, waking in the night, moulding the clay, are time-honoured sense experiences upon which creative expression has traditionally been, and still should be, based. Here we still have much to learn from early years practice. As two inspired nursery teachers write:

> Much of the daily work is sensory: the children record things in the brain through smell and touch as well as through ears and eyes. We believe that the hands are the cutting edge of the mind and that by purposely engaging all our senses, we internalise the learning and start to make sense of it: it is remembered throughout the body. For instance we tap into the emotions of smell at Epiphany, when we focus on frankincense and myrrh; when we cook chutney and make jam; when we bake bread; when we stand under an apple tree in spring and are showered with blossom; when we work with nosegays of herbs in our history programme; when we light bonfires in the autumn; when we burn incense for Divali (Rowe and Humphries, 2001, p. 162).

In his fascinating critique of post-modernity and his damming indictment of global consumer culture, *Against the Flow*, Peter Abbs (2003) attempts to put back into the arts in schools a sense of spirituality. In this vital endeavour the direct, sensual experience of the natural world still has power to refresh and awaken the ethical and aesthetic energies necessary to confront the growing vacuity of much contemporary culture.

But in the new information age we need also to offer an arts curriculum that not only aims to awaken spirituality through direct contact and celebration of the natural world, but one that is prepared to accept the dangers of the new ironic post-modern sensibility and attempts to integrate the rich variety of new virtual experiences that all pupils gather, enjoy, and are deeply engaged with, usually outside school. Genre in its new, open and social form of categorisation could provide an exciting practice-based synthesis that uses the new technologies creatively and democratically in schools, and being present within most forms of meaning-making, would demand and support the processes of reflective conversation. Multi-media production, because of its hybridity as a cultural form naturally draws across curriculum subjects, allowing formal and critical theories of artistic understanding of the way different media construct, inform and transform meaning to bleed into any discipline (Sinker, 2000, p. 213). In the face of this powerful technological and aesthetic hybridity, if we wish to reform the arts curriculum around a deep cycle of creativity and reflection that touches and engages our pupils, then it must be organised under larger epistemological categories than subjects, skills, or ‘competences’.

6. REFLECTION AND TRANSFORMATION

In reflecting upon the arts curriculum I have suggested a vital duality that should, I believe, provide the overarching categories of a reformed and integrated arts curriculum. Rather than being subject, or skills specific, as the English National Curriculum is at this historical moment, it needs to be reconstructed around wide-based themes and genres that are designed to draw on both the real and the virtual experiences of pupils, allowing them the imaginative space and support to create and then to engage in shared reflection on their own creativity. This reconstruction would allow integration of the new technologies with traditional art mediums, and of pupils' experiences of the natural and material world with literature and print texts, the latter hitherto left out of the creative arts. Here reflective conversations woven in and through artistic production that has its roots in experience and seeks to transform meaning, rather than teachers' summative evaluations simply focussed on skills or surface features, can change the shape of shared knowledge, generating deeper understandings of the creative process for teachers and young artists alike.

REFERENCES

Abbs, P. (2003). *Against the Flow*. London: RoutledgeFalmer.

Barrs, M. (1994). Genre theory: What's it all about? In B. Stierer and J. Maybin (Eds.), *Language Literacy and Learning in Educational Practice* (pp. 248–258). Milton Keynes: Multi-Lingual Matters Ltd.

Bayliss, V., Brown, J. and James, L. (2001). *Redefining the Curriculum*. London: The Royal Society for the encouragement of Arts, Manufactures and Commerce.

Bayliss, V. (2003). *Opening Minds: Taking Stock*. London: The Royal Society for the encouragement of Arts, Manufactures and Commerce.

Buckingham, D. (1993). Just playing games. *English and Media Magazine*, 28, 20–25.

Department of Education and Employment; Qualifications and Curriculum Authority. (2000). *National Curriculum: Key Stages 1 and 2. National Curriculum: Key Stages 3 and 4.*London: DfEE and QCA.

Freedman, A. and Medway, P. (Eds.). (1994). *Genre and the New Rhetoric*. London: Taylor and Francis.

Kress, G. (1997). *Before Writing: Rethinking the Paths to Literacy*. London: Routledge.

Luke, A. (1994). Series Editors Preface. In A. Freedman and P Medway (Eds.), *Genre and the New Rhetoric* (pp. vii–xi). London: Taylor and Francis.

National Advisory Committee on Creative and Cultural Education (NACCCE). (1999). *All Our Futures: Creativity, Culture and Education*. London: Department for Education and Employment (DfEE) and Department for Culture, Media and Sport (DCMS).

Osler, A. and Vincent, K. (2002). *Citizenship and the Challenge of Global Education*. Stoke on Trent: Trentham Books.

Pompe, C. (1996). 'But they're pink!'—'who cares?': popular culture in the primary years. In M. Hilton (Ed.), *Potent Fictions: Children's Literacy and the Challenge of Popular Culture* (pp. 92–129). London: Routledge.

Qualifications and Curriculum Agency. (2002). *Creativity: Find it, Promote it*. London: QCA.

Read, H. (1958). *Education Through Art*. London: Faber and Faber.

Raney, K. and Hollands, H. (2000). Art education and talk: from modernist silence to postmodern chatter. In J. Sefton-Green and R. Sinker (Eds.), *Evaluating Creativity: Making and Learning by Young People* (pp. 16–43). London: Routledge.

Robinson, K. (Ed.). (1986). *The Arts in Schools: Principles, Practice and Provision*, London: Calouste Gulbenkian Foundation, Oyez Press Ltd.

Rowe, S. and Humphries, S. (2001). Creating a Climate for Learning. In A. Craft, B. Jeffrey and M. Leibling (Eds.), *Creativity in Education* (pp. 159–175). London: Continuum.

Ross, M. (1986). *Assessment in Arts Education*. London: Pergamon Press.

Schön, D.A. (Ed.). (1991). *The Reflective Turn: Case Studies in and on Educational Practice.* New York: Colombia University, Teachers College Press.

Sinker, R. (2000). Making multimedia: evaluating young people's creative multimedia production. In J. Sefton-Green and R. Sinker (Eds.), *Evaluating Creativity: Making and Learning by Young People* (pp. 187–215). London: Routledge.

Skilton-Sylvester, P. (2003). Less like a robot: a comparison of change in an inner-city school and a Fortune 500 company. *American Educational Research Journal*, 40(1), 3–43.

Urquhart, I. (2002). Beyond the literal: deferential or inferential reading? *English in Education*, 36(2), 18–31.

LIANE HENTSCHKE AND LUCIANA DEL BEN

5 TEACHING ARTS AS REFLECTIVE PRACTICE

1. INTRODUCTION

The concept of teaching as a reflective activity is, according to Zeichner (1994), the recognition that teachers have their own theories and are able to generate knowledge about teaching. We recognise teachers' capacity for making judgements; reflecting and making decisions; and having ideas, beliefs, knowledge and experiences as the main starting point for their practice. The importance given to teachers, their actions and thoughts gave origin to a body of research on teacher thinking (Day et al., 1990; Calgren et al., 1994; Gimeno Sacristán, 1998). This body of research, and the literature derived from it, recognises teachers as the agents of their own educational actions. It views teachers as reflective professionals: practitioners who possess a specific kind of knowledge, which can serve as a basis for teaching. Furthermore, research on teacher education has shown the importance of establishing a dialogue between theory and practice as a way of understanding how teachers' knowledge is constructed and used, and how teachers' own beliefs influence the way they conceive and act in their profession (Conway, 2001; Krueger, 2001; Conkling and Henry, 2002).

But what does it mean to be reflective? According to Marcelo García (1995), the concept of reflection has been used in different contexts and with different meanings. Zeichner, in a chapter published in 1994, states that 'in the last decade, the slogans of "reflective teaching", [as well as its correlated slogans of] "action research," "research-based" and "inquiry-oriented" teacher education have been embraced by both teacher educators and educational researchers throughout the world' (Zeichner, 1994, p. 9). But Zeichner (ibid., p. 18) also points to the fact that:

> all teachers are reflective in some sense. There is no such thing as an unreflective teacher. We need to move beyond the uncritical celebration of teacher reflection and making the tacit explicit, and become interested in more complex questions than whether teachers are reflective or not. We need to focus our attention on what kind of reflection teachers are engaging in, on what it is teachers are reflecting about, and on how they are going about it.

In order to understand the complexity of this process, and contribute to discussion in the field of arts education, we present and discuss the results of a research with primary music teachers carried out in Porto Alegre, Brazil. Our focus will be on the quality or levels of teachers' reflection, especially on what sustains their reflective processes about school music education. The research consisted of a multicase study

P. Burnard and S. Hennessy (eds.), *Reflective Practice in Arts Education*, 45–54.

with three female primary music teachers, aged from 27 to 33. The aim was to investigate how primary music teachers' conceptions and actions inform their teaching practices at primary schools. It also aimed to understand how teachers construct their everyday practices and reflect upon them. Data collection involved observation of a sequence of lessons, semi-structured interviews with the teacher, and analysis of pertinent documents.

The theoretical perspective chosen to guide this work came from the body of research on teachers' thinking combined with the social phenomenology of Schutz (1973, 1976, 1979). Phenomenological approaches search for the conceptual world of the subjects in order to understand how and what kinds of meanings people attribute to phenomena and their interactions in everyday life. The social phenomenology of Schutz focuses on the ways people perceive and make sense of social phenomena. According to Schutz (1973, p. 5), 'all our knowledge of the world, in common-sense as well as in scientific thinking, involves constructs, that is, a set of abstractions, generalizations, formalizations, idealizations specific to the respective level of thought organization.' Our experience in the world is based upon these constructs. What we grasp of reality is the result of the selective and interpretative activity of human beings, based upon our previous experiences of the world and our stock of knowledge at hand.

In the process of analysis we tried to identify the fundamental constructs of each teacher's stock of knowledge (Schutz, 1973), such as their ideas about the nature of music and their general, and specifically musical, pedagogical precepts. We also identified the ways in which teachers' constructs are elaborated and how these orient teachers' reflections on their own work. In short, our data will reveal that, together, teachers' constructs constitute interpretative frames that sustain their actions as well as their reflective processes upon their practices. These interpretative frames are constructed from practice and to practice, as a dialectical process which has relevance to all teachers, particularly teachers involved in arts education. They are also permeated by personal meanings as well as derived from teachers' social setting. We will show later that, although an interpretative frame guides teachers' action and reflection, it is not free of internal contradictions or inconsistencies. Finally, we will discuss that arts teachers need to mobilise different levels of reflection in order to inform their own practices.

2. WAYS IN WHICH TEACHERS' ACTION AND REFLECTION ARE SUSTAINED: CONSTRUCTS AND INTERPRETATIVE FRAMES

Teachers' conceptions of education and their actions make sense and acquire coherence when envisaged as a whole that is guided by an interpretative frame (Schutz, 1973), from which teachers base and reflect upon their work. The existence of an interpretative frame suggests that teachers, even if implicitly, have a theory of education, from which they think about their own work and sustain or modify their conceptions and actions. Even if inconsistent, the interpretative frame of teachers is relevant, because it allows us to understand how teachers attribute meaning to and sustain their everyday practice of teaching. It is based on the constructs of their interpretative frames that teachers assume positions and make choices and decisions: they plan their classes; select the repertoire to be worked; define activities to be carried out with their students; set objectives; observe and interpret the actions and the discourse of their students; change their plans and objectives; identify strategies in order to overcome difficulties and needs; and evaluate their own work.

To exemplify this, we bring some excerpts from interviews with one of the teachers we investigated. This teacher stated many times that 'music is a non-verbal language. As such, music becomes a form of expression and thus a form of communication.' When analysing the data, we perceived that the idea of music as a form of communication was a very important one to her. Many of her conceptions and actions acquired meaning and coherence when referred back to this idea, which seemed, therefore, to constitute one of the fundamental constructs of her interpretative frame. From this idea, she reflects on how music education should be developed in school. Based on the construct that music is a form of communication, the teacher states that 'the general aim of music education is to develop a critical person, because he/she will be able to perceive the musical language and to express herself through it.' When conceived as a form of communication, the teacher can see how school music can develop students' abilities to express themselves through a non-verbal language. This conception constitutes one of the rationales presented by her to justify the importance of teaching music in primary schools.

Each construct seems to sustain and give coherence to a group of conceptions and/or actions and to teachers' reflections about teaching music in primary schools. The constructs are directed to the experience and interpretation of the situations that constitute teachers' daily practice as a music teacher. Their primary goal therefore is practical: teach music to a certain group of students, in a specific situation and context (see Schutz, 1979). The pragmatic attitude of the teachers reveals itself through a dialectical relationship between the constructs of their interpretative frame and their everyday practices of teaching. The constructs present a practical character, for they guide the teachers in their experience and interpretation of their daily practices. At the same time, it is from that experience and interpretation that the constructs will be elaborated, re-elaborated, validated, and abandoned and/or transformed by the teachers. Therefore, the constructs constitute a body of knowledge that is both directed to the practice and nurtured by it.

The dialectical relationship that characterises teachers' construction of knowledge has been emphasised by some researchers in the educational field. Elbaz (1981, p. 53), for example, maintains that:

> the teacher's knowledge grows out of, and responds to, specific practical needs; this does not mean that the teacher will necessarily incorporate the most 'practical', rather than theoretical, parts of knowledge. The teacher's practical knowledge is not a compendium of practical advice from other fields, but rather a body of knowledge oriented to a particular practical context.

Teachers' knowledge also presents an experiential character, for it 'grows out of the world of teaching as [the teacher] experiences it; it gives shape to that world, and allow him to function in it' (Elbaz, 1981, p. 58). That does not mean, however, that the teachers' knowledge is absent of theory or that they reject theoretical knowledge. Theoretical knowledge undergoes an evaluation process and later appropriation, thus becoming part of their own stocks of knowledge (see Schutz, 1979). The theories they appropriate themselves are those considered relevant to understanding the world of practice as well as to guiding and illuminating their action in, and their reflections on that world.

Because teachers' interpretative frames are constructed throughout their life, they are permeated by a personal dimension. Teachers' lived experience and the personal meanings attributed to it help them to elaborate their conceptions and actions and to commit themselves to certain constructs and not to others. But this does not mean that teachers' knowledge is constructed only from a personal standpoint, in a kind of social emptiness. According to Schutz's (1973) social phenomenology, both common sense and scientific knowledge are originated and institutionalised through human action, which includes my own actions and others'. The everyday life is lived as an intersubjective world; a world that existed a long time before our birth and is given to our experience and interpretation in an organised way, not only as a concrete and natural world but also as a sociocultural world (Schutz, 1979). According to Schutz (1973, p. 7), 'all interpretation of this world is based on a stock of previous experiences of it, our own or those handed down to us by parents or teachers; these experiences in the form of 'knowledge at hand' function as a scheme of reference'.

In this sense we can understand how one of the teachers we investigated defines the elements that constitute music as a non-verbal language: 'I love [John] Cage's definition brought by [Murray] Schafer in one of his books, which goes more or less like that: music are sounds, sounds around us, being inside or outside the concert halls.'

Inspired by Cage and Schafer, the teacher believes that 'everything that sounds in the environment can be treated as music', and that these ambient sounds constitute the basic elements for students developing their ability 'to perceive the musical language and to express themselves through it'. In this case, the teacher's reflection about what counts as music is not based on a conception created by her, but on that generated by other authors.

This means that the interpretative frame of each teacher derives not only from her own experience and interpretation of the world, but also from the multiple experiences and interpretations lived by others and transmitted to her. That is why Schutz (1973) says that only a very small part of the knowledge of each person is originated from his/her own experience; the greatest part is socially derived. By assuming the intersubjectivity of the world, Schutz 'presupposes cultures, social realities that stand prior to and are independent of individual subjectivities' (Waters, 1994, p. 52). According to these assertions, the teacher operates from practices already constructed. These practices are not given, but rather historically constructed from individual actions. The same happens with the teachers' conceptions. Although they are permeated by personal meanings, 'the thoughts about the educational action are shared, in some way, and nurtured by the culture, the reason why they acquire a radical social character' (Gimeno Sacristán, 1999, p. 101).

In sum, it is from teachers' beliefs and personal experiences, from the interaction with cultural context and from their everyday practice of teaching that teachers construct their interpretative frames, which not only guide the way they conceive and put in action the teaching in schools, but also sustain their reflections on their everyday work.

3. THE VALIDITY OF TEACHERS' INTERPRETATIVE FRAMES: INTERNAL CONTRADICTIONS AND INCONSISTENCIES

Despite the fact that the teachers' interpretative frames guide their work and function as a basis for their reflection on music teaching, these frames are not free of internal contradictions or inconsistencies. This may create some difficulties in the process of valuing teachers' own work and music as a curriculum subject in schools.

For example: the same teacher that based their action and thinking on the construct that conceives music as a form of communication, also states that: 'music is a special language because it has the power to touch the human soul'. Based on the idea of music as a form of communication, she says that in order to learn music students must make music. At the same time, based on the construct that defines music as a special language, she believes that, because music 'involves feelings, personal things and touches the human soul,' she cannot assess students' music making. Her strong belief on music's subjectivity is also revealed in the way she intervenes in her students' learning. She states that 'the student can, for instance, create his/her own treble clef,' rather than abide by notational convention. The student can also 'manipulate the musical instrument in the way he/she wants to do it.' This teacher seems to believe that there are no rights and wrongs in music; everything can be right if so considered by a student or a group of students. But by doing that, it seems that she is not helping her students to broaden and deepen their musical perception and expression, as intended by her on the basis of the construct of music as a form of communication. She seems to have relinquished her interventionary role as a teacher and the main aim of her work, which is to develop students' capacity to communicate through music. In short, the teacher uses different constructs to reflect upon her work and does not seem to be aware of the contradictions between them.

Another inconsistency related to the idea of subjectivity is that, as stated by the teacher, 'music is not like mathematics, which works, for example, with adding and multiplying.' Music, because it is considered a special language, as with all arts specialisms, deals with the emotions, suggesting that the qualities of music making and its learning outcomes depend only on private experiences, individual abilities, perceptions and responses, thus varying from student to student (Swanwick, 1994, p. 13). The subjectivity that the teacher understands to be involved with both music making and its assessment prevents her from defining what can be learned through music making (Swanwick, 1992, p. 164). Similar conceptions were also found among the discourses of the other teachers we interviewed. The above excerpts suggest that teachers do not seem to recognise the collective and shared dimension that also permeates the musical experiences and learning of the students. Therefore they do not define a body of knowledge that would enhance the musical development of their students.

The belief in subjectivity also brought difficulties when teachers were asked to reflect upon the importance of teaching music in the schools. All the teachers say they sustain their work based on a construct that defines music as a specific discipline, a unique subject, therefore different from any other subject of the school curriculum. However, when it comes to advocate the value of music to the outside world, or as part of the school curriculum, teachers normally use arguments that are used to justify any other school subject, i.e., that music can help to develop students' personality, sensitivity, psychomotor skills and reasoning. It is not a matter of questioning the capacity of music to contribute to the development of the personality, sensitivity, body and intellect, but the arguments presented by the teachers suggest that music does not seem to justify itself as a specific school subject, because its values and benefits can be achieved through other school subjects. Music can be seen as something beneficial to the students, but not necessary or fundamental to their education as a whole (Jorgensen, 1994). Teachers' rationale seems to be based on the idea that music education should serve something else and not have an end in itself. In other words, music education should be a means to an end, not specifically musical (Sparshott, 1980). This contradicts the construct that defines music as a unique subject that can contribute to the general development of the students.

When reflecting on the values of music, as with other arts in education, teachers seem to refer back to the subjective dimension of musical learning and experiences that happen inside the classroom. If, as a consequence of the idea of music as a subjective experience, it is not possible to define a body of knowledge to be developed by the student or to assess learning, then music as a curriculum subject is undervalued and loses status within the school. The teachers seem not to be able to explain in theory the needs of practice, and this results in a lack of status for music and its professionals within the school setting. The difficulty teachers have in theoretically explaining or justifying their practice seems related to the quality or the levels of their reflection.

4. LEVELS OF REFLECTION: TEACHERS' OWN INTERPRETATIVE FRAMES AND REFLECTIONS BASED ON THE SCIENTIFIC KNOWLEDGE

Teachers seem not to be aware of the inconsistencies and contradictions in their actions and reflections, because in their daily work they have 'not a theoretical but an eminently practical interest' (Schutz, 1973, p. 208). Their main interest is, above all, to teach their subject matter to certain groups of students in certain contexts, and not to question the constructs that ground and guide their pedagogical practices and their reflections on it.

According to Schutz (1976), constructs can be incoherent because people's interests shift continually throughout their experiences. Furthermore, the constructs are not entirely clear because individuals in their daily lives are only partially interested in general principles that rule their actions, mainly because, in everyday life, our aim is not to question the world but to live in it. This pragmatic attitude makes the teachers search for assumptions they consider good enough to guide their pedagogical practice. In their everyday life, they rely on one or another construct from their stocks of knowledge, as the different situations of their work require. These constructs, according to social phenomenology, are not the result of a rationalisation process or scientific conceptualisation; rather, they emerge in their everyday experience of the world. Therefore, they will not necessarily be logical, clear or consistent (Schutz, 1973, 1976).

Some of the constructs that ground and guide the work and reflection of the teachers constitute themselves in personal beliefs and therefore are thought not to need any evidence. Others are the result of their interactions with the cultural context and consolidated through arts education in general. For example, the idea that music and the arts involve feelings, emotions and sensibility, and therefore are subjective activities can be found in the writings of many authors. The same happens with the conception that the arts are beneficial to the body or to the mind. However, those who sustain these ideas do not always present arguments that justify them (Sparshott, 1980). These notions are sometimes taken as the truth by many teachers and then reproduced with little room for questioning. This seems to occur because, in our everyday life, the world is experienced as something that is given to us, in its historical and cultural forms. By being considered as something given and non-problematic, these forms are simply taken-for-granted (Schutz, 1973, 1979).

Since the inconsistencies and contradictions that exist between constructs do not emerge in the same situation, teachers can remain unaware of these problems (Wagner, 1979). In their daily work, teachers assume a pragmatic attitude, turned to the conception and concretisation of teaching in schools. Thus, they are not motivated to problematise or question the consistency and validity of these forms. That is not to say that teachers do not reflect upon their work. They certainly do, as it was revealed in their responses to the interviews. However they do it based on their own interpretative frames, without questioning its constructs. Thus, the problem seems to be the quality or the level of that reflection. If the constructs are not problematised, they will remain as unquestionable truths and teachers may have difficulties in perceiving the inconsistencies and contradictions that underlie their action and reflection.

The reflection from the teachers' own interpretative frames is a first level of reflection, the one centred on the individual subject. This kind of reflection is very important and necessary, because it makes it possible that teachers live their daily work at schools. However, it can present limitations. In limiting themselves to their own resources and inventions, teachers run the risk of going too slowly to a second level of reflection—the reflection based on scientific knowledge (Gimeno Sacristán, 1999). Searching for this second level of reflection it is not to say that the scientific knowledge is superior to the interpretative frames of the teachers. It only means that scientific knowledge can modify the ways teachers think and act, because it represents specific ways to understand and conceive educational realities (Gimeno Sacristán, 1999).

5. FINAL CONSIDERATIONS AND IMPLICATIONS FOR ARTS EDUCATION IN GENERAL

Although this chapter focused its discussion on research data from music education practices, the methodology, theoretical basis, and data, inferences of this study can be applied to visual arts, drama, and dance. The reflective process of teachers, their conceptions and actions may be similar across the arts.

Considering the dialectical character of teachers' knowledge, we can understand that practice consists of a source of reflection and transformation of the teachers' work. Therefore the experience or gains in classroom, and the knowledge of the reality of schools are conceived as fundamental to preparing teachers for their profession. Teachers emphasised during the interviews that systematic knowledge and theoretical precepts have to do with the world of the classroom; they must be related in some way to teaching practice. In other words, theories or concepts that do not refer to practice do not make sense, because in their daily work teachers' main interest is turned to practice. This suggests the need to rethink the relationship between theory and practice during initial and continuing teacher education. It is important to think that theory and practice nurture each other and therefore cannot be conceived as different domains and independent from each other. Practice is conceived as theory in action and a theory depends on the prior existence of a practice, from which it is constructed and transformed (see Pimenta, 1997). Conceived in this way, theories can become capable of fertilising practice, empowering current and future teachers to carry out their work and reflect upon it, transforming and improving it from the questioning of what is taken-for-granted.

Here a question may be raised: How can we, as teacher educators and researchers in arts education, help teachers to transform their pedagogical practice and the quality of their reflection upon it? (see Gimeno Sacristán, 1999) On a practical basis, when trying to understand and illuminate teachers' work, teacher educators should go further than simply describing their reflections, pointing out their failures or judging their work as adequate or inadequate. We need to analyse the coherence and consistency of their constructs and their interpretative frames, identifying possible constraints of their reflective processes. The constructs and the interpretative frames of teachers, as well as those produced from scientific criteria and procedures, also need to be evaluated according to their capacity to ground and orient arts teaching practices and to serve as a basis for reflection upon these practices.

Scientific knowledge or theoretical precepts are capable of nurturing the pedagogical practice of teachers, to serve as a means of confronting conceptions and actions that configure this practice. But, in themselves, they cannot change the teaching practice, for they are not directly applicable to practice. They should be evaluated by teachers in terms of their relevance and then appropriated or dismissed. They will become part of the stock of knowledge of teachers only if they are able to illuminate, explain or nurture their pedagogical practice and their reflection upon it.

If, as arts educators, we want reflective teachers working in schools, we need to help them relate theory to practice and develop strategies of reflection from the earliest stages of their professional development. In this sense, we should define strategies for initial education that acknowledge the realities of schools and classrooms. One of these strategies could be to give to future teachers the opportunity to observe, analyse and discuss the existing pedagogical practices, as a way to start their reflection process. By observing and reflecting upon the practice of others, students would be stimulated to examine their own conceptions and actions and further, confronting it with the practice of others and with scientific knowledge.

Arts education, as a human and social practice, is constituted by the actions of its participants. Thus the transformation of the pedagogical practice in schools can only occur through the actions of its participants. This points to the need to establish partnerships between researchers, teacher educators and in-service teachers, across the arts. The idea of a partnership reinforces the conception that scientific knowledge in itself cannot transform the existing practices of arts education. But theories and concepts can increase teachers' reflections about the consistency and coherence of their constructs, thus contributing to teachers transforming their own teaching practices. In the same way, from teachers' practices, researchers and teacher educators can analyse the potential of their theories and concepts to illuminate and nurture arts teaching practices. For that to happen, it is necessary to understand the experiences and the knowledge of teachers and assume the reflective character of their work, and from that help them to increase their reflection about their conceptions and actions. The actions and reflections reported here could inspire arts teachers to search for their own constructs and interpretative frames and to analyse the consistency and coherence of these constructs and frames in relation to their teaching practice.

REFERENCES

Calgren, I., Handal, G., and Vaage, S. (Eds.). (1994). *Teachers' Minds and Actions: Research on Teachers' Thinking and Practice*. London/Washington, DC: The Falmer Press.

Conkling, S. and Henry, W. (2002). The impact of professional development partnerships: our parts of the story. *Journal of Music Teacher Education*, 11(2), 7–13.

Conway, C. (2001). What has research told us about the beginning music teacher? *Journal of Music Teacher Education*, 10(2), 14–22.

Day, C.W., Pope, M., and Denicolo, P. (Eds.). (1990). *Insights into Teachers' Thinking and Practice*. London/New York/Philadelphia: The Falmer Press.

Elbaz, F. (1981). The teacher's practical knowledge: report of a case study. *Curriculum Inquiry*, 11(1), 43–71.

Gimeno Sacristán, J. (1998). *O Currículo: Uma Reflexão Sobre a Prática*. (3rd ed.), Porto Alegre: Artes Médicas Sul.

Gimeno Sacristán, J. (1999). *Poderes Instáveis em Educação*. Porto Alegre: Artes Médicas Sul.

Jorgensen, E.R. (1994). Justifying music instruction in American public schools: an historical perspective. *Bulletin of the Council for Research in Music Education*, 120, 17–31.

Krueger, P. (2001). Reflections of beginning music teachers. *Music Educators Journal*, 88(3), 51–54.

Marcelo García, C. (1995). A formação de professores: Novas perspectivas baseadas na investigação sobre o pensamento do professor. In A. Nóvoa (Ed.), *Os Professores e a sua Formação* (2nd ed.) (pp. 51–76). Lisboa: Publicações Dom Quixote, Lda.

Pimenta, S.G. (1997). Para uma re-significação da didática—Ciências da educação, pedagogia e didática (uma revisáo conceitual e uma síntese provisória). In S.G. Pimenta (Ed.), *Didática e formação de professores: percursos e perspectivas no Brasil e em Portugal* (pp 19–76). São Paulo: Cortez.

Schutz, A. (1973). *Collected Papers I.* The Hague: Martinus Nijhoff.

Schutz, A. (1976). *Collected Papers II.* The Hague: Martinus Nijhoff.

Schutz, A. (1979). *Fenomenologia e Relações Sociais.* Rio de Janeiro: Zahar Editores.

Sparshott, F.E. (1980). Education in music: conceptual aspects. In S. Sadie (Ed.), *The New Grove Dictionary of Music and Musicians, vol. 6* (pp. 54–58). London: Macmillan.

Swanwick, K. (1992). Open peer commentary, musical knowledge: the saga of music in the national curriculum. *Psychology of Music*, 20, 162–179.

Swanwick, K. (1994). *Musical Knowledge: Intuition, Analysis and Music Education.* London: Routledge.

Wagner, H.R. (1979). Introdução. In A. Schutz, *Fenomenologia e Relações Sociais* (pp. 3–50). Rio de Janeiro: Zahar Editores.

Waters, M. (1994). *Modern Sociological Theory.* London/Thousand Oaks/New Delhi: Sage Publications.

Zeichner, K. (1994). Research on teacher thinking and different views of reflective practice in teaching and teacher education. In I. Calgren, G. Handal, and S. Vaage (Eds.), *Teachers' Minds and Actions: Research on Teachers' Thinking and Practice* (pp. 9–27). London/Washington, DC: The Falmer Press.

RENA UPITIS

6. CHALLENGES FOR ARTISTS AND TEACHERS WORKING IN PARTNERSHIP

1. CHALLENGES OF ARTISTS AND TEACHERS WORKING IN PARTNERSHIP

Over the past few decades, comprehensive educational reforms have been designed to address perceived shortfalls in the teaching of language arts, mathematics, and science. At the same time, there has been a lack of commitment to arts education among educational policy-makers and leaders (Oreck, 2002). Even in schools with strong arts programmes, the political pressures to raise standardised test scores and the lack of on-going training serve to weaken teachers' efforts to teach the arts, particularly when arts specialists are no longer present to foster the arts curriculum (Stake et al., 1991). This is a deeply systemic problem. Many teacher education programmes do not provide adequate preparation for lasting engagement with the arts, yet school districts in North America have eliminated arts specialists with a single subject focus (e.g. music) and classroom teachers are required to implement extensive arts curricula that require specialised skills in multiple art forms (Upitis, 2001).

In response to these widespread deficiencies, arts partnerships have been fashioned to increase the level of arts literacy in North American and British teachers (Remer, 1996; Vagianos, 1999; Mitchell, 2000).[1] However teacher development in the arts is hindered by the virtual absence of empirical data on the impact of professional development on teaching (Oreck, 2002). There is also little research on how classroom teachers react when they find themselves working closely with artists who may not share the same educational views or culture. There is even less empirical research on the ways in which these educational partnerships affect the artists who become involved with such partnerships. This chapter identifies some of the challenges faced by teachers and artists, and artist-teachers who have been involved in educational partnerships. By artist, I refer to the musicians, dancers, painters, and storytellers who would identify art-making as their primary vocation and/or source of income, and for whom educational partnerships are a secondary occupation. By artist-teacher, I refer to teachers with substantial professional training in one or more art forms and who maintain a home studio or are otherwise active in art-making, but whose primary vocation is teaching. For the purposes of brevity, I use the collective

[1] A wide range of programs exist in the United Kingdom (see http://www.artscouncil.org.uk, http://www.tate.org/modern/eventseducation/sch_teacherstrainees.htm) and in Australasia (e.g. http://www.asilink.unimel.edu.au/aef/pd/, http://www.unisa.edu.au/art/about/partner.asp, http://www.creative-partnerships.com/people/peopleimages/64780), although it would appear that the most prolific development of arts partnerships has been in the United States.

P. Burnard and S. Hennessy (eds.), *Reflective Practice in Arts Education*, 55–66.

term 'artists' to refer to both the artists from the community as well as the artist-teachers in the schools.

2. WHAT HAVE WE LEARNED FROM THE LITERATURE?

There is a wide range of educational partnerships involving teachers, independent artists, and arts organisations. Some partnerships—such as institutes and short courses—are short-term, while others unfold over a period of several years (Babineau, 1998). Partnerships might be regional, national or international in scope (Mitchell, 2000). Regardless of the format or scope, most of these arts education partnerships claim that their aim is 'not to transform classroom teachers into arts specialists. Rather, the aim is to increase teachers' understanding of . . . the arts . . . and to promote creative teaching and learning' (Oreck, 2002, p. 2) and/or to use the arts in a 'comprehensive and complex approach to bringing about school transformation . . . meet[ing] the day-to-day needs of teachers' (Elster, 2001).

2.1. *Artist Involvement in Educational Partnerships*

One of the most imperative but understudied issues from the viewpoint of a partnering artist is whether the particular conception of the artist's art form resonates with the conception of that art form as it appears in the school. For example, in the visual arts, most school art programmes emphasise modernist conceptions of art in which Western Eurocentric traditions are key (Meban, 2002). This modernist perspective is in contrast to the postmodern contemporary art world where artists use metaphor, allegory, and the juxtaposition of media to create art that serves to critique social and political features of society (Clark, 1996; Meban, 2002). Postmodern art typically requires a different form of interpretation than what is practiced in schools. As a result, an artist with postmodern sensibilities may be uncomfortable working in a school setting. This was the case for Meban (2002) when she became an artist-in-residence at an elementary school and found herself censoring the content of her work. Meban claimed that this self-censoring resulted in shifts in the style and purpose of her art-making with students, and therefore affected the nature of the educational experience. Her accommodations 'resulted in a studio program that emphasised the basic skills of drawing and painting with little attention paid to the social function of art.'

The extent to which the issues relating to the artistic process are encountered in an artist's work with educational partnerships will depend on how deeply the artist is involved in the partnership itself. A recent publication titled *Creating Capacity: A Framework for Providing Professional Development Opportunities for Teaching Artists*, based on the reflections of educators and administrators involved in nine high-profile arts organisations in the United States, delineates a continuum of artist involvement in educational settings (Gradel, 2001). At one end, artists may be involved in schools by giving performances or creating exhibits for students and teachers, but the artist is not expected to engage audiences in interactive learning experiences. An artist acting in this capacity is considered a 'performing artist'. Next in the continuum is the 'interacting artist', where, in addition to performing and exhibiting, the artist engages audiences in pre-performance or post-performance discussions and may also be involved in interpreting the artistic work within the educational context. The 'collaborating artist' may perform or exhibit his or her work and engage in discussions of that work, but is also engaged more deeply in the school setting as an artist-in-residence, planning instructional and assessment strategies with classroom teachers. Finally, the 'master instructional artist' is deeply involved with curricular planning with the school partners, acting as a leader in programme design and mentoring other artists. Some of the challenges that the contributors to this document identified for artists involved in educational partnerships were the need for more time to plan and communicate with teachers, difficulties in planning assessment strategies that resonated with the school system, and conflicts between individual artistic endeavors and philosophies of the educational settings, of which the latter echoes Meban's (2002) concerns. These types of challenges have also been identified by other researchers such as Bumgarner (1994) and Patteson et al. (2002).

2.2. *Teacher Development in the Arts*

Richardson (2003) summarised features that researchers and developers have identified as important for effective teacher development. These include creating programmes with long-term follow-up, generating situations that encourage collegiality, fostering agreement among participants on the goals of the programme, acknowledging participants' beliefs and practices, and making use of outside facilitators—which, in the present context, would be the partnering artists. Morrow (2003) endorsed Richardson's view that professional development should be continuous and long-term, and also stressed the importance of creating opportunities for teachers to be reflective and for teachers to engage with research-based pedagogy. Australian educators have also stressed the importance of reflection as part of the professional development process (Australian National Board of Employment, Education and Training, 1993).

The general literature on teacher development has also documented how institutional influences have an effect on the success of educational partnerships. Some of the these influences include availability of resources, time for planning and development, support of administrators, school commitment to professional development, and district and provincial/state policies regarding curriculum and testing (Fullan, 1991; Sarason, 1999; Patteson, 2005).

In terms of teacher development in the arts, additional issues arise. Researchers have questioned how teachers are to carry out what is often seen as the extra burden of professional development in a field that is not their own, in addition to the pressures of keeping up with the mandated standards of education (McKean, 2001). McKean also queried whether the people providing arts partnerships do more than just stimulate an interest in the arts, provocatively asking whether partnerships are a poor substitute for addressing the paucity of full-time arts specialists in schools. Rowlett (1986), a school principal whose teachers were involved in arts partnerships with the Kentucky Center, claimed that in order for an arts programme to thrive, the programme required the full support of administrators as well as the school staff, with particular individuals being identified as the 'champions' for the programme.

Like others (Fullan, 1982; Sarason, 1999), Rowlett identified the importance of procuring appropriate funds and materials, and supporting professional development of teachers through financial support and release time. Rowlett also noted that the objectives of the particular arts partnership had to be clearly articulated, in keeping with the strong sentiments expressed by Bumgarner (1994) and Richardson (2003). However, the area that Rowlett emphasised most in terms of arts partnerships was the need to involve the greater community. Indeed, the involvement of the community for successful teacher development and school change is perhaps more important in arts partnerships than in other forms of professional development because the arts involve a performance aspect that is less apparent in other disciplines, and further, such performances or exhibitions often need to take place in specialized venues in order to be effective.

In the following section, four case studies are described to give a fuller sense of some of the key partnership problems identified in the literature. The case studies are organized to highlight both the shared concerns and benefits of arts partnerships for artists and teachers, as well as the unique experiences of the two groups.

3. AFFIRMING THE IMPORTANCE OF ARTS PARTNERSHIPS: FOUR NORTH AMERICAN CASE STUDIES

Reflections of participants from four North American arts partnerships were examined in order to provide examples of the challenges faced by teachers and artists working in partnership. All four partnerships shared the broadly stated aim of enabling teachers to enliven their work through the arts. They differed in structure; two programmes were school-wide, while the others drew artists and teachers from within a geographically bound region. They also differed in that two partnerships emphasised using the arts in combination with other subjects, while the other two partnerships emphasised the teaching of skills specific to particular art forms. There were other differences in terms of longevity, funding sources, and whether the scope was rural, urban, regional, or national. Together the four partnerships encompassed virtually the entire spectrum of North American, British, and Australasian educational partnerships involving teachers and artists. A description of each of the partnerships follows.

The Kentucky Center for the Arts[2] was established in 1983 as a center for the performing arts and offers the Kentucky Institute for Arts in Education in Louisville and Arts Academies in six regions throughout the state. The primary aim of these partnerships is to help teachers implement the core arts curriculum. The Canadian Learning Through the Arts (LTTA) programme, founded in 1994, operates throughout Canada and in the United States, Italy, Singapore, and Sweden.[3] It is a school-wide initiative with artists and teachers involved in joint planning and teaching to integrate the arts throughout the curriculum. Teachers as Artists (TAA) was developed in

[2] http://www.kentuckycenter.org/

[3] http://www.rcmusic.ca/

Ontario in 1996 as a school-wide partnership to help teachers become beginning artists so that they might bring more arts-based experiences into their classrooms.[4] The Creative Arts Learning Partnership (CALP) was established in 2001 in the Greater Toronto area, drawing teachers from across the region to take part in workshops conducted by members of creative arts organisations. Its goals are to help teachers with the Ontario Arts Curriculum as well as to infuse the arts into other aspects of their teaching.

4. DOCUMENTING TEACHERS' AND ARTISTS' CLASSROOM EXPERIENCES

Data were collected from teachers and artists who had been involved in one of the four educational partnerships for at least two years and as many as five years, and were obtained through a combination of surveys, interviews, and written and oral reflections. Open-ended questions focused on teachers' and artists' classroom experiences, their perceptions of teaching and learning, and their views on how the educational partnerships affected their personal and professional growth. Artists and teachers were also encouraged to reflect on how the mandated curricula affected their work. Free-writing exercises were used to elicit written reflections from teachers immediately following some of the art-making sessions. Informal conversations were also recorded.

Program directors, school principals, and site administrators were surveyed and interviewed, and their views on partnerships and political and institutional factors were used to triangulate the findings related to teachers and artists.

A set of data codes based on prior analytic work examining teachers' beliefs and practices was used to begin analysis (Patteson et al., 2002). Additional open codes were added based on the literature and on the data. At this stage, some codes were collapsed or eliminated, and the remaining codes were grouped into families. These families of codes were used to organize the results reported in the following section of the chapter. Further details regarding the data collection protocols, sample sizes, and analysis methods are beyond the scope of the chapter and are detailed elsewhere (Smithrim and Upitis, 2005).

5. SHARED REFLECTIONS ON ARTS EDUCATION BY ARTISTS AND TEACHERS

There were a number of shared issues for artists and teachers, providing common ground from which to strengthen the educational partnerships. The most significant of these was that artists and teachers generally agreed about the importance of an education rich in the arts. Artists and teachers talked about how the arts helped children understand concepts, both those that were arts-related and those that came from other disciplines. Artists and teachers observed that schools do not always allow children

[4] http://www.educ.queens.ca/~arts/

to explore the full range of their abilities and claimed that the arts should be more prevalent for this reason. Teachers and artists identified the importance of physical involvement in the arts, commenting on the power of movement and embodied learning. This observation is in keeping with the growing field of research on embodied knowledge, where researchers have demonstrated that people learn through their bodies in profound and lasting ways, particularly in the arts (Bresler, 2004).

Despite the public rhetoric about the arts enhancing achievement in other subjects, not a single artist and, indeed, very few teachers, suggested that this was a central benefit of arts education, despite the political pressures that teachers face in terms of raising test scores. Rather, the benefits they identified had to do with attitudes, physical and emotional knowledge, and the social cohesiveness of communities.

6. SHARED CHALLENGES

It would appear to be a perennial and universal lament among artists and teachers that there is not enough time to plan arts encounters for students. As one artist explained:

> [W]ith more planning time and more flexibility in format, I feel my knowledge and experience as an artist would be put to much greater use. In addition I believe that the teachers would be more comfortable being more involved and would also get more out of the process.

Artists also indicated that they could not always predict the amount of time that a certain process might take, and that the fluid nature of art-making did not accord well with the 'forty-minute class time-tabling'. Some teachers observed that the arts required a qualitatively different kind of planning time than other subjects, stressing the importance of 'uninterrupted time with a professional artist'. Teachers and artists also claimed that there was not enough time for art-making in general, reporting that they wished for more opportunities to become so deeply immersed in the arts that they might encounter a sense of timelessness (Patteson, 2005). One artist-teacher stated:

> When I'm involved in art-making, I lose all track of time. But that's not the reality in the classroom. So, when I do art with students, I have no clock in my classroom. I want students to be in another space.

This artist-teacher also described how she negotiated large blocks of time for art-making, thereby overcoming some of the limitations of the school time-table.

Artists and teachers suggested that the very success of a partnership could be its downfall, when extending the partnerships to larger populations resulted in the 'watering down' of the original programme. Participants from two of the partnerships that had experienced such expansion hotly expressed this view. Both groups lamented the loss of professional development time, noting that there was lower attendance at after-school workshops than when workshops were offered during the day. Also, the quality of the programming suffered when the professional development was offered in the shorter after-school sessions. As one teacher said: 'There isn't time, any more, to get to sit for three hours with [an artist], you know, just sit with them and just discuss whatever you're working on,' offering the informal opportunities for reflection that the artists and teachers both craved.

The final commonly experienced challenge was that the physical spaces in schools limited what could be taught. Many participants in the school-based partnerships related that it was difficult for them to find spaces for dance and drama, appropriate tables and lighting for art-making, and rooms with good acoustics for music-making (Upitis, 2004). Predictably, in those partnerships where the rehearsal and performance spaces of the arts organisations were utilised, this issue did not arise, and indeed, artists and teachers commented favourably on the learning environments.

7. REFLECTIONS AND CHALLENGES SPECIFIC TO TEACHERS

In spite of the many benefits of taking part in the arts partnerships, there were some teachers who found that the partnerships added more burden than pleasure, particularly in the early stages. One teacher commented that 'We are all stressed and this was another thing to do' while another stated that 'Working with artists is hard—they don't seem to have any sense of how a classroom operates.' Still others suggested that they would prefer to be audience members rather than participating directly in art-making activities. A sizeable group—especially in the first few years—were frustrated by their own lack of arts skills, indicating that working with artists made them 'more aware of how talented some people are.' Although such claims diminished in frequency and severity over time, these issues should be seen as significant initial challenges, suggesting the need for reflection on the dynamics of both classroom and studio life for the participants. Indeed, in one of the arts partnerships where teachers had worked with artists for five years and had been given frequent opportunities for oral and written reflection and informal conversation, teachers offered informed views about the complexities of working as an artist, reflecting on such challenges as maintaining creative energy, facing political hurdles, and identifying the very real struggles that many artists encounter in procuring sufficient resources to maintain their practices. Teachers spoke of how their views of art-making and the artistic process had been expanded, commenting on how they had come to see artistic work as a mixture of creative freedom and a deeply disciplined approach. This was in sharp contrast to teachers with only two years of involvement, who were more likely to reflect on such issues as the importance of process over product (or vice versa) or about how they viewed artists as eccentric or in some other way romanticised the lives and work of artists.

There was overwhelming evidence that teachers were integrating the arts into their teaching, largely as a result of being able to work in close community with their colleagues. Teachers stated that the arts partnerships had 'helped them to make connections between different subject areas' and that they used 'the arts in many other subject areas rather than just the art strands.' One teacher described how she was 'more confident and able to give the children more experience with the arts,' claiming that the arts partnership had provided fertile ground for creating conditions of collegiality and bringing positive changes to the school community. Several teachers commented on how the partnership had helped to break down the isolation that is often experienced by teachers, and that a 'learning community' had been established because the partnership allowed enough time to 'make [a community] last and grow'. Still others commented on how they had enjoyed collaborating with colleagues because of the 'spirit of sharing' and reflective practice that had developed.

Not surprisingly, there was evidence in the data that teachers experienced challenges when administrative support was lacking. Areas of concern included the loss of the initial enthusiasm expressed by administrators, the ongoing struggle to secure resources for arts teaching, and the need for recognition of the time required to work with artists and plan for arts activities. However, it was abundantly clear from the comments that strong personal support from administration was more important to the teachers than extra resources. Indeed, wider community support was considered essential in order to sustain the impulse of the arts partnerships.

The final significant challenge identified by teachers involved in all four partnerships was their concern that they would not be able to sustain their arts involvement once they no longer had the regular support of the artists. While some teachers indicated they had planned ways to 'keep working with the arts after the programme ends', others feared competing priorities would emerge and that many of the inroads that they had made would be lost.

8. REFLECTIONS AND CHALLENGES SPECIFIC TO ARTISTS

While most of the artists described positive ways in which their artistic practices had been influenced by taking part in the arts partnerships, some artists claimed that their art-making was, in some sense, curtailed by the partnership. One poet indicated that she 'did not write a word while involved in the teaching,' stating that the kind of work involved in poetry writing was of a different quality to the work involved in teaching poetry writing. One visual artist was vehement that the arts partnership had no bearing on her work as an artist, and, indeed, claimed that the partnership was detrimental to art-making for her and for the students themselves. She stated that she was 'reluctant to return to the school system as an artist,' claiming that schools stifle the true artistic process. Indeed, it is possible that this view was not more prevalent because those artists whose work might clash with school expectations may have elected not to take part in a partnership. It is also the case that these artists may not have been selected by the program directors to take part in the educational partnerships.

Just as teachers found that some artists 'had no idea about classroom life,' some artists, too, found it challenging to work in classroom environments. A sizeable portion of artists did not hold teachers in high regard, and some chose to leave the educational partnerships because they felt that their work as artists was not valued by teachers, or was so distorted by the educational system that they were no longer producing art. One artist stated that: 'I think most teachers are closed-minded and do not teach the students well.' This artist felt that she was treated badly by teachers, and that her art-making was neither understood nor respected. A number of artists held a less harsh view of teachers, and whilst they found that teachers' views of art and art-making were limited, they felt that this was a result of teachers being intimidated by the arts, and that: 'with a little encouragement and skill-building, they will address the critical creative and hands-on work with enthusiasm.'

Still others claimed that they had become 'more conscious of, and sensitive to, the needs and struggles that educators face in their daily practice.' Artists talked about developing patience and flexibility in the context of classroom life, and indicated that they were more effectively able to modify their instruction, having watched experienced teachers adjust to given situations. Some artists mentioned the importance of learning about classroom management and about how teachers had helped them understand the complexities of the human relationships that exist within classrooms. That these artists succeeded in coming to appreciate the complexities of classroom life does not mean that, at least in the initial stages, the challenges were not considerable. Rather, their appreciation of teachers' skills and daily struggles is an indication of their having overcome some of their own challenges by engaging in classroom interactions with teachers.

Another common experience of artists related directly to the mandated curricula. Some artists felt that their work with students and teachers was compromised by curriculum expectations. Rather than being free to pursue an art form and artistic processes, they were concerned about how their work with the students would relate to the curriculum, to assessment, and to standards. As one artist put it: 'We're too worried about curricular links . . . isn't instilling a passion for something in a child as important as some stupid math concept?' One artist suggested that it helped her to deal with the contradictions between her professional work and educational partnerships by remembering to differentiate 'theatre as an art form' from 'drama in education.'

9. IMPLICATIONS FOR EDUCATIONAL PARTNERSHIPS

In what is now a classic work on educational change, Fullan (1982) outlined the importance of both formal and informal interchanges between teachers (and in our case, this can be extended to teachers and artists), and argued that professional development should be considered as a continuous undertaking. These sentiments were expressed by the participants in the four arts partnerships, and it would appear that the more that arts partnerships encompass these features, the more likely they are to be successfull.

One observation made by Fullan that is problematic in the context of arts partnerships is that successful programmes should focus on job-related tasks that teachers must complete. Certainly it was the view of many of the artists that their work was more effective when they were able to make curricular links with the teachers. Ironically, the need to connect professional learning to job-related tasks may be the very thing that distances authentic art-making from art-making in the classroom. There is little doubt that the so-called 'authentic learning' experiences, which allow students to genuinely engage in the processes of practitioners, can lead to meaningful and long-lasting learning (Lave and Wenger, 1991). Yet, moving toward more authentic learning practices is fraught with challenges, given the present political and social realities of schools. This makes educational partnerships with artists of all kinds (modern, postmodern) in various roles (performing, interacting, collaborating, instructing), and in places of all kinds (the artist's studio, classrooms, performance venues in the community) all the more important if arts partnerships are going to be truly effective in bringing the arts to students and their teachers.

Given the complexities of the artists' roles, it is not surprising that artist selection was something that all of the administrators felt to be crucial to the success of their partnerships. The administrators indicated that they had refined their criteria for selection over time, and had determined that successful artists had to be willing to take on the role of an artist-educator, to engage in professional development, and to understand their art form well enough to be able to share their art form with teachers and students. The administrators also indicated that the artists needed to be willing to build relationships with teachers and students, and to read, understand, and interpret curriculum documents and research, so that they could work together with teachers to find the means to approach the mandated curricula.

I close with the observation that one of the most important vehicles for experiencing success in the arts partnerships was the opportunity for participants to reflect on their experiences, beliefs, and practices. Over time, artists and teachers developed strategies to overcome some of the initial challenges that they experienced, and these strategies were developed through ongoing relationship-building. The reflective tools used to gather data—written responses, informal conversations, interviews—all had their place in this process. There was no particular tool that was more effective than any other, rather, it was important that participants had a variety of ways in which to express their frustrations and joys, and that they could do so over an extended period of time. As the teachers and artists noted, it all comes down to having enough time and space to explore, plan, and work with colleagues, so that informed and sustained changes to personal and professional practices can be achieved.

ACKNOWLEDGMENTS

This work was supported by a grant from the Social Sciences and Humanities Research Council of Canada. Data were gathered throughout Canada and in the United States, and I am grateful to the members of our Queen's University research team who participated in the research design and data collection. I am also grateful to the administrators from the four partnerships for accommodating numerous site visits. The chapter was written while I was a Visiting Fellow at The Australian National University, and my colleagues in Musicology generously offered feedback and support.

REFERENCES

Australian National Board of Employment, Education and Training (1993). *Workplace Learning in the Professional Development of Teachers. Commissioned Report No. 24.* Canberra: Australian Government Publishing Service.

Babineau, N. (1998). Partners in the arts: the orchestra as community resource. In B. Roberts (Ed.), *Connect, Combine, Communicate* (pp. 223–236). Sydney, NS: University of Cape Breton Press.

Bresler, L. (Ed.). (2004). *Knowing Bodies, Moving Minds*. Dordrecht: Kluwer Academic Publishers.

Bumgarner, C.M. (1994). Artists in the classrooms: the impact and consequences of the National Endowment for the Arts' artist residency program. *Arts Education Policy Review*, 95(3), 14–30.

Clark, R. (1996). *Art Education: Issues in Postmodernist Pedagogy*. Reston, VA: National Art Education Association.

Elster, A. (2001). 'Learning Through the Arts™': program goals, features, and pilot results. *International Journal of Education and the Arts, 2*(7). Retrieved 1 February 2005, from http://ijea.asu.edu/v2n7/.

Fullan, M. (1982). *The Meaning of Educational Change*. Toronto: OISE Press.

Fullan, M. (1991). *The New Meaning of Educational Change*. New York: Teachers College Press.

Gradel, M.F. (2001). *Creating Capacity: A Framework for Providing Professional Development Opportunities for Teaching Artists*. Retrieved 1 February 2005, from The John F. Kennedy Center for the Performing Arts, Washington, DC, http://www.kennedy-center.org/education/partners/creating_capacity.html.

Lave, J. and Wenger, E. (1991). *Situated Learning*. Cambridge: Cambridge University Press.

McKean, B. (2001). Concerns and considerations for teacher development in the arts. *Art Education Policy Review*, 102(4), 27–32.

Meban, M. (2002). The post-modern artist in the schools: implications for arts partnership programs. *International Journal of Education and the Arts*, 3(1). Retrieved 1 February 2005, from http://ijea.asu.edu/v3n1/.

Mitchell, S. (2000). *Partnerships in Creative Activities among Schools, Artists, and Professional Organisations Promoting Arts Education*. Lampeter, UK: The Edwin Mellen Press.

Morrow, L.M. (2003). Make professional development a priority. *Reading Today*, 21(1), 6–9.

Oreck, B. (2002). *The Arts in Teaching: An Investigation of Factors Influencing Teachers' Use of the Arts in the Classroom*. Paper presented at the AERA Annual Conference, Seattle, April.

Patteson, A. (2005). *Present Moments, Present Lives: Teacher Transformation through Art-Making*. Unpublished doctoral dissertation, Queen's University, Kingston, Ontario.

Patteson, A., Upitis, R., and Smithrim, K. (2002). *Sustainable Teacher Development in and Through the Arts*. Proceedings of the International Society for Education Through Art 31st World Congress, New York, August.

Remer, J. (1996). *Beyond Enrichment: Building Effective Arts Partnerships with Schools and your Community*. New York, NY: ACA Books.

Richardson, V. (2003). The dilemmas of professional development. *Phi Delta Kappan*, 84(5), 401–405.

Rowlett, H. (1986). *Implementing the Arts*. Paper presented at the American Educational Research Association Annual Conference, San Francisco, April.

Sarason, S. (1999). *Teaching as a Performing Art*. New York: Teachers College Press.

Smithrim, K. and Upitis, R. (2005). Learning through the arts: lessons of engagement. *Canadian Journal of Education*, 289(1 and 2), 109–127.

Stake, R., Bresler, L., and Mabry, L. (1991). *Custom and Cherishing: The Arts in Elementary Schools*. Urbana, IL: National Arts Education Research Center.

Upitis, R. (2001). *A Vision for Arts Education in Canada*, proposal to the Conseil des Ministres de l'Education (Canada)/Council of Ministers of Education, Canada, April.

Upitis, R. (2004). School architecture and complexity. *Complicity: International Journal of Complexity and Education*, 1(1), 19–38.

Upitis, R. and Smithrim, K. (2002). *Learning Through the Arts: National Assessment*. Toronto, ON: The Royal Conservatory of Music.

Vagianos, A. (1999). *Professional Development and Training for Teachers and Artists*. Toronto, ON: Laidlaw Foundation.

SECTION 2

TOOLS OF REFLECTION

CHARLOTTE J. PEEL

7. GAME FOR REFLECTION?

Reflections on the Development and Use of a Reflective Tool

1. INTRODUCTION

In this chapter, I tell the story of the development of Game, an artwork, research method and reflective tool. I tell how Game emerged firstly as a means to reflect on my practice as a visual artist and educator, and of how it developed as a research method and reflective tool—used by artists and children in gallery workshops. I discuss possible applications of Game as a reflective tool in the classroom and offer strategies for teachers to experiment and develop ideas for creating an imaginative tool of reflection in their own practice.

I see my activities as a visual artist and educator as part of one creative practice. As an artist, I work across art forms—often collaboratively—in the creation of objects, installations and performance. My practice as an educator is also collaborative. I work in partnership with other practitioners—including teachers and artists—in the development and delivery of education projects in schools, galleries, museums, the community and higher education. It is from the perspective of my creative practice as an artist and educator that I write the story of developing and using Game. This is interwoven with my personal reflections on this process (my voice reflecting on practice) as inset paragraphs.

2. REFLECTING ON MY PRACTICE

Game 1 (2002)

Materials: 100 blank playing cards, photographs, tracing paper, pencil, and photo mount spray
Activity: recording my day, inventing rules, playing with routines
Participants: 6 MA students, 2 lecturers
Played: 28 to 30 August 2002, Art, Design & Museology Studio, Institute of Education, University of London.
Duration of play: 18 hours over 3 days
Context: MA Module, Learning and teaching in art and design

Here, in my reflective voice, I relate my experiences during a workshop at the Institute of Education that stimulated me to reflect on my practice in new ways. This studio-based workshop, developed by Prentice (1995) provides a conceptual, experimental

P. Burnard and S. Hennessy (eds.), *Reflective Practice in Arts Education*, 69–82.

and supportive framework for art and design educators to reflect on their own creative behaviour and ways of working:

> Have you ever tried to change the ways in which you do things? Do you recall what it was like? I arrive at the studio. Six of us are participating in a three-day workshop. We are together in one large room where we each have our own studio space. We all have a background in art, craft or design and in education. For three days we work alongside each other—investigating an aspect of teaching and learning in art and design through our own creative practice. We all have favoured ways of working. This workshop disrupts our routines—it frames the structures we have to work in and around: time, space, people, seminars, tutorials. It challenges the way I would have approached this project, if I had been on my own in a personal space. This disruption to the ways that I would usually work, and the knowledge that I have to investigate something publicly within this time frame, make me feel at first uncomfortable, but I feel that this is necessary in order to take a fresh look at things very familiar to me.
>
> I bring 100 blank playing cards with me to the workshops. To begin with, I am not sure how I am going to use them but am interested in their material quality and the ways in which I can handle them. As a way of starting, I decide to invent a rule to record my day using the cards—to record what I am doing, thinking, feeling or participating in every ten minutes throughout the day. I record on the blank cards time and action and interaction, posting each one into a box. As the game develops the rules I set myself become more playful and I begin to collect the workshop experience in different ways. I invite others working within the department to also give me rules to follow. This is the most interesting part as suddenly I am opening myself up to act in new ways that I wouldn't have thought of or chosen for myself. And so a game starts growing in response to the environment it is in and the people who interact with it. The cards themselves, and the sequences they are placed in as I begin to arrange them in my studio space, become a record of the three days of play, of repeated journeys and daily routines. The record of the workshop itself becomes the artwork. I call this artwork Game I.

The aim of the workshops was to deepen our understanding of the conditions necessary to support and nurture creative behaviour in teaching and learning by reflecting through and upon our own creative behaviour. The physical and conceptual framework of the workshops supported us in developing a reflective practice that involved disrupting habitual ways of working and responding, and gave validity to taking risks and trying things in new ways. Although this may feel uncomfortable, Dewey (1933)—who conceptualised reflection and reflective thinking in education in the early twentieth century—identified uncertainty and ambiguity and the consideration of alternatives as key factors in stimulating reflective thought.

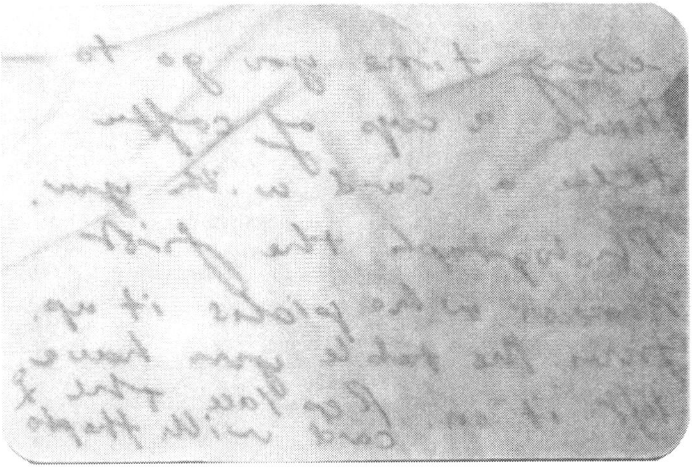

Figure 7.1. [Game I (2002), Rules][1]

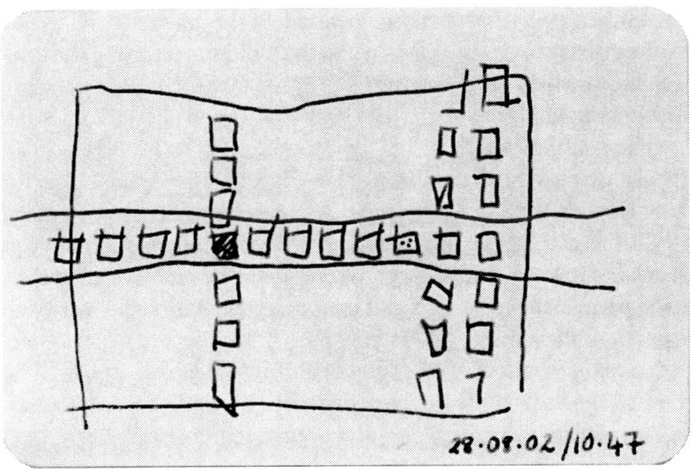

Figure 7.2. [A Conversation][2]

The most significant thing I took from these workshops was a strategy for taking a fresh look at my practice through developing a creative and experimental approach to reflection. I continued to develop this approach within a research project, the process of which is discussed in the following section.

---

[1] A rule given to me by a player, which (following another rule) I re-wrote backwards and layered over a digital photograph taken at the time. I decided to layer the cards with image and text on translucent papers because it evoked a feeling or memory.

[2] A drawing made during a conversation with another player where we discussed a possible structure for arranging the cards.

3. THE DEVELOPMENT OF GAME AS A RESEARCH METHOD AND REFLECTIVE TOOL

Game II (2003)
Materials: blank playing cards, photographs, pencils, index box, glue Activities: making rules, collecting observations, playing with systems, reflecting with children and artists Played: January to March 2003 at Wednesday Club, Kettle's Yard, University of Cambridge Participants: 14 children and 2 artists Duration of play: 12 hours over 8 workshops Context: MA Dissertation, Art and Design in Education

Game II was developed as a research method in the context of case-study research which sought to investigate the nature of the engagement between artists and children and their meaning-making in gallery workshops. Particular strands of enquiry were framed around the following research questions:

- How are children and artists making meaning in the gallery?
- How are the artists engaging children and the children engaging the artists—what sorts of things are they doing/saying?
- How does interaction between artists and children in the gallery stimulate and extend understanding/experience of the artwork—for both?

I conducted a case study of the Wednesday Club, an after-school club for children aged 8–11 at Kettle's Yard in Cambridge. A core education activity in the gallery, Wednesday Club is run by two artists and comprises a course of eight weekly workshops each academic term. The aims of Wednesday Club are to enable children to:

- explore the permanent collection and temporary exhibitions;
- make artwork of their own;
- work with practising artists.

The period of the case study covered one term of workshops. Fourteen children (three boys and eleven girls) aged 7, 8 and 9 attended the workshops. In close consultation with the artists, I joined the group to observe and investigate the research questions. I talked with the children about why I was there and was an active presence in the group, engaging fully with the artists and children throughout. What follows is a description of the gallery environment and of the exhibition that Wednesday Club activities were focused on throughout the duration of the case study.

Kettle's Yard is a house with a permanent collection of twentieth-century visual art and objects arranged in a domestic setting and an art gallery showing an exhibition programme of twentieth-century and contemporary visual art. A dedicated education room adjoins the house and gallery. Wednesday Club workshops occur in all the different spaces within Kettle's Yard. During the term of Wednesday Club workshops of my case study, the majority of the workshops were held in the gallery itself (directly in front of the artworks) with some parts of the workshops developed in the education room.

Connect 4
Tally Charts
Windows
Flats
Televisions
Roads
Ladders
Train Tracks
Fleas

Figure 7.3. Game II (2003), Children's initial responses to Karshan's drawings

The gallery exhibition *Linda Karshan: marks and moves* (Kettle's Yard, 2003)[3] was the focus of the Wednesday Club workshops during the case study. Karshan's large-scale drawings record personal rhythms that she feels and carries in her body. She starts a rhythm by counting, walking, pacing and turning and then continues the rhythm to make the drawing. In the process of making a drawing she transforms something physical into something visual. The children were exploring the concept of personal rhythms and patterns in the workshops and Game II developed within this context.

3.1. Research Process

Game II evolved as a research method and reflective tool in response to all those participating in the case study and to the contexts of the exhibition and the gallery. Here I write reflectively on this process. I describe how I drew upon my arts practice to record my observations on the blank playing cards, and the rules and systems I set myself to collect and organise these observations in different ways. I discuss how I used Game II to reflect on the observations I had been making and how it developed to encourage the reflections of the artists and children.

My aim was to create detailed records of how I observed the artists and children engaging with each other and making meaning in the gallery. I wanted to record small moments of their engagement with one another in detail—a record rich with atmospheres, feelings and moods; dynamics, actions and interactions; spaces, sounds and environments. I imagined this record as something fluid and layered.

Thinking of strategies to record these tiny moments that are so rich, complex and transient made me think of the processes that I use to document ephemeral artworks. Documentation of this kind of artwork is often the only remaining trace of it, and as

[3] An exhibition of recent drawings and prints (etchings and woodcuts) by American-born artist Linda Karshan.

an artist you try to evoke the experience of it in as rich a way as possible. Both endeavours involve trying to record the traces and residues of something transient and complex. Both involve an evolving 'reciprocal relationship' between the artist/researcher and the developing artwork/research (Prentice, 2000, p. 529). Both involve recording observations, describing experiences and atmospheres, interpretation and reflection.

Game II comprises five reflective tools, each of which could be used independently. Three of these tools were developed to aid my reflection as a researcher, and could be developed further as tools for teacher reflection; two of the tools were used to reflect with children.

Researcher reflection:

(i) *Three-part book*

(ii) *Flick book*

(iii) *Index box*

Reflecting with children:

(iv) *Memory books*

(v) *Memory table*

3.2. Tools for Researcher Reflection

These tools were developed to help me reflect upon what I had been observing in the workshops. For each tool I invented a rule to challenge myself to look at the workshop in different and fresh ways. Although the rules I set myself limited what I was recording, they also ensured that I collected different modes of evidence and did not just privilege one mode (for example just writing down what was said). When we observe an event what we take from it is always a personal response, and selective. We need to find ways to challenge the routine ways in which we observe and listen so that we may think differently about a familiar situation. With all these tools I was also experimenting with different holding forms for the playing cards, inventing systems to sort and classify.

(i) Three-part book

Rule: For one workshop, record the ways in which the artists are engaging the children. Record these observations as they occur using the following categories:

- Look
- Say
- Do

Extensions of rule:

- Invent new categories to record observations e.g. mood, sounds, atmospheres, actions, pauses, gestures, interruptions.
- For one workshop, record the ways in which the children are engaging the artists.

I use the blank playing cards to construct a three-part book. Each page of the book is made out of three cards, one at the top, one in the middle and one at the bottom. They are joined at the left-hand side by a spine and mounted on a stiff backing, so that cards can be flicked over and easily written/drawn upon. On the top cards I record observations relating to 'looking', on the middle cards 'saying', and the bottom cards 'doing'. This framework enables me to reflect on one mode of evidence in light of another.

(ii) Flick book
Rule: Every seven minutes, for the duration of one workshop, record what you observe happening on a blank playing card. Fix the cards in time sequence.

Each card records a different moment in time. I document something going on at that time either with a photograph or by making a drawn or written note. I develop the photographs and make a playing card of each one. I also make a playing card of each written or drawn note and then fix the cards into the time sequence in which they were recorded by binding them into a small book. As I flick through the book the workshop is animated through word and images. I am able to reflect upon how something unfolded over time.

(iii) Index box
Rule: Invent a classification system to catalogue the playing cards collected in as many different ways as you can.

As the research progresses, I make a growing pile of cards, each capturing a tiny slice of something I have observed. I decide I want a system that is more flexible for holding the cards. I experiment with an index box, personalising the index dividers in playful ways. Organising and reorganising the cards, and inventing the categories, becomes itself a way of reflecting on what has occurred. This process enabled me to make connections between different observations and was open-ended. The multiple possibilities of organising the cards also broke the cycle of always trying to fix things down.

3.3. *Tools for Reflecting with Children*

Up to this point, I had used Game II as a tool to collect and reflect on my observations of how the artists and children were engaging with one another. I began to develop the research process in response to the workshops and my interactions with both the children and the artists. I extended Game II as a research method, and invited artists and children to join in play. I felt it was important that the research should be engaging with the research questions from their perspectives, and Game II became a fun way of inviting their reflective participation with these experiences. Extending the use of the tool in this way gave voice to both the children and artists in the research.

(iv) Memory books
I was able to lead the first half of a Wednesday Club workshop and introduced the idea of *Memory books*: individual tools of reflection. I showed the artists and the children all the playing cards I had collected so far and discussed with them that what was missing was their accounts of the workshops: their meanings. To start the workshop, we discussed the idea of memory. I asked the children:

- What is a memory?
- Where is a memory?
- How can you record a memory?

One of the children talked about how he thought different memories came together in your mind to create new memories—where your original memory is changed.

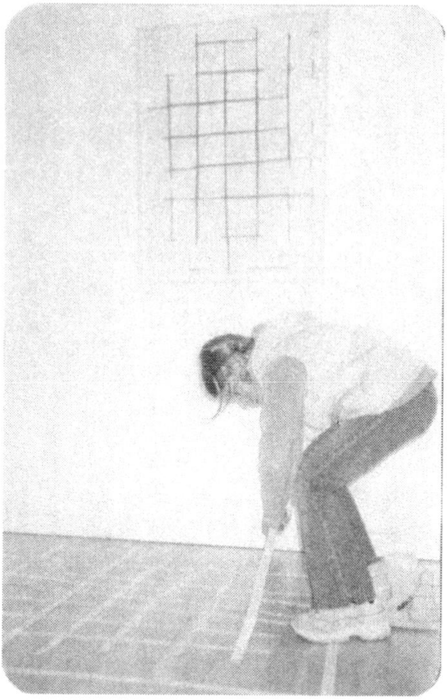

Figure 7.4. Game II (2003), A child's creative response in front of a Karshan drawing

His observation captured well the idea that memories are constantly reconfigured as we remember them, as we make sense of them and connect them to other things that we know.

I give blank playing cards to each of the artists and children and invite them to create a memory book of their strongest memories of the workshops. I ask them to record each memory on a playing card and then to find a way of combining their cards (memories) together—to create a memory book. I provide a variety of joining materials but leave it open as to how they want to do this. Participants are able to choose how many of these cards they wish to use, with an option of having more. Some cards become fixed in a sequence, including a comic strip book and a flick book; others are joined loosely together by threads and suspended. One set of cards, delicately constructed to form a card house, blows down.

Developing the research process to give visibility to the meanings and perspectives of children was akin to how the artists set up the workshops, and is an empowering experience. The artists planned activities in the gallery that often involved the children making interventions in the gallery space in front of the exhibited artworks. Encouraging the children's creative responses directly in front of the artworks makes visible and values their meanings. For that moment, when their work exists in relation to the exhibited work, it becomes part of the work and even makes a new work.

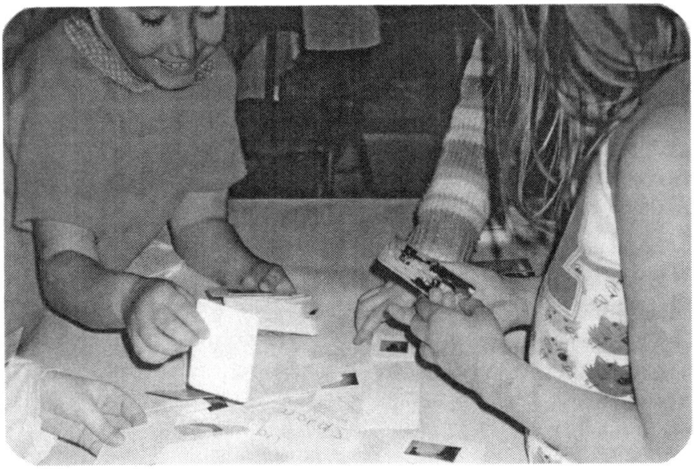

Figure 7.5. Game II (2003), Children using the memory table

In the same way the children's observations and meanings were made visible in the research alongside my own.

(v) Memory table
After turning she starts where her hand falls
Getting faster
Final arrow points towards direction of turn
(My observation of a child making a rhythm drawing, 2003: *Memory table*)
The rhythms keep on coming
they just do . . .
and the kids got it.
(Karshan, 2003: *Memory table*)
Marks, rhythms, titles, words
(Parent, 2003: *Memory table*)
Signs to explain words
(Child, 2003: *Memory table*)

At the Wednesday Club private view, where parents, grandparents and siblings can come and see the artwork made in the workshops, I set up an installation in the education room within the gallery. On a table are arranged a pile of transformed cards and a pile of blank cards. I invite all the participants and their families attending the private view to contribute further memories or observations to the growing pile, asking them to shuffle and rearrange the cards to create their own stories of the workshops. With each new arrangement a new story is told. Through this process of story 'making' and 'telling', we engage reflectively with our experiences as well as with each other.

Spread out together on the table the cards begin to evoke a rich patchwork of experiences and interactions. Players can alter the sequence of how things happened;

create collisions and juxtapositions that could make something appear in a new light. As I manipulate the cards I increasingly begin to notice the spaces or 'gaps' between; somehow they highlight the fact that the documentation can never offer a complete record—making even more evident the complexity of human experiences. I find that the gaps give the cards the possibility of change and of new connections between them. The gaps are pauses for reflection.

I wanted the documentation to exist in its relationship with its participants and to develop *in situ* in the education room within the gallery. To this end, I decided to keep the form of the documentation open, inviting participants to add, layer, change, shape and form it—setting up a conversation between their voices and mine—a document of dialogue and exchange. This problematised the record in keeping with the idea that many different meanings can be made of one experience and that it could never be a complete record.

3.4. *Opportunities*

> Meaningful learning results when a person is able to actively construct and find personal meaning within a situation (Falk and Dierking, 2000, p. 41).

The particular focus here is on making meaning using the reflective tools, and the possibilities of this for learning. Discussion focuses on *Memory table* as a reflective tool which invites shared meaning making, and which holds the possibility of extending the experience of the workshops for all involved.

Memory table engaged children and adults as co-reflectors. Establishing a reflective dialogue between teacher and learner, where meanings can be shared and different perspectives discussed, could have rich potential for learning and for empowering children. *Memory table*, as a reflective tool, made visible both the artists' and the children's (teachers and learners) experiences and meanings. Through using the table they were able to share their stories and see from another point of view. Each card had equal status and everyone's ideas and meanings were valid.

In the context of art and design education in school, Addison and Burgess (2000a) identify this as the foundation of a 'critical curriculum': 'it is essential that you develop the classroom as a site for dialogue, a place where talk is productive and meanings negotiable' (p. 43). They communicate a compelling case for encouraging more participatory and discursive interactions and interventions in the classroom, where both teachers and learners have agency (Addison and Burgess, 2000b, pp. 28–32).

4. POSSIBILITIES FOR CLASSROOM USE

I have discussed how Game was developed in two contexts: an art and design studio (Game I) and a series of gallery workshops (Game II). It wasn't formulaic—each time it grew and changed in response to the context and to the people interacting with it. Each context has its own atmospheres, expectations, roles and relationships. This is important to keep in mind when thinking about the application of any of these tools in another context. They worked the way they did because they were developed in response to the things going on around them. Any of the components of Game II could be developed independently as reflective tools in other contexts, if approached in an open and flexible way. In the final section, I suggest some further starting points for developing a tool of reflection in your own practice.

4.1. Finding your own way

Developing an experimental approach to reflecting upon practice was an important personal and continuing outcome of this research. I feel it is important that teachers are able to find a way to develop a tool for reflection that they can make their own. Central to this is recognising that it is valid to take risks and try things in new ways (and to fail).

I identify my reflective process as moving in a cycle through the following stages:

- Recognise
- Reorganise
- Reflect

Within each of these stages I offer a few starting points for developing a tool for reflection in your own work—to take a look at your classroom practice in new ways. Within each stage imagine ways in which you could involve children as co-reflectors.

4.1.1. Recognise Start with the familiar. Look closely at things that are already in your environment—identify formats, usual patterns, habitual routes and ways of working. Find imaginative ways to record your routines and ways of working. Think about the possibilities of drawing upon your own arts practice and processes to do this:

- Draw the shape or pathway of a lesson. Immediately reflect back on the line/shape—what happened where the line bends, curves, breaks, gets fainter or heavier? Do any of the lines/shapes repeat?
- Make a sound recording of a visual lesson or a visual recording of a music-making lesson.
- Record sixty-seconds of ambient sound in your classroom at a time given to you by *someone else*. Listen back to the recording straight after the lesson, even if it is of nothing, and use it as a starting point to write or draw about what you hear.
- Make a recording (this could be a photograph/written note/drawing/sound recording) of what you are doing at exactly the same time (e.g. at 10:17 or 14:23) each teaching day for a week. Look at this series of recordings as a group. What do you notice?
- Invent 'rules of play' with your class for recording and thinking about a daily routine.
- Try the old practice of tying a knot in a handkerchief to remember something. For one lesson, tie a knot in a piece of string every time you do a certain thing (decided on beforehand) e.g. moments when you paused or gave an instruction or asked a question. At the end of the lesson recall this series of actions.

4.1.2. Reorganise Find a way of breaking the cycle (keep it small and possible). Turning things around and disrupting the formats we follow could spark different ways of responding and reflecting for both you and your class. Starting points for 'breaks' could include:

- Changing the atmosphere of the room e.g. through lighting or sound.
- Changing flow—how you and others move around the classroom.
- Rearranging the room so you are observing and interacting with your class in a new way.
- Altering the pace or rhythm of a lesson or workshop.
- Changing the way you start or finish a lesson.
- Being given a rule for observing your class in a way you might not choose for yourself.
- Start a personal collection of reflection cards. On each one invent one instruction or rule to change something you are doing. Every so often, pick one of these cards at random and follow the rule.

4.1.3. Reflect Take time to reflect (including with your class). What happened? What stood out? What was surprising? Did it unlock something for you? For somebody else? Where has it taken you and your practice?

5. GAME FOR REFLECTION?

In this chapter I told the story of how a tool for reflection was developed and used by both adult and child artists in gallery workshops. I recalled how I drew upon my own arts practice to devise tools for personal reflection and how these were then extended to be used by others. A key aim in developing a tool for reflection was to nurture the reflective practices of children, to give them voice as meaning-makers alongside the voices of adults. I discussed how a reflective tool, such as Game II, could invite a co-reflective relationship between teacher and learner. I offered possibilities for the application of Game II in the classroom and further starting points for inventing new reflective tools. The emphasis here is placed on the importance of the practitioner making the ideas their own.

Game is a useful metaphor to keep in mind when developing a tool of reflection. To be 'game' suggests our willingness to participate in something—to act reflectively means 'being game' to take a fresh look at our practice, however vulnerable this may make us feel at times; 'game' implies rules of play that are agreed by all those participating, whether individually or with others; very importantly, 'game' also suggests play and playfulness—something enjoyable. One child added a playing card to the *Memory table* on which she had drawn herself arranging the cards on the table. Her speech bubble reads: 'This is fun.' Through developing a reflective classroom practice that is playful and that engages with the perspectives, experiences and meanings of children there lies the potential to fire learning through engaging with yourself and the children in new, exciting and enjoyable ways. You are invited to continue the Game.

REFERENCES

Addison, N. and Burgess, L. (2000a). Learning in art and design. In N. Addison and L. Burgess (Eds.), *Learning to Teach Art and Design in the Secondary School* (pp. 20–56). London: RoutledgeFalmer.

Addison, N. and Burgess, L. (2000b). Contemporary art in schools: why bother? In R. Hickman (Ed.), *Art Education 11–18 Meaning, Purpose and Direction* (pp. 14–36). London: Cassell.

Dewey, J. (1933). *How We Think: A Restatement of the Relation of Reflective Thinking to the Educative Process*. Washington, DC: Heath and Company.

Falk, J.H. and Dierking, L.D. (2000). *Learning from Museums: Visitor Experiences and the Making of Meaning*. Oxford: AltaMira Press.

Prentice, R. (1995). Learning to teach: a conversational exchange. In R. Prentice (Ed.), *Teaching Art and Design* (pp. 10–21). London: Cassell.

Prentice, R. (2000). The place of practical knowledge in research in art and design education. *Teaching in Higher Education*, 5(4), 522–534.

JOANNA GLOVER AND JANET HOSKYNS

8. REFLECTION AND EVALUATION

Tools for Learning by Arts Practitioners

1. INTRODUCTION

As music educators and practitioners currently teaching in higher education, we have been involved in evaluating and researching a number of projects that employ musicians and other artists to work with young people, with the general aim of widening access to a broad range of opportunities for participation in music making. As a result of government initiatives since 1999 there has been a massive increase in the number of funded projects involving young people and artists across the United Kingdom. In England and Wales, both the Department for Culture, Media and Sport (DCMS) and the Department for Education and Skills (DfES) have been setting up systems to encourage and develop the creative industries in the United Kingdom as well as to ensure that the recommendations of the National Advisory Committee on Creative and Cultural Education (NACCCE, 1999) are implemented. Many of these projects are funded in partnership with Youth Music in England, Wales and Scotland (www.youthmusic.org.uk).

In this chapter, we draw on experiences from several such projects in rural and urban locations in England. As researchers and evaluators, our role is to bring an external perspective to projects that are often working entirely outside institutional frameworks, and to work in partnership with project leaders to evaluate the quality of their work and to monitor the extent to which projects are meeting targets, agreed in planning with their funders. In addition, we believe that our role is to help project managers and practitioners develop a culture of reflective practice that will become part of the project's legacy. For all concerned, the genuine and intrinsic motivation towards developing such practice is the desire to constantly seek ways to do things better. Most of those involved in Youth Music projects want to be responsive to young people's needs and to be innovative and creative in developing sustainable projects of high quality. There can, however, be considerable difficulties in translating this desire into effective practice, for many different and often understandable reasons. In working with teams of musicians, and as practitioners ourselves, we share layers of reflection to find the most productive and meaningful ways to carry out evaluation, or to create a climate for continuing development.

Reflective practice and evaluation can sound turgid and dull to those who are anxious to get on and make things happen; the *doers and practitioners*, as opposed to the *thinkers and philosophers*. 'Don't ask me to evaluate this as well as plan it and do it' is an opinion commonly expressed by all kinds of practitioners in the arts, sport and education, as well as those involved in business and finance. Artists often say to us,

P. Burnard and S. Hennessy (eds.), *Reflective Practice in Arts Education,* 83–94.

'I need to start doing this to see how it goes—I won't know until I start'. Writing as a community musician, Bick (2004, p. 15) admits:

> I have a very ambivalent attitude to evaluation. Throughout every working day . . . I am asking myself whether I am doing things in the most effective ways; whether the direction of my work is on the right track. When I am working with groups I am constantly looking at faces, observing actions and asking questions to check whether I am really helping them in their music making, or just getting in the way.
>
> This is the core of evaluation, and is surely a normal part of life for any human being. I am wary, however, of making this reflective process explicit. Firstly because it would make it much more time consuming and secondly because the process can become highly inhibited if I begin to get concerned about what other people will think.

Nevertheless, Bick goes on to discuss ways of making evaluation relevant, directly helpful, low cost and informative. So practicalities, methods, and also concerns for how best to make use of reflection can all be problematic for practitioners who naturally hold widely differing views on these matters. The idea of planning one's evaluation procedure can seem intrusive and unhelpful when an idea is at the devising and implementing stage. However, our observation suggests that progress and development are not automatic unless reflection and action are used in conjunction with each other. Without built-in evaluation and reflection there is the potential for repeating mistakes eternally.

Much evaluation and reflection occurs on the hoof and is done intuitively, particularly by experienced practitioners (Bick, 2004). However, as Woolf (2004, p. 9) suggests 'evaluation is a powerful tool for learning. It is a structured way of thinking about what happens during your project, and why'.

Evaluation and reflection therefore need to be planned into the structure of the project so that improvements can be made, funding bodies can be assured about the way in which money was spent, and all participants can be involved in reviewing the process. Moriarty (2001, para 2.1) differentiates monitoring, which involves 'the regular measurement of progress against objectives', from advocacy 'which tends to highlight strengths'; evaluation—'a learning process which also involves considering failures and weaknesses'; and documentation—'a record of activities and events'. She sees evaluation as demanding 'reflection, critical analysis, recommendations and further action'.

The first edition of Woolf's (1999) *Partnerships for Learning* was subject to some criticism since it was not felt to support a philosophy for reflection and evaluation. Ross (2003, p. 75) states 'Woolf's Guidelines document (1999) offers the ways and means but is distinctly short on the philosophy that must underpin evaluation'.

In this chapter, we consider some tools that will support the evaluation process and embed it in the present and future work of the participants, whatever their role.

2. CONTEXTS FOR MUSIC PROJECTS

When a project is set up, project proposers, leaders, managers and participants all bring with them expectations and experiences which are part of the fabric of the project itself and support the evolution and building of the project over time. Before considering how to evaluate a music project, it may be important to give some thought to those who are running it and to what they bring with them. Projects normally involve practising artists, and artists often move between different project contexts. A number of the artists we have worked with run a portfolio career where they may work partly in education or social services, at developing their own music or arts related business and also participate in a number of performing activities: gigs of one sort or another.

The musicians in Youth Music projects come from a wide spectrum of musical backgrounds. Different musical pathways are characterised by different ways of learning and talking about music, and different patterns of interaction and status between 'novices' and experienced musicians. Musicians working alongside each other in a project may each have learned their skills through a different mixture of self-teaching, alone or with peers, formal or informal tuition, apprenticeship, periods of part or full time study and learning 'on the job' through regular performing or participation in groups or bands. Rock and pop, folk and traditional, classical and jazz musical styles are each rooted in different learning styles and teacher-learner relationships, as are different instrumental or vocal traditions. Each tradition brings with it a form of discourse, practice and learning assumptions that musicians import into their work with young people.

Our research indicates that these perspectives profoundly affect musicians' reflections on what they do and their evaluation of project work as a whole. Personal aims and a sense of mission strongly colour how musicians set about their work with young people and also the vision they have of the outcomes.

For a musician working with under 12-year-olds in a year long out of school project based around creating a traditional folk band, there was a clear contrast between her musical skills and expertise in this genre and her own experience of music education as a child. With much self-awareness she not only articulated this contrast, but used it to build a working approach that embodied her own beliefs. She expected the young people to listen musically and socially, and gave participants the skills and confidence in their ability to do so. They had plenty of opportunities to self evaluate and a voice in determining how their band developed as they went on to play at local festivals and in street processions. This musician described how her vision emerged from a desire to improve on her own experiences, as is often the case when workshop leaders start out:

> My approach relates quite a lot to my own musical background and educational experience in that I had quite a negative experience of music at school and it very nearly put me off music for life. So I feel very strongly that music needs to be taught in a very positive way a really interesting,

> exciting, creative, fun—definitely fun—way. I also wanted results. I wanted to push them. I wanted them to really do their very best. I didn't just want it to be mucking about. I wanted them to have that feeling that they really could be good at what they were doing. So it was a kind of mixture.
>
> The whole technical approach to music was a big turn off for me in the reading of the music and that kind of thing so I actually approached the group by ear—everything we did we played by ear. I wanted to encourage them to listen and to stretch their ear muscles and improve that side of their ability.

This musician already has a framework of strong personal beliefs that may, or may not, resonate with the outlook of the project or of other practitioners. The following observations illustrate motivations that three more musicians brought to different age-range settings within the same project:

> I saw the workshops as a way of engaging young people and encouraging new young people (into a Youth Centre).
>
> I love music myself—see it as an excellent youth work resource.
>
> I was brought up on the punk rock attitude that anyone can play and it's not about musical prowess.

These viewpoints are not incompatible, but without communication and discussion that enables ideas to be made explicit and a working approach negotiated, there can be serious misunderstandings that in turn affect how the project is evaluated and developed further.

Musicians may be more or less aware of how they perceive work with young people through the filters of their own experience. There may be a closer or looser 'fit' between what musicians are aiming to achieve in a youth music project and the pathways they themselves have travelled in their own musical apprenticeship. We have also found many instances where musicians leading workshops are working with someone trained in a quite different field, for example youth work, social work, early years teaching, childcare, child psychology, mental healthcare or administration. Professional training in any of these areas has its own frameworks, jargon and expectations of reflection and evaluation. It can be powerfully positive to collaborate across 'disciplines' in this way, but it also requires time and effort to make sure that everyone understands each other and can agree roles. So in developing a culture of reflective practice within a group of practitioners with disparate experiences, part of the richness, but also the hazard, lies in being able to negotiate understanding across different ways of relating and communicating. In the sections that follow, we have tried to identify some key features of approaches to evaluation and how these evolve from the preferences, previous experiences, life stories and professional training of those who are principally involved in leading them.

2.1. *Project Evaluation: Leadership and Theoretical Underpinning*

Projects are initiated in a number of ways of which there are three we have observed typically.

1. They may be created by the influence of one artist wishing to work with a particular group of people (young children and their families, prisoners, youngsters in youth clubs etc.) and this then develops into a project.
2. An organisation, such as a nursery, school or youth club decides to employ a composer, performer(s) or other artist in residence for a limited period to work with particular groups of young people.
3. A consortium of artists is put together in order to provide intensive workshops in a designated geographical area and then local groups are invited to bid to be allowed to host such workshops and use them to develop their own musical or artistic culture. The scale of a project may range from a few weeks in one setting to many small projects co-ordinated over two or three years and taking place across a much wider area.

If reflection and evaluation are to become embedded in a project from the beginning, a project manager working in any of these formats must from the outset facilitate discussions involving all practitioners towards evolving an overall philosophy as well as practical measures through which to carry it out. Some theory and reflection at the beginning can help artists to see the context for the activity and make sense of it, not only for themselves, but also for the participants and their adherents. This means approaching reflection and evaluation from a grounded perspective where the theories are developed out of the activity.

Activity theory has been used in a number of studies of collaborative and distributed learning and has been particularly influential and useful when applied to both schooling and workplace training (Russell, 2002). When considering projects such as those we have been evaluating, where consortia are formed and used both as a network for distributing funds, and then as a structure within which evaluation of activity takes place, it seems that activity theory can be very helpful. A distributed learning environment is one where learning occurs not only as part of collaboration but emerges between the participants (Engestrom, 1990). Arts projects such as those described above can be understood as distributed learning environments. For example, in distributed learning environments, 'do individuals or groups of individuals understand themselves as part of a disciplinary or learning community focused on a common object?' (Russell, 2002, p. 323) It seems clear to us that the groups and individuals making up consortia rarely understand themselves to be part of a wider group or learning community at the outset. Where this is recognised, or where this understanding gradually evolves, the groups are much stronger and are able to develop and evaluate progress towards agreed goals. We have witnessed major misunderstandings that can emerge when the director of a consortium is not fully cognisant of the aspirations of the individual project managers and musicians who work alongside them. This can lead to an incoherent experience for participants and a sense of frustration amongst the musicians who feel unable to make progress. One project coordinator expressed concern that they had not been able to recruit more participants from disadvantaged backgrounds (Hoskyns and Glover, 2004, p. 6).

Projects such as the innovative mixing of music with media and skateboarding (Fenton, 2004) demand careful preparation, and the opportunity to respond to evaluation and change throughout. In order to do this, detailed planning was deliberately kept to a minimum. The project partners felt it was important to respond according to the dynamics of the moment. It certainly challenged the practitioners and they needed to shift their roles to accommodate new developments. Despite this, a great deal of reflective practice was evident, and many ideas for future projects emerged. One partner reflected how the 'personality', 'skills' and 'faith' of practitioners was one of the most effective successes of the project. It clearly shows that members of the group understood their roles as part of a new learning community and were able to evolve their practice through a shared understanding of the goals they hoped to reach.

Another aspect of activity theory concerns understanding how subjects, rules and communities interrelate. Many of our participant musicians had not had the opportunity to understand and agree the rules of working or to disembed the underlying assumptions of the participants in the individual projects. Where this process took place and was open and supportive, then again, outcomes were much clearer and better understood. As can be seen above, the shared understandings and the trust and faith of the partners was a vital ingredient in the many successful outcomes.

We have found attitudes towards evaluation which range from the very negative: '*Don't want it and can't see the point'* where it is done under duress if at all—through to very positive—'*we incorporate evaluation as part of the whole process, with funding for every aspect; newcomers are formally inducted'*.

Although very obvious, it is surprising how often musicians 'on the ground' in projects are either unaware or have completely lost sight of the project's original aims and objectives, or those of the funding body. So although they may be very clear as to what they are aiming for themselves, they are not able to connect their reflection or evaluation to the core objectives of a project.

2.2. Tactics to Support Reflection and Revaluation

Some of the ways in which reflection and evaluation can occur are listed below:

- Talking
- Writing
- Gathering evidence
- Troubleshooting
- Using external observers

Many of the musicians we worked with found that all of these came naturally to them and that elevating these factors to the status of reflective or evaluative tools seemed to over emphasise these evaluations.

2.2.1. Talking Given the complex nature of developing a culture of evaluation in such settings, it is necessary to build funded time into projects to meet, talk and find effective channels for sharing problems and successes and for enabling less experienced practitioners to encounter or work alongside those who are more experienced. For example, musicians leading a songwriting workshop for young people with a range of disabilities reported:

> We were left alone with these special young people, without any information about their problems and difficulties, and we thought in retrospect that it would have been very good to have somebody from their support team on hand to support us and the young people. Despite this, the day was a very productive day, and I would consider that this was 'workshopping at its best'. We discussed with the staff at the centre our concerns about support staff, and this information was submitted to the relevant party.

Such exchanges help to build the sense of a learning community, whether the project is large or small. If such opportunities are available, they help to promote both individual and shared reflective practice. They also make it possible to conduct formative and summative evaluation 'conferences' at appropriate time intervals—occasions on which to look back and forward, at what has been achieved, difficulties encountered and what to do and aim for next.

The following are two examples taken from projects we have worked on:

1. In one of the very first Action Zones there were examples of musicians comparing notes across two different strands of activity. These discussions helped the musicians to develop day-to-day workshop management techniques. By comparing notes musicians were able to share ways of dealing with one hour sessions, which they found challenging, since everything had to be ready for action within the single hour. Additionally, these meetings enabled strand leaders to intervene and recognise what some of the issues were. This model allowed musicians who were new to the whole concept of workshops and outcomes to be inducted into ways of analysing their own activity and development, to recognise what was going on in their sessions and to learn what to expect.
2. A large project linked with a conservatoire had a kind of pyramid structure. Tutor meetings were regularly convened where tutors could feed back their concerns and successes, thus sharing good practice. It was also expected that teams of tutors and other participants would meet to plan and review progress. As Renshaw (2004, p. 3) suggests: 'All teachers, students and young people in education need to be valued and feel that their voices are heard within an ethos of shared responsibility and mutual interdependence'. Where this happened and communications were good, participants had a much clearer focus for their activities and roles were fulfilled.

2.2.2. Writing It can be very helpful to encourage every practitioner working on a project to plan some means of capturing ideas routinely in writing or audio / video diaries in order to track what happens as a project unfolds. For example:

1. Comments books were employed by the Early Years strand in a Youth Music Action Zone, where a team of six artists worked in more than twenty early years settings

weekly over periods of six weeks or more. All those working with the young children were encouraged to comment or note any progress or particular activity that they had observed either during or after a session by making an entry in the book. Initially these tended to contain praise and mentions of a complimentary nature, such as:

> Absolutely fantastic—the children enjoyed it so much and haven't stopped talking about it all week, asking when A is coming back.
>
> Wonderful to see the children interacting with the music man.
>
> As the project progressed, more analytical comments were made, which could be used to identify future objectives or action:
>
> It was a real revelation to see the children responding.
>
> It was lovely to see them thinking about how to express their ideas through movement of their bodies.

In the most useful examples, the books also gave evidence of practitioners developing understanding: (observing the range of responses within an activity): *'some were more comfortable with this than others'*.

2. Professional and young apprentices in the conservatoire linked project were required to keep logs or diaries of their work. These were useful both as a way of sounding-off about things that went wrong but also for reflecting on why things went wrong and what might be done about them. These logs were received by the Project Management team as well as by the researcher. They enabled the management team to intervene if necessary to ensure smooth continuation of the projects.
3. Regular consultation with the young participants about project preparations, plans and their own future aspirations, seemed to engender a positive attitude to diary writing which all participants undertook. Here it can be seen that the processes of writing or recording comments not only supports the artist's own day to day reflection, but also builds a record of stages gone through and important occasions. This becomes an important source of data for overall review and evaluation.

2.2.3. Gathering evidence Much of the success of reflection and evaluation depends on the key skills of observation and evidence gathering. These might appear to be the first rather than the last concern. However, in order to carry out data collection of any kind, the prerequisite is to have some idea of what is being looked for and why. Observing participants, interviewing those who have feedback to give, devising tools for collecting participants' experiences and viewpoints, or measuring progress—all this is skilled work and it is meaningful only to the degree to which someone can make sense of what is collected. At the outset of any project musicians often need a good deal of help to plan observation and other data collection opportunities into their way of working so that this does not cause overload or diversions from the main objectives once projects are under way. There is no point collecting too much if there are no resources to handle it. Video recording every workshop, for instance, is of no value unless someone has time to watch it all, or it is carefully cued and dated for spot reference later. Watching a video of an activity with the participant group, however, can add value for young people in evaluating their own progress as well as for the workshop leader.

2.2.4. Troubleshooting Schön (1983, p. 68) outlines a process of working through problems towards a better understanding:

The practitioner allows himself to experience surprise, puzzlement, or confusion in a situation which he finds uncertain or unique. He reflects on the phenomenon before him, and on the prior understandings which have been implicit in his behaviour. He carries out an experiment which serves to generate both a new understanding of the phenomenon and a change in the situation.

Schön's notional cycle of action—breakdown—reflection—action shows how practitioners (in his case designers) engage in their task until they experience a breakdown in the situation. It is this that forces a 'down tools' for reflection and problem solving. It is the finding of a solution that causes our understanding of a task to grow and change. Activity Theory too helps us by enabling 'understanding and evaluating where and why they [the projects] work or break down. If something unexpected—or messy—happens when people use those environments, Activity Theory can provide analytical lenses to understand what has occurred' (Russell 2002, p. 324). The tactics of troubleshooting by searching out fundamentally better practice inevitably bring with them a growth in the capacity for productive reflection.

2.2.5. Using external observers In many of the projects with which we have been involved the researcher or external evaluator has had an impact on the process of the project, in the sense that participants, musicians and coordinators have requested information from the researcher and have often wanted to establish some form of dialogue. This role can be misunderstood by participants and artists and on occasions external visitors influence the course of a project. This can be both positive and negative, depending upon the extent to which the visitor is drawn into the whole project and is able to reflect appropriately on what goes on. It is important to be clear at the outset with all project practitioners how far external evaluation is going to be interventionist and to build in feedback or review meetings accordingly.

Celebrity visitors, visits from funding bodies or publicity and media can also distort project work. Government Ministers and other VIPs have regularly been invited to view the work of projects with which we are involved. They too can alter the direction of the project if their advice is sought and acted upon. In some cases this happens just because of who they are, not because of the relevance of their advice to the particular participants. Equally, such advice may help to improve the self-esteem of project workers and participants so that they value the project more because it has been in some way 'externally approved'.

Each of the above tactics can contribute considerably to the quality of reflection and evaluation in a project. None can be effectively implemented without planning that draws funding into the project to provide time for such activity. They also require good organisation, strong leadership and encouragement as well as the practical management to establish good channels of communication. Where more experienced practitioners are involved alongside 'novice' musicians both can benefit from the challenge of having to consider, articulate and act on different points of view.

3. A COMMON APPROACH?

A common approach to evaluation can be adopted, as Woolf's 2004 publication shows, through the use of examples. Application of Activity Theory suggests that the approach must be based on a common framework and understanding of the rules that govern the work in the project and that unless these are both agreed and, more importantly, adhered to, outcomes are likely to be unfocused. The nature, personalities and life histories of the artists involved in such projects will also have a major effect on the overall outcomes, so it is important to have worked them into some kind of underpinning philosophy at the outset, even if as work proceeds it is changed and amended. Overall it is important to recognise that whilst approaches to evaluation and reflection will differ from project to project, a crucial factor is that time and opportunities for it to occur should be planned from the beginning. Renshaw, (2004, p. 100) encourages us to consider how change might be effected, suggesting that:

> strong visionary leadership needs to create an environment in which honest, open critical dialogue is respected and actively encouraged. Each person's voice has a right to be heard. Without this commitment to a conversation that is premised on the making of connections, most artists, teachers, students and managers will remain trapped in their silos, resistant to moving into uncharted territory.

The opportunity for all participants to talk, discuss, reflect and evaluate is essential to the success and future development of any project.

REFERENCES

Bick, M. (2004). How am I doing? *Sounding Board: Journal of Community Music*. Spring Edition, 15–17.

Engestrom, Y. (1990). *Learning, Working and Imagining: Twelve Studies in Activity Theory*. Helsinki: Orienta-Konsultit Oy.

Fenton, E. (2004). *SK8/dSK8 Sept 03–04 Evaluation Report*. Cornwall Youth Music Action Zone: Cornwall.

Hoskyns, J. and Glover, J. (2004). *REMIX Bristol and Gloucester Youth Music Action Zone Final Evaluation Report*. Birmingham: University of Central England.

Moriarty, G. (2001). *Sharing Practice: A Guide to Self Evaluation for Artists, Arts Organisations and Funders Working in the Context of Social Exclusion* (p.8). London: Arts Council England.

National Advisory Committee on Creative and Cultural Education (NACCCE). (1999). *All Our Futures: Creativity, Culture and Education*. London: Department for Education and Employment (DfEE) and Department for Culture, Media and Sport (DCMS).

Renshaw, P. (2004). Connecting conversations the changing voice of the Artist. In M. Miles (Ed.), *New Practices New Pedagogies* (pp. 99–116). London: Routledge.

Ross, M. (2003). Education programmes in arts organizations. *Music Education Research*, 5(1), 69–79.

Russell, D.R. (2002). Looking beyond the interface: activity theory and distributed learning. In H. Daniels and A. Edwards (Eds.), *The RoutledgeFalmer Reader in Psychology of Education* (pp. 309–325). London and New York: RoutledgeFalmer.

Schön, D.A. (1983). *The Reflective Practitioner: How Professionals Think in Action*. London: Temple Smith.

Woolf, F. (1999/2004). *Partnerships for Learning; A Guide to Evaluating Arts Education Projects*. London: Arts Council of England.

LINDA ROLFE

9. USING LEARNER JOURNALS IN TEACHER EDUCATION IN THE ARTS

1. INTRODUCTION

One approach to providing a vehicle for reflection is through a learner journal, which is an accumulation of material that is largely based on the writer's processes of reflection (Moon, 1999a). Journals are used in professional education and development in different disciplines for various reasons, for example, to capture thinking, connect knowledge and ideas, and stimulate creativity. Whilst their use in education is generally accepted as an acknowledged learning tool it is also recognised that reflection is intellectually challenging. A feature of initial teacher training (ITT) in England over recent years has been the appearance of the terms 'critical reflection and 'the reflective practitioner'. They are frequently used to describe approaches to training that are designed to foster student teachers' metacognition and help them to reflect on their learning (Schön, 1983, 1987; Hatton and Smith, 1995). Pre-service teachers need to learn to reflect on their learning experiences. They need to identify areas of strength which they can build upon; to monitor their progress over time and set realistic targets for their professional development; to analyse their experience and place it in a wider context related to the theory of teaching and learning; and to develop awareness and understanding of how their personal and professional development leads to an individual philosophy of teaching. However, although a variety of approaches have been used as strategies to develop reflection in pre-service teachers not all appear to be appropriate for stimulating reflection, and there is little research evidence to show how effective they are (Hatton and Smith, 1995).

Drawing on personal experience and insights drawn from a small-scale research project, this chapter introduces a tool for facilitating reflective processes. The context in which this tool is developed involves trainee dance teachers. Questions arising include: What have they learned from the experience? Is a reflective journal a useful or valuable means of achieving the teaching Standards?[1] Is the ability to engage in reflection during training, something that may usefully be extended into future professional practice? What are the factors that may help trainees to reflect in order to learn, or learn as a result of reflection? How might teacher educators encourage

[1] It is now a requirement in England that everyone involved on an (ITT) course should meet specific criteria for effective teaching laid down by the Teacher Training Agency (TTA); these are called the Standards for the Award of Qualified Teacher Status (QTS) (www.tta.gov.uk).

The Standards require trainees to, 'have the capacity and commitment to analyse and reflect on their own practice' (S1.7) so this has to be a requirement in ITT courses.

P. Burnard and S. Hennessy (eds.), *Reflective Practice in Arts Education*, 95–106.

reflection in trainees? These are some of the questions that prompted this investigation and provide a focus for this chapter.

2. OPPORTUNITIES FOR REFLECTION IN TEACHER EDUCATION

Teacher education programmes are increasingly emphasising the need for students to develop as reflective practitioners. Hatton and Smith (1995) in their research at the University of Sydney, Australia, reported on a review of literature on reflection which focused on strategies to assist in the development of pre-service teacher training programmes. The research project identified types of reflection which were defined and applied to an analysis of student writing. Overall the most common type of reflection was descriptive, this often led on to dialogic reflection where further issues and alternative explanations were discussed. They also indicated that a powerful strategy for fostering reflective action was to engage in dialogue with another person as a 'critical friend'. This provided an opportunity to talk, question, even confront a trusted person, in order to examine planning for teaching, implementation and its evaluation. The importance of having opportunities for verbal interaction with others to facilitate reflection was identified as highly effective by student teachers. Research by Francis (1995) also recognises the significance of collaborative learning and critical friendship to enable students to articulate, shape and clarify ideas: 'Sharing develops confidence in self as learner and the positive reaction of peers contributes to valuing of personal experience and confidence in the capacity to generate knowledge' (p. 240).

A further effective strategy was found to be the inclusion of a written record as a stimulus for further reflection at a later date (Hatton and Smith, 1995).

It would seem that whilst opportunities for reflection do exist, they need to be an integral part of the training programme. The following section examines whether reflective writing in a learner journal as a means of giving rise to learning can be supported by relevant theory.

3. LEARNER JOURNALS

Moon (1999a/b) identifies four significant theories which examine ways in which journal writing might lead to learning. It is suggested that journal writing favours learning through *the promotion of conditions for learning* and the *encouragement of reflection*. There is a requirement for time and intellectual 'space' to write the journal. This can be particularly difficult to achieve whilst on an ITT course, (or in any number of arts education contexts), where the demands on time are onerous and require skilful management in order to meet the many diverse challenges. Therefore, as well as the recognition that journal writing needs to be located within a philosophical framework and address the institutional expectations of students, it is also important to develop consciously the attitudes and skills of reflective writing with time allocated to writing on the course (Francis, 1995).

It is generally recognised that the writer should take decisions about the subject matter that is relevant for them, with the journal providing a focusing point encouraging them to set out their ideas coherently. This may help them to make sense of a particular situation or piece of information. The expression of emotion or feelings may be included and this is considered to lead to a more complete and effective form of learning (Boud et al., 1985). Affective responses to events can be either positive or negative factors in the learning process. Attending to feelings when re-evaluating an experience can help trainees to understand whether they need to be engaged with, put on one side or retained and enhanced so that learning can proceed.

Journal writing also enables students to deal with situations that are not straightforward. King and Kitchener (1994) coin a useful word for this as 'ill-structured'. They define ill-structured problems as those that 'cannot be described with a high degree of completeness', and 'that cannot be resolved with a high degree of certainty', where experts 'may disagree about the best solution even when the problem can be considered solved' (p. 11). Moon (1999b) suggests that we 'tidy up' in higher education, by providing 'ready made' material such as handouts and lecture notes, thereby removing the training ground of material that is ill-structured, challenging and problematic (p. 21).

This is, however, not a totally accurate description of the course that the dance trainees, referred to in the present study, experienced. In this context they were frequently required to use seminars and practical workshops, together with educational research and literature, which they then structured to apply specifically to teaching and learning in dance. The learning was often experiential and based upon a model of cognitive apprenticeship to teach students thinking and problem solving skills (Brown et al., 1989). A constructivist view of learning was adopted which stressed that learners construct their own knowledge and therefore construct their own view of the world (Richardson, 1997).

Metacognition is defined as 'knowledge and cognition about . . . anything cognitive' or 'anything psychological' (Flavell, 1987, p. 21) and journal writing has been associated with improved capacities for metacognition, (McCrindle and Christensen, 1995). Metacognitive capabilities have also been related to an individual's capacity to study effectively or to learn (Ertmer and Newby, 1996; Hadwin and Winne, 1996). It seems that learning is enhanced when students become more aware of their own thinking whilst they read, write and problem solve in the journal. This has the potential for their development of a greater awareness of the learning process and an increased ability to set realistic learning targets for the future. It might seem, therefore, that the development of metacognitive abilities may be a further explanation for the support that journal writing provides for general aspects of learning. In Australia, Dart et al. (1998) focussed on the analysis of learner journals written by students on a one year Graduate Diploma in Education. Their findings indicated that the majority of students found keeping a learner journal aided reflective and metacognitive thinking, as well as providing a means for the reconstruction of experience. Arts educators may find this a particularly useful approach due to the practical nature of many learning tasks which can offer limited chances to capture activities, monitor events or evaluate outcomes in a written form. Through the journal students may reflect on the nature of their learning, determine the cognitive strategy adopted for the task, and this may in turn affect future performance.

In journal writing the language is closer to speech and thus different from normal academic language and it may be that the learning acquired is different. 'Informal language' can make it easier to think about events and the notion of removing barriers to writing through the usual requirement to use formal language has been a focus of research with reference to school children (Parker and Goodkin, 1987, p. 16). Once acknowledging the notion that writing is a powerful way of learning, the means by which this learning occurs become clearer. For example:

> During the 1st term at University I wrote in my journal when I felt I had a particularly interesting day, so I wouldn't forget valuable experiences.
>
> Writing my lesson evaluations helped me to reflect on my teaching and realise the extent of my own development as a teacher.

As much of our knowledge about learning is still evolving and based upon hypothesis the following study aims to provide a clearer idea of what happens when someone writes reflectively in a journal and how the process can be supported during a training programme.

4. PROCEDURE

The nine trainees in this study were enrolled in the Secondary Postgraduate Certificate of Education (P.G.C.E.) Dance course at the School of Education and Lifelong Learning at the University of Exeter. The trainees were all female and their ages ranged from 21–27 years. They held first degrees in Dance or Arts degrees which included 50% dance content. Five of them started the course immediately after gaining their degree, coming from different institutions, whilst the other four had a variety of work experiences prior to training. One had worked as a dance artist in education, another had professional work at Covent Garden Theatre in London, one had worked in retail and another was employed as an entertainment officer on cruise ships. This range of training and different backgrounds brought a rich and valuable diversity of experience to the course.

The ITT course is a one year (36 week) programme, see Table 9.1.

The trainees were asked to keep a reflective journal at the start of the course in October. This could be presented in any form of notebook and the amount or frequency of writing was not prescribed. To encourage entries at any time or place trainees could use handwriting, rather than word processing if they found it simpler. It was explained that this was an expectation of the course and that the writing would form the basis of a 3,000 word reflective paper which would be formally assessed in the following April. It would thus reflect upon 6 months of their journey towards becoming qualified teachers. On completion of the assignment all trainees completed a questionnaire that asked them to comment on: how they managed the reflective writing process; what helped them to reflect in order to learn or learn as a result of reflection; and how the reflective writing helped them to learn about teaching and learning.

TABLE 9.1 Pattern of training and reflective writing

Term 1 Oct.–Dec. (weeks 1–12)	Term 2 Jan.–April (weeks 13–24)	Term 3 May–July (weeks 25–36)
2 weeks in schools to observe practice (Primary and Secondary)	12 weeks in secondary school 1 working alongside experienced teachers	12 weeks in secondary school 2 working alongside experienced teachers with more independent teaching
10 weeks in university, including dance subject knowledge, pedagogy and professional studies	3 seminar days at the university	3 seminar days at the university
Journal started week 3	Journal completed week 24 Assessed assignment Questionnaire	

4.1. Guidance and Support for Reflective Journal Writing

During Term 1, when the trainees were based mainly at the university, there were three sessions targeted at supporting their reflective writing:

1. Handouts were provided designed to provide information, guidance and promote discussion about reflective writing. One of these gave an introduction to this activity, and included what reflective writing is not, such as straightforward description, simple problem solving or conveying information. A series of questions prompting reflective writing were also offered, together with questions to encourage more profound reflection, for example:
   - Are there others, or the views of others who are relevant to this matter, and in what way?
   - Is there relevant formal theory?
   - If you step back from this issue does it look different?
   - Do you notice that your feelings about it have changed over time, or in the course of writing this, suggesting your own frame of reference has changed?

   It was also suggested that working with a peer might be helpful, taking turns to ask prompting questions and then revising the writing.

Another handout was designed as an exercise in reflection, using a teaching scenario based on a dance lesson as the basis for three versions of reflective writing. The trainees were also provided with a framework to help identify different types of reflective writing (Moon, 1999a). Trainees were given time to read and discuss the three different accounts and in pairs asked to identify the features of each, to explain how they fitted into the framework and to justify their decisions with reference to the content of the reflective writing, and how it applied to the framework.

2. The group were asked to bring an example of their reflective writing to share with a peer and then to discuss the work with others. This was a strategy to build confidence in their ability to write reflectively and to share any concerns or identify useful writing approaches.

3. Trainees were provided with prompts for writing and asked to write in their journal during a session. It was hoped that this would encourage and motivate trainees to make entries. For those experiencing difficulties it was an opportunity to talk to peers or the tutor and seek guidance or reassurance.

In Term 2 the trainees returned to the university for three seminar days. On the second seminar day, time was dedicated to sharing extracts from their journals that they found interesting or significant. There was also an opportunity to discuss the structure of the assignment which would be based upon the journal, and identify examples from personal experience and the literature that may be relevant.

5. ANALYSIS

A grounded theory approach was used to evolve categories and concepts from the data in the journals. The categories were refined and developed by repeated reading of the journal entries which were analysed across each of the two terms to allow developmental changes in trainees knowledge to be identified. The questionnaires provided additional data, but in the main the answers were brief.

5.1. How Did the Reflective Journal Help Trainees Learn about Teaching and Learning in Dance?

What follows is an account of the different purposes served by the journal which characterise the apparent nature of the learning that occurred.

5.1.1. Development as a learner and a teacher The majority of entries in this category were made in term 2 during the school placement, although a few students also wrote some comments in term 1, whilst at university. Many of the entries recorded students' beliefs about what they needed to achieve in order to become an effective teacher. They identified strategies used by experienced teachers, whom they observed, which they felt could be part of their own pedagogical practice. Early on in the course Kirsty wrote:

> I really enjoyed watching the 2 classes, I discovered that good teaching includes variation, understanding pupils' needs, giving encouragement and praise when needed. The teacher was also not negative towards wrong answers but questioned the student further and asked the rest of the class what they think. I hope to take and learn from these observations to employ in my lessons (T1 week 3).

Four weeks later the same student, who had been accompanying a pupil to observe them in all their lessons on one day, wrote:

> Today I have been following a pupil around to their lessons It has been interesting to view each teachers managing strategies. An English teacher used humour and a relaxed atmosphere to gain control and input from the students. This is something I would like to use and would feel comfortable with (T1 week 7).

These two entries demonstrated how Kirsty had started to develop a picture of what kind of teacher she aimed to become and was capturing evidence of what that might look like in practice. A few students adopted a more analytical stance, where they were asking questions in relation to the teaching approach or the learning task. For example at the beginning of the school placement Jenny wrote:

> Her (school tutor) behaviour management is on the ball—how does she know when things have gone too far? These judgemental decisions seem the most difficult and daunting elements of teaching (T2 week 1).

There is further evidence of deeper thinking when Suzie wrote a series of reflections at the start of the placement, not unsurprisingly for a beginning teacher, all focused on learning how to manage a class. Over the first few weeks there were regular entries on how to maintain control, for example:

> My most worrying part of teaching is class management, I feel I cannot achieve 'teaching' as I would like because behaviour, dealing with varying needs and listening skills are always being addressed. I feel I will not be able to gain control of a class (T2 week 2).

Further examples included:

> Teaching full lessons I must be assertive and show the pupils what is expected (T2 Jan week 3).
>
> The main thing I need to consider is a command that enforces pupils to stop and listen to my instructions (T2 week 4).
>
> At present I am working on the pitch and pace of my voice and varying it to suit the activity and instructions (T2 week 5).

The final entry about this dimension of teaching from Suzie was:

> I am realising that until a positive learning environment is maintained learning for the pupils will not develop. I must be consistent in enforcing strategies and concentrate on classroom conduct to maintain authority (T2 week 7).

This implied that Suzie was starting to take a more holistic view of her teaching and was able to examine previous ideas and feelings, perceive the relationship between events and arrive at an insight into the issue she was processing. There was also a sense of her development in this dimension as her experience in the school expanded.

There are fewer entries relating to students' development as learners, however, Kirsty did start the course by reflecting on her previous experience in higher education:

> I related back to when I started my degree and I realised I had similar fears to what I have now, I know that new things are going to be scary but

> its best to have a go at it . . . . I need to go through the work, talk to teachers and friends and share fears (T1 week 1).

By acknowledging her feelings and re-evaluating the experience of learning in a similar context she has attempted to use it to inform subsequent activity. Acknowledging the affective dimension of her experience may also enable Kirsty to engage more openly with her responses in her future career.

Most statements relating to students' development were made in term 2 during their first school placement. This was a very demanding and challenging period of their training. Most students worked from 8.00 a.m. until at least 4.00 p.m. in school, and then spent many hours preparing lessons and collecting evidence of meeting the Standards through completing course paperwork A large percentage of their time was directed towards meeting the demands of the real world of the classroom and the placement. It is therefore significant that they still made time to make journal entries and this could indicate that this had become an important activity for them. Throughout the writing there was evidence of an approach that demonstrated both reflective and metacognitive abilities.

5.1.2. Links between theory and practical teaching experience There were very few journal entries in this category and the majority of students made no connections at all between theory and practical experience over the two terms. In two cases there was a list of references and quotations with no reflective comment, and in others a practical experience of teaching was given and a link made to appropriate literature:

> The mixed ability approach certainly seems to correlate with the schools ethos of integration. I'm not really sure which approach is best.
>
> Reference to the literature states that a major number of research reports have failed to show any particular advantages in terms of academic attainment for either streamed or mixed ability grouping (T2 week 10).

5.1.3 Practical information on teaching and learning in Dance The majority of entries in this category were written in term 1, with the number tailing off during the school placement in term 2. Several of the entries commented on ways to improve practice by reflecting on teaching activities, for example, 'I need to work on my level of pupils' understanding through questioning' (T1 week 5). Others were practical descriptions of how to use, for example, differentiation or explanation within teaching, Shelley wrote:

> I used differentiation . . . we gave out pictures for the children to use in their sequence, the more able had difficult ones and the less able easy pictures, some children finished the tasks so we gave them cards with repetition, canon, unison and they added that to their sequence . . . this was a really good session and I learnt how to use differentiation (T1 week 7).

The reflection was largely descriptive, however, one entry related to classroom management proceeded to analyse the episode of teaching and provide possible strategies on how to improve future practice. Two instances, written by Moira, demonstrated how observation of an experienced teacher provided information about the skills required to develop pupils' learning through questioning and the use of subject specific language:

> I noticed that the dance teacher always tried to slip in 'dance specific terms' throughout the class. She also directed questions to test knowledge, understanding and make sure they were all listening (T1 week 3).
>
> The teacher used questioning to test and generate understanding and ideas. Dance specific vocabulary was used throughout the lesson but more so at the beginning and end in relation to analysis/discussion of the pupils' work (T1 week 6).

The distribution of statements in this category were almost all found in the journal in term 1. This is understandable as students were starting a new course designed to qualify them as teachers and they therefore felt a need to record information about practical ideas on what and how to teach. Initially they had only the practical experiences provided for them to draw upon. As they progressed through the course their personal beliefs begin to emerge as they shift to writing about their development as a learner and a teacher.

5.1.4. Feelings and emotions It is also possible to examine the journal entries from the perspective of students' statements about their affective development. It is interesting to note that the majority of entries in term 1, made whilst at university, related to themselves as learners. Once on school placement in term 2 the emphasis shifted to reflecting upon themselves as trainee teachers. The comments relating to their feelings about themselves as they progressed through the course ranged from near exhaustion and anxiety to a growing sense of confidence and enjoyment. Early in the course trainees commented as learners:

> Right now I'm feeling as though I have a hundred and one things to do and just no time at all to complete them, it's as though I never get to the end of my list it just keeps growing and growing (T1 week 4).
>
> This was my worst day at University, I felt like quitting, the workload is increasing and every time I feel up to date more work comes along. . . . I came home today and cried, felt like an idiot but it helped (T1 week 5).

Or again:

> In order to overcome my anxieties I need to think positively, have confidence in myself and work hard (T1 week 5).
>
> Talking to other trainees helped put my fears at ease (T1 week 6).

Towards the end of their first school based work placement in Term 2 trainees made the following sorts of comments reflecting upon themselves as teachers:

> I'm really enjoying teaching-perhaps because I'm teaching my own units of work, perhaps because I'm building better relationships with pupils, or perhaps because I'm just feeling more confident (T2 week 9).

> Walking into a class I was taking was daunting, now it's more of a routine (T2 week 9).
>
> I'm feeling really confident teaching classes to most of the groups now. I am particularly pleased with the relationship I have established with my difficult year 8 group described previously. I'm at a stage where I am sensitive to the pupils' needs and can adapt the lesson to meet their needs–whether in terms of pace (increase or decrease), include extension tasks to challenge or adapt tasks to encourage. From having been my most dreaded class of the week, the class is my most enjoyable to teach (T2 week 10).

The writing about the affective dimension takes little account of the inter-relationship between feeling and cognition, and the complex interaction that occurs during reflection. There are few connections between the ideas and feelings which are part of the original experience and those that have occurred during reflection.

6. DISCUSSION ON THE BENEFITS OF KEEPING A JOURNAL

Trainee teachers appear well placed to develop as reflective practitioners as they are continually being required to evaluate their performance by a variety of means: writing, reading, talking, listening and observation. For most students keeping a journal seemed to aid reflection and metacognitive thinking, and the assignment provided further opportunities to reconstruct their experiences and deepen their reflection. In the journal the descriptive phase often provided the context for an event, providing a basis for a shift in the perspective within the writing where more issues and alternative reasons were explored at a later date. This fits within the hierarchical framework of types of reflection proposed by Hatton and Smith (1995), with higher levels of reflection in this study only being mastered through the writing required in the assignment. They also found that the descriptive mode was more easily mastered and utilised than either the more exploratory or demanding critical forms and hence features most in the journal, which was not being assessed. This was found to be the case for the majority of students in this study, with the journal acting as a means of capturing events and ideas as they happened. However, it is also important to recognise that we all learn in different ways and as Pat commented:

> I didn't find the journal particularly helpful apart from reminding me of particular events. Perhaps if I'd been more consistent in making entries it would have been more helpful (Questionnaire T2).

This supports previous research findings which emphasised the need for courses to provide adequate time and an encouraging environment which establish a commitment to journal writing (Francis, 1995; Dart et al., 1998). Trainees may also need reassurance that reflective writing is a skill that needs to be practised and developed over time. As one trainee wrote: 'I could think reflectively but not write reflectively'. One of the changes to the course resulting from the study will be to provide trainee teachers with the explicit skills that aid reflection. Specific tasks linked to the reading of key articles from the literature on reflection, and how it can be developed through writing a journal will be designed. This may promote writing with more dialogic reflection. There will be paired and small group discussion to clarify understanding related to reflection on practical experience, such as the microteaching episodes in term 1 to encourage connections between theory and practice. They will also be introduced to the notion of 'critical friend' in order to develop familiarity and confidence in critical and collaborative processes at the outset of the course (Francis, 1995; Hatton and Smith, 1995). Finally, greater account will be given to the importance of trainees recognising that feelings and emotional responses to events can be either positive or negative factors in the learning process, (Boud et al. 1985).

7. SUMMARY

1. Reflecting on beliefs

The students' journals recorded their developing beliefs as they progressed as teachers and although this cannot be attributed solely to the need to maintain a journal it does seem likely that it provided a focussing point, and opportunities for the development of metacognitive abilities. It was in the assignment that connecting theory with practical teaching experience occurred. The application of theoretical information to their own learning and teaching was not consciously included in the journals, where the emphasis was mainly on their developing skills and knowledge of teaching.

2. Reflecting on concepts

This could suggest that the promotion of a constructivist view of learning, which enables students to begin to construct their own concepts of teaching and learning, is enhanced through providing structured writing opportunities, such as essays and curriculum tasks, which arise from deeper reflection-on-action drawing upon a journal (Moon, 1999a). As trainee teachers of dance, who may be expected to be familiar in dealing with more abstract ideas and creative approaches to their work, there appeared to be little significant transfer of this experience to writing their journal. It would be very interesting to compare their writing with non-arts specialists.

3. Reflecting on learning

Most trainee teachers feel overwhelmed with course work and the reality of school placements, and few are likely to engage voluntarily in reflective writing. However, the results of this study suggest that by deliberately fostering and encouraging trainee teachers to write reflectively, their learning is likely to be developed and this may then prepare them to carry the practice into their professional careers. It is important to enable them to realise that their personal experience provides valuable and valid evidence upon which they can develop opinions and beliefs about teaching, which will be part of their professional journey.

4. Learning to write reflectively

The need for teachers to be reflective is a commonly held tenet among teacher educators and researchers, and although more research is needed to explore fully what form that reflection should take journals may be useful learning tools. Longitudinal research into this is essential to provide more conclusive evidence.

5. Writing as dialogic reflection

The ability to engage in discourse with one's self, to step back from events and explore possible alternatives is important for students to develop. Through the journal it was possible for them to analyse factors, make judgements and attempt to provide a rationale to reach useful outcomes of learning, or more material for reflection. Developing this deeper level of reflection should form part of planned objectives for ITT and arts education programmes.

REFERENCES

Boud, D., Keogh, R., and Walker, D. (1985). *Reflection: Turning Experience into Learning*. London: Kogan Page.

Brown, J., Collins, A., and Duguid, P. (1989). Situated cognition and the culture of learning. *Educational Researcher*, 18(1), 32–42.

Dart, B., Boulton-Lewis, G., and Mc Crindle, A. (1998). Change in knowledge of learning and teaching through journal writing. *Research Papers in Education*, 13(3), 291–318.

Ertmer, P. and Newby, T. (1996). The expert learner: strategic, self-regulated and reflective. *Instructional Science*, 24, 1–24.

Flavell, J. (1987). Speculations about the nature and development of metacognition. In F. Weinett and R. Kluwe (Eds.), *Metacognition, Motivation and Understanding* (pp. 21–29). Hillsdale, NJ: Lawrence Erlbaum.

Francis, D. (1995). The reflective journal: a window to preservice teachers, practical knowledge. *Teaching and Teacher Education*, 11(3), 229–241.

Hadwin, A. and Winne, P. (1996). Study strategies have meagre support: a review with recommendations for implementation. *Journal of Higher Education*, 67(6), 1–17.

Hatton, N. and Smith, D. (1995). Reflection in teacher education-towards definition and implementation. *Teaching and Teacher Education*, 11(1), 33–49.

King, P. and Kitchener, K. (1994). *Developing Reflective Judgement*. San Francisco, CA: Jossey-Bass.

McCrindle, A. and Christensen, C. (1995). The impact of learning journals on metacognitive processes and learning performance. *Learning and Instruction*, 5(3), 167–85.

Moon, J. (1999a). *Learning Journals: A Handbook for Academics, Students and Professional Development*. London: Kogan Page.

Moon, J. (1999b). *Reflection in Learning and Professional Development*. London: Kogan Page.

Parker, R. and Goodkin, V. (1987). *The Consequences of Writing: Enhancing Learning in the Disciplines*. New Jersey: Boynton/Cook.

Richardson, V. (1997). Constructiveness teaching and teacher education: theory and practice. In V. Richardson (Ed.), *Constructivist Teacher Education* (pp. 3–14). London: Falmer Press.

Schön, D. (1983). *The Reflective Practitioner*. San Francisco, CA: Jossey-Bass.

Schön, D. (1987). *Educating the Reflective Practitioner*. San Francisco, CA: Jossey-Bass.

JANE CHEUNG AND ETON KUNG

10. REFLECTIVE USE OF DIGITAL TECHNOLOGIES IN THE ARTS

1. DIGITAL TECHNOLOGIES IN EDUCATION

The application of digital technologies in arts and music education has been developed in recent decades. There has been abundant research on this topic as well as different kinds of teaching materials developed for use. Williams and Webster's (2006) illustration on the use of music technology in music making as well as computer-aided music instruction is a typical example in this field.

Technology in music education seems particularly strong in facilitating the learning process when students are engaged in creative activities, and research in this area can be categorised into three groups (Kung, 2002). The first investigates compositional processes in discrete stages (Bennett, 1976; Kratus, 1989; Levi, 1991; Wilson and Wales, 1995; Kaschub, 1999); the second focuses on the measurement of 'creative thinking in music' (Webster, 1987, 1989, 1990; DeLorenzo, 1989; Fung, 1997) and the third studies the qualitative aspects of children's compositional processes in the context of technology (Bamberger, 1977; Hickey, 1997; Ladanyi, 1997; Emmons, 1998).

Although the three categories are not directly related to using technologies as reflective tools, it is found from the project below that digital technologies can help students to realise musical ideas most effectively during the creative process. When a student is engaged in a compositional process, creating and manipulating ideas through interaction with the technological environment, and developing ideas until achieving a final product, he or she is actually going through a reflective process. This chapter begins with a brief explanation of reflective practice and discusses some educators' views on using technologies to empower learners to compose and to develop self-learning and reflective practice. This is illustrated with a project conducted by the authors with some pre-service music students using music technologies to enhance their composing as well as using the Discussion Board of the elearn Blackboard Platform to reflect on their processes and products. The chapter finally concludes with consolidating the reflective use of digital technologies in helping learners analyse their work, and develop self learning, critical observation and creative thinking.

2. TECHNOLOGIES TO ENHANCE REFLECTIVE PRACTICE

Schön (1983, 1987) argues for the reflection-in-action behaviour of solving problems through rapid thinking and trial and error that brings about on-the-spot experiments and spontaneous responses. He also encourages the reflection-on-practice approach

P. Burnard and S. Hennessy (eds.), *Reflective Practice in Arts Education*, 107–122.

to look back on what has happened, to develop one's self-knowledge and the ability to analyse situations in order to improve. Practice is a constructive process to develop workable solutions to situations. Argyris (1993) and Argyris and Schön (1978) also argue that reflective practice requires both thought and actions as integral processes, where context and culture are important in shaping the reflective process. Digital technologies can be utilised as tools for reflection in arts education in many ways. Jonassen (2000) not only provides models to integrate technologies with the learning process to develop mindful learning, but also simulation programming which can enhance problem-solving and engage learners in constructive and critical thinking about their learning. As reflective tools for evaluation, Montgomery (2003) believes that such applications can actively engage the learner's intellect, leading to an increased understanding that promotes reflective practice among pre-service educators. Davidson (1990) considers the computer as a compositional tool that provides an environment for exploration, verification and confirmation. Students can perceive musical knowledge, compose their own pieces and reflect on them in a flexible, integrated manner without following a rigid sequence. The 'Playback' and 'Save to file' features allow students to engage in problem solving over long periods of time, and to reflect on the development of their musical ideas.

3. HOW LEARNERS DEVELOP REFLECTIVE PRACTICE THROUGH TECHNOLOGIES

Digital technologies can play a significant role in empowering learners in the process of self-learning through Internet support. Goethals et al. (2004) promote the opportunity to integrate different subject areas to stimulate a variety of end products and allow the learners to make wise choices, to engage in critical observation and to be able to separate the observed event or behaviour from its expectation and interpretation. Sequencing and multimedia software allow the integration of different arts, which provide an effective environment for trial and error, integrating audio, visual and media to create multimedia products and musical compositions, and linking concepts across different subjects. To develop the learners' emotional growth, it is important to emphasise the need for trial and error and risk taking experiences, as well as innovative and critical thinking. Learners are encouraged to acquire technical skills and develop problem-solving skills, to work as a team and to scrutinize their practice critically. To facilitate social development, learners require an environment of support that enhances open communication, critical dialogue, shared insights and peer problem solving. Learners are encouraged to value individual differences with appropriate skills to resolve conflicts. Wilson and Jan (1993) recognize that reflective practice supports learners in their endeavours to set their own goals. It empowers learners to make their own decisions and reflect on what they have done well and what they need to improve on.

The *Discussion Board and functions* of the elearn *Blackboard* Platform allows learners to communicate with each other, to reflect critically on their action and to improve with innovative strategies (see Figure 10.1). The following sections give

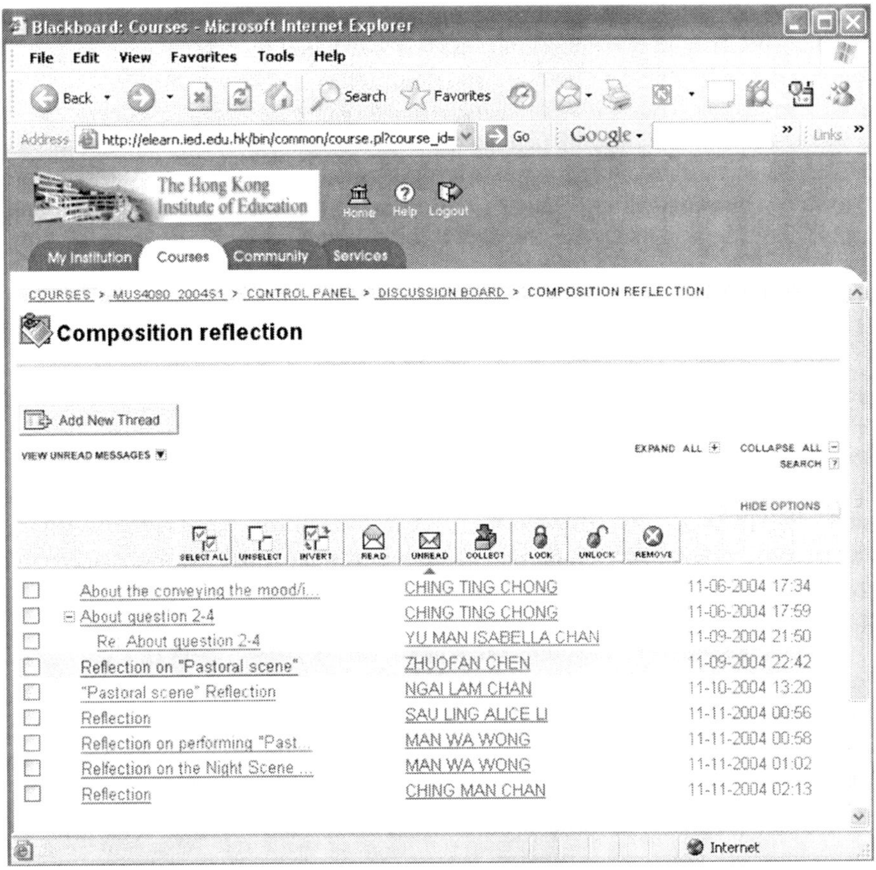

Figure 10.1. [Discussion of the elearn Blackboard Platform]

more concrete examples of how digital technologies have enhanced student teachers to learn and reflect.

4. DIGITAL TOOLS FOR COMPOSING AND REFLECTION

This project was conducted with a group of fourth year music students in the Hong Kong Institute of Education pre-service Bachelor of Education (Honours) (Secondary) course. Prior to the project, the students attended a module on Materials and Structure and a Music Composition module, where they experienced various composition techniques. They also used technologies for various purposes such as music arrangement and creating a music score. Composing or creating has not been a common practice in the secondary schools of Hong Kong, it was treated only as an additional activity until the new Arts Education Curriculum Guide (CDC, 2002) and the Music Curriculum Guide (CDC, 2003) were published, which promote the integration of performing, creating and listening activities in schools. Hence with limited experience in composing, student teachers found themselves lacking confidence and often found it difficult. In this project, music technologies were incorporated both in their creative music making and in reflecting on the creative process and product, with a view to developing students' creative and critical thinking, to promoting an interest in composing and to developing a systematic way of keeping records of creative thinking. Students worked in their peer groups to explore sound, compose music using acoustic and digital instruments, and critically reflect on the creative process and product critically.

4.1. Arranging and Record Keeping

The first assignment used visual images as a starting point. Each group chose a scenic picture either from a calendar or supplied by the teacher e.g. a night scene in Cape Town or a pastoral scene, and discussed some prominent features of the picture, the mood it conveyed and how these could be best represented and expressed in sound. The teacher put particular emphasis on obvious objects or mood that they could imagine and represent, using rhythmic or melodic motives and their development, the general mood of the music conveyed, and the choice of instruments to represent them. Dynamic contrasts and suitable musical form were in mind when constructing the piece. The students chose and explored their instruments, including the electronic keyboard, and were actively engaged in experimenting with melodic lines, rhythmic motives, harmonic ideas, instrumental timbre, different tempi, dynamic contrasts, and different moods and styles. The students were so much engaged in their own musical venture that they filtered out the noise made by other groups. When the students were engaged as active composers, listeners and performers, the teacher facilitated their learning by raising relevant questions: 'Is it a quiet time of the night in Cape Town or a busy time? How would you express some African flavour? Think of an event that happens, is it joyful or mournful? What is in the foreground and what is in the background?' 'Imagine you see some creatures on the pasture, express them musically, develop and extend these ideas to a musical whole.' 'Listen critically to the contrast of timbre and expression, and try to give some structure to the piece.' This helped to arouse students' creative thinking, aural discrimination, critical judgement and personal enquiry. Alternatives were sometimes given, which required their independent decision making. The first compositions were performed and recorded, the digital files were posted onto the Assignments section of the elearn platform, together with the visual stimuli for everybody to view and listen to after the lesson. Students were encouraged to reflect and improve on their creative works through group discussion and answering four questions on the Discussion Board:

(a) Do you think your group has conveyed the mood/ideas/message that you wanted to express?
(b) Is the music coherent? How?
(c) With what are you most and least satisfied?
(d) Can you suggest how you can further revise, extend or improve your work?

In the second session, they revised their works through discarding, adding, extending and contrasting. The second musical impressions were also posted onto the elearn platform for comparison, reflection and critique.

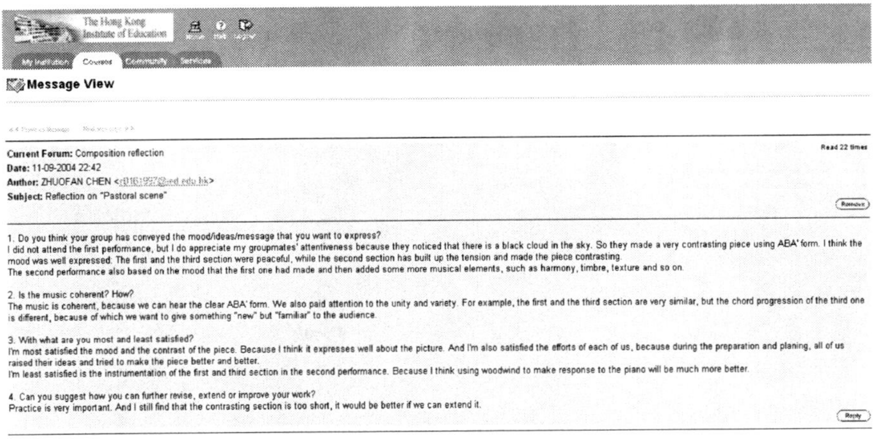
The Hong Kong Institute of Education

My Institution | Courses | Community | Services

Message View

Current Forum: Composition reflection
Date: 11-09-2004 22:42
Author: ZHUOFAN CHEN <s0161997@ied.edu.hk>
Subject: Reflection on "Pastoral scene"

Read 22 times

1. Do you think your group has conveyed the mood/ideas/message that you want to express?
I did not attend the first performance, but I do appreciate my groupmates' attentiveness because they noticed that there is a black cloud in the sky. So they made a very contrasting piece using ABA' form. I think the mood was well expressed: The first and the third section were peaceful, while the second section has built up the tension and made the piece contrasting.
The second performance also based on the mood that the first one had made and then added some more musical elements, such as harmony, timbre, texture and so on.

2. Is the music coherent? How?
The music is coherent, because we can hear the clear ABA' form. We also paid attention to the unity and variety. For example, the first and the third section are very similar, but the chord progression of the third one is different, because of which we want to give something "new" but "familiar" to the audience.

3. With what are you most and least satisfied?
I'm most satisfied the mood and the contrast of the piece. Because I think it expresses well about the picture. And I'm also satisfied the efforts of each of us, because during the preparation and planing, all of us raised their ideas and tried to make the piece better and better.
I'm least satisfied is the instrumentation of the first and third section in the second performance. Because I think using woodwind to make response to the piano will be much more better.

4. Can you suggest how you can further revise, extend or improve your work?
Practice is very important. And I still find that the contrasting section is too short, it would be better if we can extend it.

Reply

Figure 10.2. [Reflective comments on composition]

In the last session of the first assignment, students arranged their compositions with the sequencing software SONAR on a MIDI keyboard. They worked either in groups or individually: in fact many of them preferred to work independently with headphones. The teacher helped them solve some technical problems or find their desirable sound. Some students worked section by section and layer by layer, but most of them worked track by track with the chosen timbre. They worked quietly and again shared their completed work on the platform. They reflected on the musical experience; their views on using technologies to assist music composing; the creative process and the final products. Their reflections were posted on the discussion board so that their peers could share and comment (see Figure 10.2).

4.2. Developing Critical and Aesthetic Thinking

One of the visual images was a peaceful pastoral scene taken from a visit to the South Downs in West Sussex, the United Kingdom.

Penny tried to explain how the music composition evolved from the visual stimuli (see Figure 10.3).

> When we got the picture we tried to decide an appropriate mood for it first. We wanted to convey a peaceful and relaxed mood. We selected some instruments that we thought appropriate and a moderate tempo. Then we thought of adding some contrast because it would be quite boring with just one mood. We looked at the picture closely and found a black cloud. We based on what we observed and felt, and started to create two contrasting sections, one was like a tempest.

She reflected on their thinking process, which led to a decision that influenced their action, and finally produced the piece of creative work.

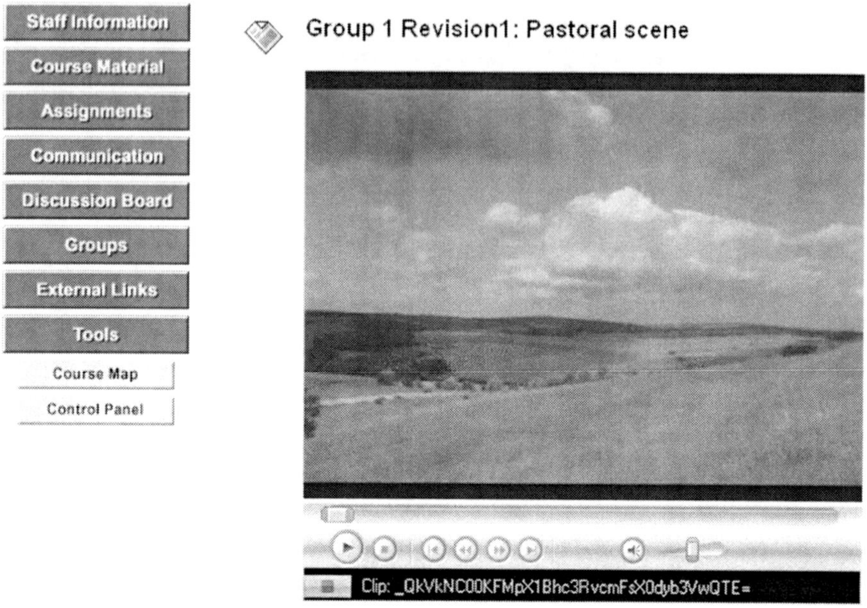

Figure 10.3. [Pastoral Scene]

Jennifer also reflected on how they worked with the digital technology: 'We used the flute and the clarinet from the instrument list to play the melody, replacing the original instruments we used. We chose the woodwind instruments because of their warm tone, which we thought was most suitable to convey a pastoral scene' (see Figure 10.4).

Aesthetic qualities very often guided their musical choices in composing. 'In the first performance, we felt that the second section was too short and the changing mood was not obvious,' said Penny, 'and after some revision with a change of instruments and added imitation, we have made an extension of the section and the changing mood was more obvious.' Jennifer believed that their composition was coherent: 'We could hear the music with a clear ABA form and we were conscious of achieving unity with variety. The first and the third sections were very similar, but the chord progressions of the third section were different, so that we could hear something new but familiar.' Isabel agreed that technologies had helped her develop creative thinking and aesthetic awareness. She reflected: 'After these sessions, my creative thinking and aesthetic thinking have been enhanced through using the computer. After completing some musical phrases, I would see these as a whole, to connect all the phrases smoothly and aesthetically. I used the dynamics to balance and make the contrast between phrases. These sessions have been useful in learning to compose.'

The software facilitated the creative process of developing musical ideas, which was reflected in Jennifer's remarks: 'I divided the music into three parts, and recorded it part by part (i.e., section by section), layer by layer' (see Figure 10.5). She further

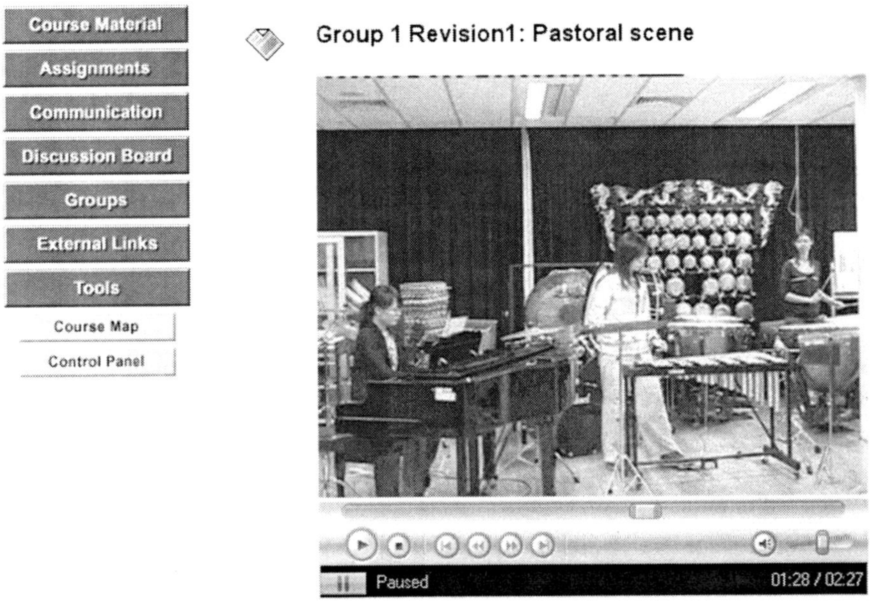

Figure 10.4. [Group One Revision One]

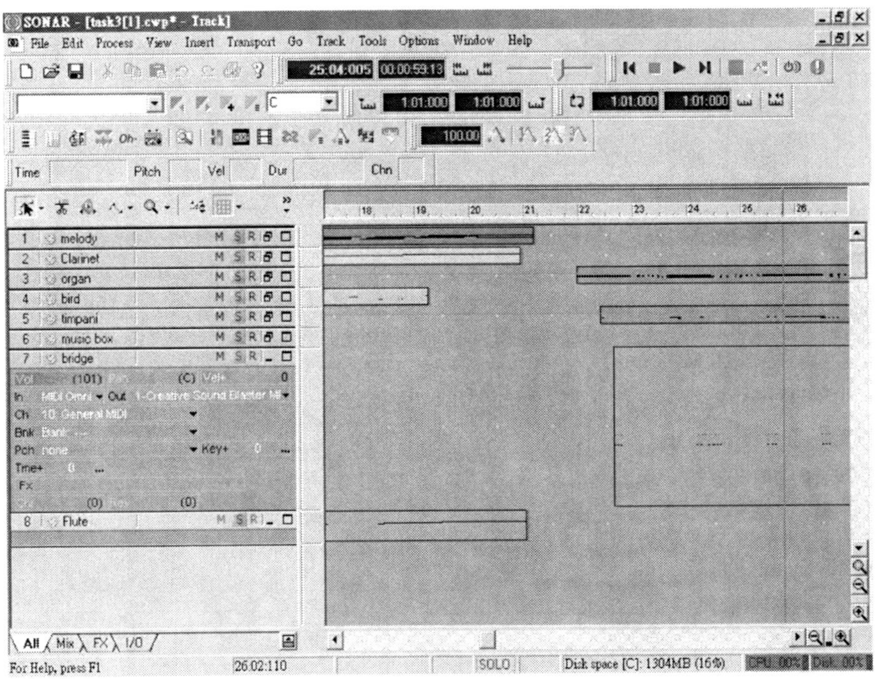

Figure 10.5. [SONAR score]

described the advantages of computer technology:

> I can record my ideas immediately using the record function . . . it is easy to listen to my composition and revise it too. . . . I think using the arts is a good way to stimulate young people's creative thinking. . . . From my previous experience, the most difficult thing is to think of an idea, but now, every visual stimulus can be a source of musical imagination for me.

She also wrote:

> By using the MIDI keyboard, we could add some sound effects like the blowing wind, the bird calls and add as many instrumental effects as we like through layer recording, which we could not have done with the three of us using only limited instruments.

Penny also held a similar view:

> Technologies are helpful, I can create the sound that I imagine in my mind through the computer because it sounds real, and I can revise and extend the ideas, e.g. the dynamics and tempo. It would be quite difficult for me to make the musical expression without the computer, because I could not control the other classmates during the performance. We had technical difficulties in playing real instruments to express the music.

Alice also agreed with the others:

> The computer is useful and convenient for me to compose, I have tried to explore more musical elements. I have improved in composing using the computer, the music sounds richer with more attention to the elements like melody, rhythm, formal organisation, change of timbre and dynamics.

Sandra analysed the changes made to the revised version and how they could do better:

> In the revised version, we used improvisation and added new melodies, which made the piece more musical. However, if we could use the flute for the melody, the melodic line would sound much clearer. I agree with Penny that we could do more with the dynamics both within a section and between sections.

Jennifer also wrote positively about technology: 'I think ICT is a good way to develop our creative thinking, it gives me new insights about teaching music in the secondary school, where creativity is less emphasised.'

Technology has proved to be a user-friendly and effective tool for composing, however, despite the many advantages in using technologies to compose and reflect on the learning process, some students were very aware of the problems and issues that they encountered with technologies: 'The tone colour from the MIDI keyboard was quite different and some expression marks could not be interpreted either' (Sandra). 'The percussion section of the computer was not always reliable, the sounds were unstable. We chose the cymbals to express the wind but it eventually changed to some other sounds' (Isabel).

It is hard to perform a piece if the instruments chosen turn out to be either out of tune or their timbres cannot be predicted during a recording or a performance. Penny enjoyed creating music with her friends using acoustic classroom instruments:

> The computer did not allow me to communicate or share the composing process with other students when we worked individually. I quite enjoyed communicating with my friends during the creating process using classroom instruments because we could discuss with each other.

4.3. Creating Multimedia Products

In another assignment, students under took two tasks in which they were presented with a sequence of silent video animations (the first lasting 15 seconds, the second lasting 60 seconds) composed of movement and the transformation of lines and shapes in two colours (red and blue). Students first watched the video, analyzed the movement and structure before creating appropriate musical material to synchronize with the images. Cakewalk SONAR sequencing software, which is capable of creating sound to synchronize with video images, was used as the main tool for these multimedia tasks.

Before working on these tasks, the teacher introduced to students the relationship between visual and musical elements, and how they could correlate to each other as shown in the Table 10.1.

Students were asked to reflect on the relationship between the visual stimuli and their creative musical expression in sound for *Task 1* and in addition, the use of technologies in learning music and the arts in *Task 2* (see Figure 10.6).

TABLE 10.1 Possible relationships between musical and visual elements for understanding artistic elements from an integrative learning approach

Visual image	Musical sound
Lines	Melodic lines and contour
Shapes	Relations between shapes
Form	Musical form
Texture	Polyphony
Colour	Key, tonality, timbre
Contrast	Dynamic contrasts e.g. *p*, *f*, *crescendo*, *decrescendo*
Pattern/Rhythm of appearance of objects/order	Rhythm/melodic and rhythmic pattern, tempo change e.g. *ritardando, accelerando*
Objects in space (two-dimensional)	High and low (registers)
Types of objects e.g. dots, lines, rectangles, etc.	Single notes, sustained notes, phrases, note clusters, etc.

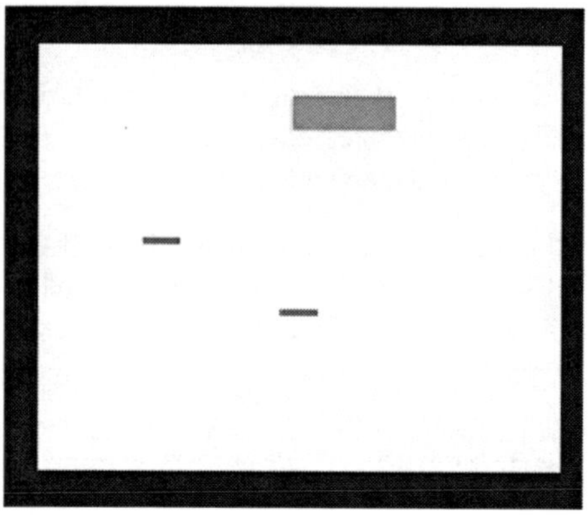

Figure 10.6. [Visual stimuli]

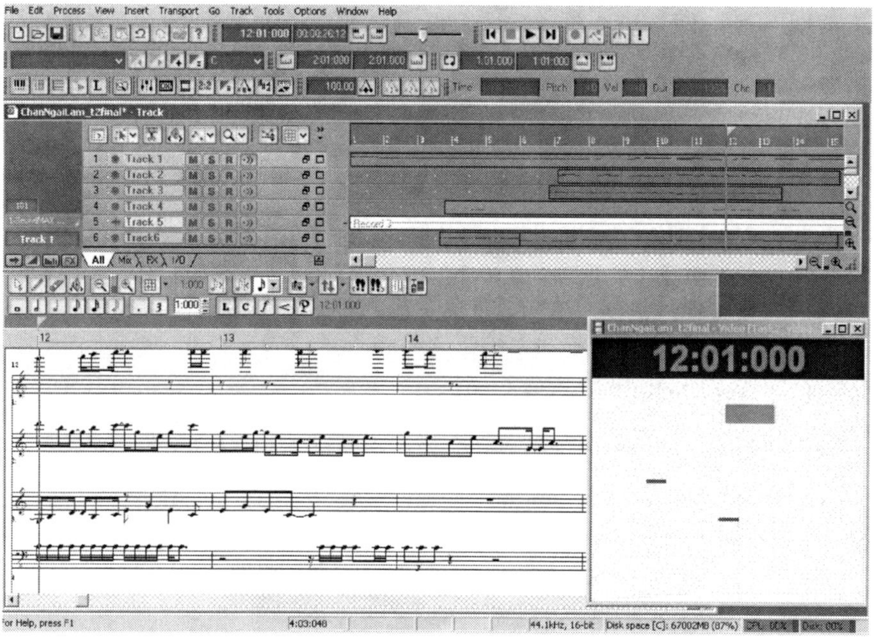

Figure 10.7. [Composition with visual stimuli]

Penny explained:

> The jump (of an object) from a higher position to a lower position makes me feel the pitch dropping from high to low, . . . the mood is quite relaxed, . . . I have tried to create a relaxing mood by using an active rhythm and a melody in a major tonality.

Moreover, when seeing the object change and move, the students were able to connect them with continuous changes in musical elements. Isabella said: 'as the size of the circle is increasing, I use more notes, even running notes to represent them.' Jennifer also commented: 'I want to create peaceful background music to represent the white background of the video. But frankly speaking, I'm not satisfied with the melody I created. It needs improvement.' It was obvious that the visual stimuli were able to arouse imagination, creative and critical thinking in sound.

4.4. A Fast Route to Communicate

The computer is an effective tool for students to learn from each other. 'We could see other classmates' creative products on the elearn platform,' said Penny. 'The computer and the MIDI keyboard have helped me to express my feelings and ideas through music,' Alice also admitted. She further added: 'Not only have we saved time in composing without having to write down the notation, we can express our feelings directly.' It is clear that technologies have provided opportunities for students to express their ideas, and for students to share and comment, which ultimately leads to the construction of knowledge and understanding. The advantages of displaying their composition process and product electronically and providing them with an environment to share feedback are unique, and helped learning to occur more efficiently.

4.5. Self and Peer Assessment

The reflection showed critical evaluation of their performances and their personal strengths and weaknesses in composing. Penny was not satisfied with their group performance:

> I was less satisfied with the performance because we did not have enough time to practice, and our lack of cooperation affected our performance. We could have done more about the dynamic contrast, and put more thoughts on the choice of instruments. Nevertheless, I was satisfied with the structure and the mood of the piece because it gave me a peaceful feeling first before it got agitated.

Jennifer was more appreciative and reflected:

> I was satisfied with the joint effort because during the planning and rehearsal stage, all of us made constructive suggestions and we all tried to improve the piece together. I was less satisfied with the instruments used in the first and third sections during the second recording, because I thought using the woodwind to answer the piano phrase would be much better. I still found the B section too short, it would be better to extend it a bit. Also, practice is most important.

Alice agreed with Jennifer that they needed more practice: 'Our cooperation at the end was bad, we were not together, and we needed more time to practise the final part in order to improve.' Sandra too, was not happy with their collaboration and communication: 'We seemed to be playing different chord progressions at the end, hence more communication was needed both during the rehearsals and at the performance.'

5. REFLECTIVE USE OF DIGITAL TECHNOLOGIES

5.1. *Technologies as 'Facilitators'*

Technologies helped students to explore, express and develop their musical ideas in an integrated and effective way. As facilitators, they helped students to stretch their imagination to new heights. The sequencing software provided a convenient tool for students to develop and record their musical ideas instantly without having to spend extra time notating it on paper or inserting the notes using notating software. The 'playback' function and the instrument resource bank were extremely user-friendly, not only for students to choose their desired timbre, chord progression or the appropriate mood through trial and error, but also to help them listen critically to what they had created. Creating music with visual stimuli provided an opportunity for students to broaden their perspective to understand the relationship between various artistic elements. This integrative approach to experiencing the creative process provided motivation for creativity that led to innovative art works with which the students have seldom engaged. Students seemed able to construct a piece where the musical flow was induced by the continuously changing impact of the visual objects. Using visual elements to stimulate music compositions facilitated students' artistic and imaginative thinking. Technologies provided tools for reflection which added a new dimension to their understanding, as reflected in their discussion.

5.2. *Technologies as 'Catalysts'*

While students were working intently on computers to create and edit their music, they were involved in a process of trial and error experimenting, quick thinking and spontaneous responses. In this, the metaphor of 'catalyst' applies to the potent technologies, which were used in many guises as a means to create, expand, communicate, appraise and reflect. The powerful functions of the MIDI keyboard and the computer facilitated decision making and the on-the-spot reflection-in-action behaviour. The Assignment section of the elearn platform, where students' finished or unfinished products could be uploaded for open appreciation, provided further opportunities for musical analysis, reflection, comparison and critical thought. This helped their self-knowledge and ability to analyse artistic situations. With the teacher's guiding questions on coherence, communication, quality and suggestions for improvement, the Discussion Board provided yet a third channel for students to reflect critically on their creative process and products. The environment was most effective for learning in the sense that students could access their own compositions at any time, so that they could look back at what they had done; to reflect on the creative process, their strengths and weaknesses, and suggest new strategies to improve their work. This integral process of reflection and action was effective in relating theory to practice, to developing self learning strategies and to developing an attitude of responsibility for their own learning. Moreover, students were able to evaluate their peers' performances and recommend ways of improvement. Hence the Discussion Board not only served as an effective self-assessment tool, it also provided a common ground for reflection. Using these reflective tools gradually enhanced students' musical knowledge, skills and attitudes as independent learners.

5.3. Technologies as 'Enhancers'

Technologies, including multimedia, are fast changing and resourceful, they are used to evaluate and enhance students' creative works as well as to increase their curriculum time. Nowadays, young people communicate with each other through various digital means. They use mobile phones with digital camera functions to capture precious moments and send photographs to friends electronically. They send messages through short messaging service; contact one another through instant messaging and remember each other's important dates and events by sending e-cards to different parts of the world. The use of the Discussion Board of the e-learn platform to communicate with the rest of the class, and to reflect on their own progress for professional development, is much in line with how they communicate with each other in their daily lives. These tools further extend the formal curriculum time where students can discuss and share new knowledge and experience according to their learning styles. This enables the teacher to respond appropriately to their doubts and concerns beyond lecturing hours.

5.4. Technologies as 'Role Reverser'

Reflective practice brings about a paradigm shift in the roles of the teacher and the learner, where the learner/practitioner is responsible for solving problems and becoming active in creating his/her own learning agenda. The role of the teacher has changed to that of a facilitator, providing directive questions to guide students' personal enquiry, supporting their professional growth. While the learners take greater responsibilities for their own learning, the teacher facilitates their learning by providing a secure environment that encourages active reflection and action. The students find relevance and pleasure in their learning and their reflections on creative experiences was a musical self-discovery. This approach paves the way for the paradigm shift of encouraging students to take charge of their own learning and making their musical experience meaningful. The reflections have demonstrated students' abilities to solve musical problems, develop sensitivity to aesthetic qualities, engage in the integral process of reflection-in-action at work, become self-critical, analyse their creative process and appreciate the use of digital technologies to compose. It has also shown the effectiveness of technology as a creative environment. Learners gradually learn to make intelligent use of technologies to enhance their arts experience through active reflection and practice. Teachers should be aware of the advantages and issues brought about by digital technologies to guide students learning through these powerful tools.

6. CONCLUSION

This chapter has tried to illustrate how digital technologies can act as reflective tools to facilitate learners to develop artistically and think reflectively. Digital technologies can extend the provision of a creative environment for the learners to develop their artistic knowledge, skills and attitude, to enable learners analyse their own creative processes and products. Learning thus occurs when learners create, revise and develop ideas either by engaging in compositional processes or reflecting through discussion. While young people are generally receptive to new technologies, educators could be more confident to take advantage of digital technologies to develop innovative strategies for achieving a student-centred curriculum, in order to fully develop the learners' aesthetic sensitivity and support their professional growth in the arts.

REFERENCES

Argyris, C. (1993). *Knowledge for Action: A Guide to Overcoming Barriers to Organisational Change*. San Francisco, CA: Jossey-Bass.

Argyris, C. and Schön, D. (1978). *Organisational Learning*. Reading, MA: Addison-Wesley.

Bamberger, J. (1977). In search of a tune. In D. Perkins and B. Leondar (Eds.), *The Arts and Cognition* (pp. 284–319). Baltimore, MA: Johns Hopkins Press.

Bennett, S. (1976). The process of musical creation: interviews with eight composers. *Journal of Research in Music Education*, 24, 3–13.

Curriculum Development Council (CDC). (2002). *Arts Education Key Learning Area Curriculum Guide (Primary 1–Secondary 3)*. Hong Kong: CDC.

Curriculum Development Council (CDC). (2003). *Music Curriculum Guide (Primary 1–Secondary 3)*. Hong Kong: CDC.

Davidson, L. (1990). Tools and environments for musical creativity. *Music Educators Journal*, May, 47–51.

DeLorenzo, L.C. (1989). A field study of sixth-grade students' creative music problem-solving processes. *Journal of Research in Music Education*, 37, 188–200.

Emmons, S.E. (1998). *Analysis of Musical Creativity in Middle School Students through Composition Using Computer-assisted Instruction: a Case Study* (Doctoral dissertation). The University of Rochester, Eastman School of Music, New York. Dissertation Abstract International, 59/02 (University Microfilms No. 9825697).

Fung, C.V. (1997). Effect of a sound exploration program on children's creative thinking in music. *Research Studies in Music Education*, 9, 13–19.

Goethals, M., Howard, R., and Sanders, M. (2004). *Student Teaching. a Process Approach to Reflective Practice*. (2nd ed.). New Jersey: Pearson.

Hickey, M. (1997). The computer as a tool in creative music making. *Research Studies in Music Education*, 8, 56–70.

Jonassen, D.H. (2000). *Computers as Mindtools for Schools*. (2nd ed.). Upper Saddle River, NJ: Merrill.

Kaschub, M. (1999). *Six Grade Student's Descriptions of Their Individual and Collaborative Music Composition Processes and Products Initiated from Prompted and Unprompted Task Structures* (Doctoral dissertation). Northwestern University, Dissertation Abstract International, 60/06. (University Microfilms No. 9932187).

Kratus, J.K. (1989). A time analysis of the compositional processes used by children 7–11, *Journal of Research in Music Education*. 37(1), 5–20.

Kung, E. (2002). Case studies of students' compositional processes and products with and without the use of sequencing software. In J. Drummond and D. Sell (Eds.), *Conference Proceedings to Taonga of the Asia Pacific Rim NZSME and ISME Regional Conference 2001* (pp. 247–258). Auckland: New Zealand Society for Music Education (Inc.).

Ladanyi, K.S. (1997). Insights into process of musical composition facilitated by digital music equipment. *Bulletin of the Council of Research in Music Education*, 131, 33.

Levi, R.G. (1991). *A Field Investigation of the Composing Process by Second-Grade Children Creating Original Language and Music Pieces*. Unpublished doctoral dissertation, Case Western Reserve University.

Montgomery, L.A. (2003). Digital portfolios in teacher education: blending professional standards, assessment, technology and reflective practice. In D. Lamont Johnson and C. Maddux (Eds.), *Technology in Education. A Twenty-Year Retrospective* (pp. 171–186). New York: The Haworth Press Inc.

Schön, D. (1983). *The Reflective Practitioner*. New York: Basic Books.

Schön, D. (1987). *Educating the Reflective Practitioner*. San Francisco, CA: Jossey-Bass.

Wilson, J. and Jan, L.W. (1993). *Thinking for Themselves*. Portsmouth, NH: Heinemann.

Wilson, S.J. and Wales, R.J. (1995). An Exploration of children's musical compositions. *Journal of Research in Music Education*, 43(2), 94–111.

Webster, P.R. (1987). Conceptual bases for creative thinking in music. In J. Perry, I. Perry, and T. Draper (Eds.), *Music and Child Development* (pp. 158–174). New York: Springer-Verlag.

Webster, P.R. (1989). Creative thinking in music: the assessment question. In C.P. Dooane and J.W. Richman (Eds.), *Proceedings of the Sun Coast Music Education Forum On Creativity* (pp. 40–74). Tampa, FL: University of South Florida.

Webster, P.R. (1990). Creativity as creative thinking. *Music Educators Journal*, 76(9), 22–28.

Williams, D.B. and Webster, P.R. (2006). *Experiencing Music Technology*. Belmont, CA: Thomson Schirmer.

JODY L. KERCHNER

11. TOOLS FOR DEVELOPING REFLECTIVE SKILLS

> Reflective thinking requires the continual evaluation of beliefs, assumptions, and hypotheses of the data. The resulting judgments are offered as reasonable integrations or syntheses of opposing points of view. Because they involve ongoing verification and evaluation, judgments based on reflective thinking are more likely to be valid and insightful than are beliefs derived from authority, emotional commitment, or narrow reasoning.
>
> (On John Dewey's (1933) reflective thinking model, King and Kitchener, 1994, p. 7).

In order to design effective lessons, arts educators must develop reflective thinking skills with which they carefully consider their students' cultural contexts, fears, skills, interests, and contributions to the classroom dynamic. A primary pedagogical goal for mentor teachers and teacher educators is to lead and model the dance of reflection: on values that guide their teaching, shared roles as teacher and learner, presentational style, methodology, sequence, artistic authenticity, students' backgrounds and abilities, and classroom dynamics.

In this chapter, I explore ways in which arts educators, both novice and experienced, can further develop their reflective thinking and teaching skills. Specifically, I present four tools—river journeys, metaphor sculptures, portfolio goals, and videotaped teaching reflections—that have guided my music education students in their quest to develop reflective thinking and teaching skills. The chapter begins with a discussion of environmental conditions and habits of mind or personal traits necessary to engage with reflective thinking tools (in reflective thinking). While the examples I use to illustrate the reflective thinking tools come from a music education perspective, I make suggestions later in the chapter for applying each tool to other arts education domains. Developing and refining reflective thinking skills empower arts educators to monitor and assess their own teaching.

1. A TOOL FOR REFLECTING ON SELF

Reflective thinking is similar to looking at your image in a mirror. You might look at yourself and find exactly what you expected to see. Or, depending on your self-concept, the perception of your image might be clouded by mental or emotional distortions. Or, perhaps your surroundings (i.e., bright light, color schemes, clarity of the mirrored glass, magnification of the glass) influenced the specificity of detail you were able to see. Depending on what you were looking for as you glimpsed into the mirror, you

P. Burnard and S. Hennessy (eds.), *Reflective Practice in Arts Education*, 123–136.

might have focused on seeing the whole picture of yourself or on a minute detail while ignoring other features. Presumably, the more you looked into the mirror, the more image details came into your awareness.

The same is true of developing reflective thinking skills as an arts educator. While there are many aspects about teaching on which educators might reflect, they typically begin focusing only on one or two elements of the classroom or their methodology. Novice arts educators often have the opportunity to request mentor teachers to assist them in their quest for gaining multiple perspectives about a particular teaching situation or challenge. Depending on the mentors' reliability for providing objective observational feedback, novice teachers might have their perceptions of their teaching confirmed, rejected, or expanded by the mentors' feedback.

There are times, however, when mentors' observational feedback remains 'unnoticed' by novice teachers. It is not until the novice teachers are willing to 'see' for themselves what is happening in the classroom that the teachers begin to look closely at their teaching methodologies, materials, and the classroom environment in order to analyse their efficacy in serving all students. In a conducting class that I teach, I often ask the students to watch themselves in a mirror as they conduct a musical passage. I remind the students to analyze what they see and to make adjustments, until they see what they want to see from their conducting gestures. While I might have suggested that their conducting gestures needed clarity or definition, it is the young conductors' self-realizations and analyses that convince and propel them to change their gestures for the purpose of effective and efficient music-making and communication. As with any skill, reflective thinking can be practiced. The more arts educators engage in reflective thinking, the more they can move from analyzing the general to analyzing the specifics of their teaching.

2. CHARACTERISING REFLECTIVE PRACTITIONERS IN ARTS EDUCATION

Being a reflective practitioner involves the acts of thinking and teaching, knowing and doing. One might make a case that reflective thinking is inseparable from reflective teaching. Thought, either conscious or subconscious, is inherent in action. Therefore, to be a reflective practitioner who reflects-for-action, one must engage in reflective thinking *and* teaching. The end product is not reflective thinking itself, but rather the teaching and learning that occurs.

Reflective practitioners are teachers who move beyond the simple utilitarian questions that arise from their daily teaching and typical teaching routine. They seek to discover perspective on who is learning, why they are/are not learning, and how best to present the artistic material so that it is accessible for all students. Reflective practice is a holistic viewing of 'recognizing and responding to challenges in the classroom' (Norlander-Case et al., 1999, p. 9).

Reflective practitioners do not look for 'quick fixes' in dealing with classroom challenges. Instead, reflective practitioners use reflective thinking skills, intuition, artistic experience, and content knowledge to create solutions to teaching and learning challenges in the moment or during their analysis, reflection, and planning after the class has occurred. These teachers examine, with a depth of thinking and feeling, their own biases and pre-judgments about teaching, learning, the artistic medium, their students, and the classroom culture. Reflective practitioners 'give themsel[ves] up to the action of the moment to be researchers and artists in the laboratory of practice, the classroom' (ibid., 17).

Teacher educators and mentor teachers expect novice arts educators to demonstrate the ability to be pedagogical technicians. Technicians effectively implement research-based arts education methodologies and artistic content knowledge in their classrooms. In addition, teacher educators seek pre-service arts educators who are humanistic, compassionate, and creative. They are the teachers who are capable of designing lessons full of questions, hands-on artistic engagement, and enjoyment.

Pre-service arts educators also need to possess and refine the following professional habits of mind—personal traits that are fundamental to effective and efficient teaching and reflection.

1. Trusting in oneself and others (i.e., students, administrators, colleagues, community members).
2. Curiosity for learning about self and others in the teaching-learning partnership.
3. Openness of mind in order to challenge thinking patterns and teaching behaviors and to modify existing teaching strategies or classroom environments.
4. Sharing thoughts and feelings about teaching and challenges with mentors, other colleagues, and possibly students (depending on the particular thoughts and feelings).
5. Supporting other colleagues who are engaged in reflective thinking and teaching. Supporting students as they develop their higher-order thinking skills and reflective thinking about their own artistic performances.
6. Observing all interactions with students and the artistic material in the classroom environment.
7. Listening to mentors, colleagues, students, and self in order to understand and learn about the teaching-learning partnership.

Having the personal and professional traits outlined in this section of the chapter implies that arts educators are open-minded, willing to amend practice and perception, and curious about the teaching-learning partnership. Arts educators who demonstrate curiosity, artistic content knowledge, compassion, and professional habits of mind occupy fertile ground in which the seeds of reflective thinking skills can flourish.

In the next section of this chapter, I will describe and discuss the nature of four 'tools' that teacher educators, mentors, and pre-service arts educators might find useful in developing reflective thinking and teaching skills. Each tool and its respective tasks are not goals in and of themselves. Rather, the goal is to nurture dialogue between experienced and novice arts educators in order to initiate positive change in the classroom. Furthermore, this reflective thinking results in meaningful teaching and learning experiences for both arts educators and their students.

3. TOOL 1: RIVER JOURNEYS

At the beginning of the first semester of their first year in college, I present my music education students with the *Music Education River Journey* task, based on Pamela Burnard's (2004) 'critical incident charting'. On a blank piece of paper is a drawing of a winding river. At each bend in the river, the students list and/or describe pivotal moments in their music history that ultimately led them to pursue a career in music education.

This is an exercise in the students' identifying and acknowledging their music education background, while also comparing their experiences with other students' backgrounds. In order to reflect on and appreciate other people's (i.e., colleagues' and students') experiences that contribute to a class dynamic, pre-service teachers should explore their own significant experiences. After all, these experiences shape how they teach, what they value, how they think, and what they embrace as preconceptions, biases, assumptions, and skills.

Examples of my students' significant turning points in the direction of their music education journeys include:

- Piano lessons
- Participating in honors choirs
- Teaching choral ensembles
- Arriving at college
- Sneaked in the attic and played around on my mother's cello
- Not being allowed in 6th-grade band (I was only in 4th grade)
- My 6th-grade recital
- Entering high school jazz ensembles
- Mr. Ramsey and Ms. Newton, my music teachers
- Auditions
- Commercial jingles on television
- Taking a music aptitude test
- Parents forcing me to take an instrument
- Taught my own student private lessons
- Loved singing in church choir
- Attending a community music school
- Attending music camps
- Enjoying performance at solo and ensemble contests
- I heard Beethoven's 6th Symphony
- Performed as a soloist and my life was changed
- My mother always practicing playing her violin at home
- Music was used in schools to help us learn languages
- I heard a gospel choir and they were very powerful. I was struck by the way they breathed together and the force of their joy in their singing.
- I went to Ghana and was deprived of piano lessons
- Grandfather gave me his old violin—oooh, green, plush case lining!

The *River Journey* task can also be adapted for pre-service arts educators who reflect after they teach a lesson in the classroom. In order to complete this task, they identify those significant moments or turning points that influenced the efficacy of teaching and learning in a particular class or rehearsal. Then, each 'turn' in the river is analyzed for future classroom action and adaptation.

Pre-service arts teachers also could use the *River Journey* task to trace their development of self-concept from being a freshman arts education major to being a student teacher. The question sparking reflection might be: What points in the arts education program or in the student-teaching semester were significant in developing your concept of self as arts educators?

From the students' descriptions (see Figure 11.1), it seems that private music teachers, family members, and music-related events (i.e., auditions, solo and ensemble

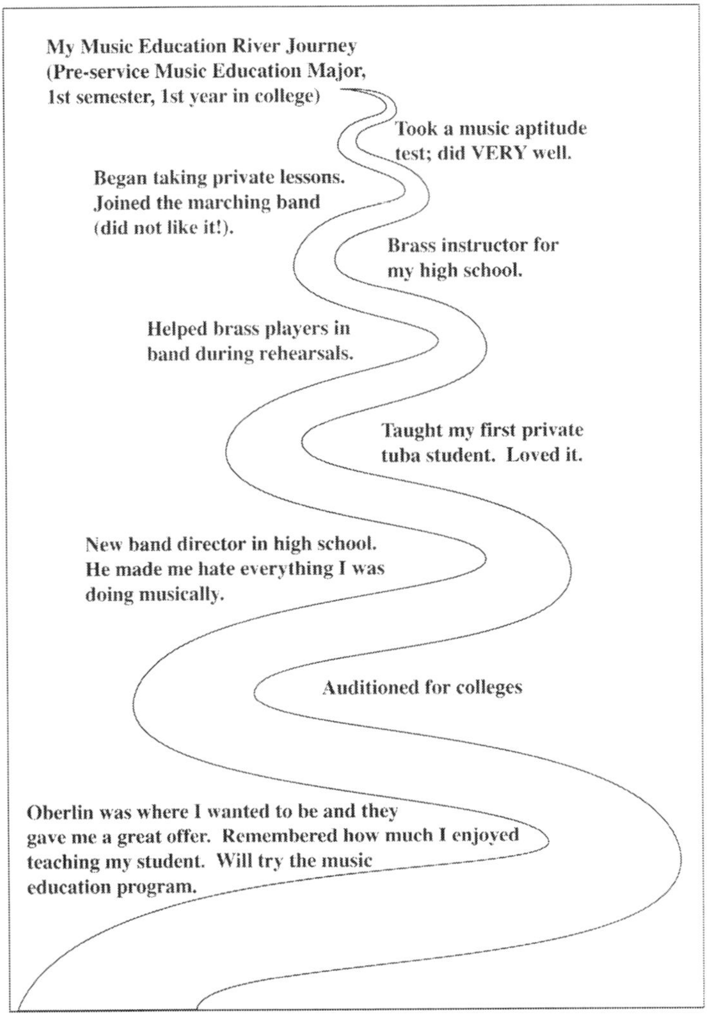

Figure 11.1. [My River Journey]

performances), and early teaching experiences were formative in bringing the students to the point of considering music education as a career option. Also interesting is that the pre-service students included those people and events in their life journeys that were negative influences. All listed events and people contribute to informative one-on-one teacher-student and class discussions. Students enjoy finding commonalities among their past and present music journeys.

As for my river journey (see Figure 11.2), the first step was to review the videotape of the second-grade classroom situation. Plotting my river journey assisted me in planning for future teaching in that general music class. Clearly I under-estimated

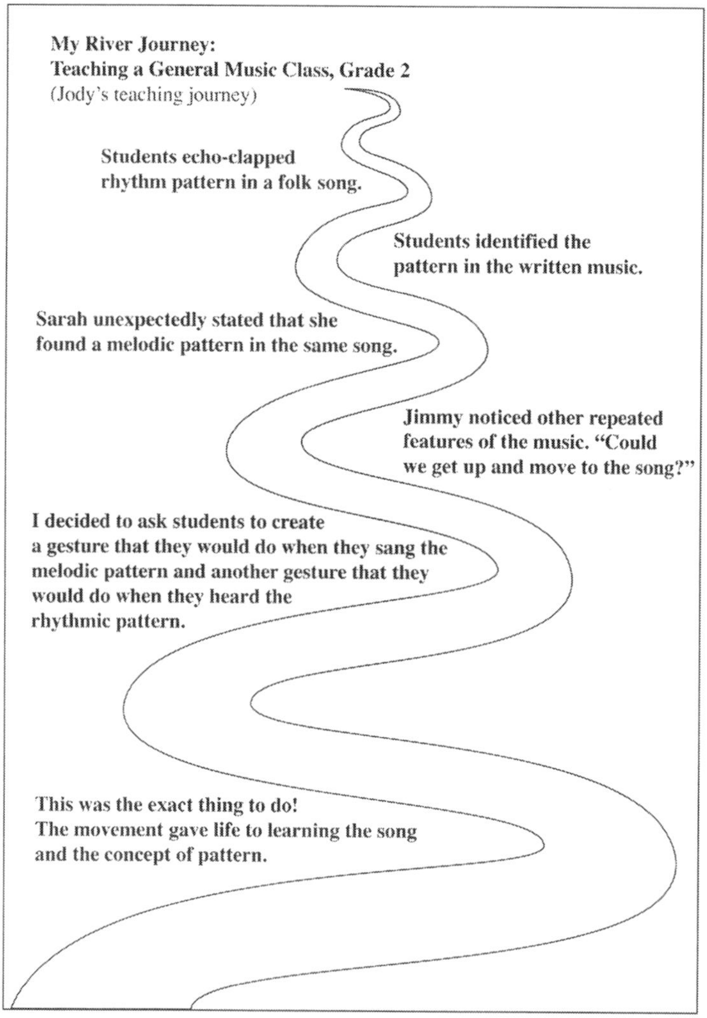

Figure 11.2 [Jody's teahing journey].

how much the students were able to discern by listening to, performing, and reading the music. The students informed me that, while the focus of the class was rhythmic pattern, they were 'ready' to find other types of patterns in the music. They also informed me that they wanted to move to the music. Being a guest teacher in the classroom, I did not know whether or not the students would be comfortable creating musical movements. They were! In my subsequent interactions with the students, we engaged in many more experiences that involved creative movement, and we explored musical concepts at more advanced levels than I had originally anticipated.

4. TOOL 2: METAPHOR SCULPTURES

My music education students are required to take the course, *Practicum Experiences in School Music*, during the second-semester of their first year in college. It is in this class that they participate in their first field experience in the local public schools. Students assist cooperating teachers in music classroom settings; most students teach brief lessons or rehearsal segments by the conclusion of the semester.

During the final meeting of the class, I invite my students to create metaphor sculptures that represent themselves at this particular point along their teaching journey. Using colored clay, students sculpt metaphorical figures of themselves as developing music educators. I encourage students to use metaphors to describe their actions, their feelings, and their observations in the classroom. Metaphors assist people in making connections between the concrete and the abstract. Often, the imagery created from clay unleashes the vivid essence of students' reflective thinking. Conversely, searching for appropriate labels and professional verbiage can stifle or sterilize the complex nature of students' thoughts and ideas. Sometimes, students find it easier to create images of themselves in non-verbal ways, before they describe verbally who they are and who they want to be as educators.

Arts educators could also use this activity to reflect on the 'actors' roles' that are played out in the classroom. Which sculpture would represent the role of the teacher? Of individual students? Of a group of students? Perhaps pre-service arts teachers could create 'before and after' sculptures: 'These are the respective roles that my students and I played during this lesson today. Here is the role that I want to play in our lesson tomorrow.'

The following is a list of the verbal descriptions that accompanied my pre-service music education students' multi-colored clay metaphor sculptures.

- I am a patchwork quilt; I am learning to combine so many different elements, on my way to making something beautiful.
- Parallel-parking: it's ok if you start over.
- My ideas are as fuzzy as a dandelion flower's fuzzy seeds.
- My love for observation is like a heat wave.
- Recent enlightenment has opened me up to see more light like a flower that opens in the light and closes in the dark.

- A mirror—simply reflecting the things given to me, shown to me, the things I experience.
- I am a budding leaf. As the leaf grows, it takes in carbon dioxide from the atmosphere and makes oxygen through photosynthesis. Similarly, I can gather information from my experiences and reflect upon the thoughts and ideas. As I develop, I can give back to society through teaching students to love music, just as the leaf gives oxygen back to the environment.
- I'm on an Easter egg hunt, and I think music education is my golden egg.
- I feel like a tourist in Rome. I am interested in embarking upon grand exhibitions of artistic excellence, yet I do not have a complete picture of that artistry.
- I'm a sponge.
- I'm a ball of dough that has yet to be baked or shaped into a cookie.
- I'm a butterfly just about to leave the cocoon. I want to test my wings.

The depth of emotion cannot be captured adequately with words. The use of verbal metaphor and/or metaphor sculptures allows pre-service music educators to use concrete referents in order to make the essence of their abstract, ineffable affective states known. Some pre-service students do not feel comfortable 'owning', let alone sharing, their emotions. Placing their emotional states or observational characteristics in a three-dimensional clay figure helps students to depersonalize and share their ideas and feelings about themselves as future teachers more readily. The figures, that might look cute, odd or funny, provide a safe prompt for talking about becoming a teacher. How many students would admit in classroom conversation that they were scared, even anxious, about becoming an educator? Embedded in the metaphor sculptures and their descriptions, however, are fascinating descriptions of the pre-service teachers' anxiety, wonderment, excitement, ideological views of growing into being a teacher, and the constant practice of teaching skills.

5. TOOL 3: PORTFOLIO GOALS

Each year, I ask my third-year collegiate music education majors what they want to learn in their secondary-school music methods course. They consider the skills and knowledge they want to acquire in order to become an effective music educator at the secondary-school level.

Since a benchmark trait of reflective thinking is the willingness to question and to solve challenges, I ask my pre-service music education majors to find two 'problems'. That is, they examine past music and pedagogical experiences and formulate two goals that they work towards achieving during the semester (Kerchner, 1997, 2004). Typically, writing the two goal statements is more difficult than actually working toward the goals and showing evidence of their progress. Students often are accustomed to being told what they 'should' improve or what they 'need' to achieve. The process of stating two goals requires students to determine for themselves what they want to work on or which areas of knowledge that they would like to explore.

The first of the goals addresses some facet of the students' presentational/teaching style. Students consider which aspect(s) of their presentational style need improvement in the classroom. Examples of students' presentational goals have included:

- Effective oral communication
- Posing various types of questions based on Bloom's taxonomy
- Using multi-sensory methods
- Incorporating movement
- Use of vocal inflection
- Facial involvement
- Using various forms of student feedback
- Flow of speech
- Looking at individual students around the classroom

The second goal addresses a topic (e.g., artistic technique, methodology, classroom management issue, special needs students, folk arts, unit planning, artists' health issues) that pre-service arts educators want to explore. It is common that when students begin their exploration they find too much information, thus they refocus and revise their goals. Another frequent occurrence is that students find more interesting paths to follow than their original content goal topic. Again, goal revisions are possible.

Goals are listed in broad and general terms. In their goals essays, however, students state the goals, describe their reasons for choosing them, specify possible means for tracking progress in achieving the goals, and describe possible 'synthesis' products. At the conclusion of the semester, students meet with me and show 'evidence' of their progress toward achieving their goals. In that meeting, students reflect on the process and product they experience in pursuing the goals. They also prescribe related or tangential paths for future inquiry, based on their original goals explorations.

An excerpt from Justin's presentational goal statement is given below:

> My first goal is to become a more effective communicator. In education, communication with students is extremely important. It is essential that the passion and enthusiasm of a teacher are clearly shown in a way that students feel important. Addressing a crowd is not easy for me, as I often stumble over words and hesitate. It is necessary for me to plan what I will talk about, since I'm not comfortable speaking extemporaneously.
>
> This class will offer the perfect setting to help me become a more effective communicator. Working with adolescents in the youth orchestra will give me the opportunity to get in front of a section or group of musicians and give lesson segments. Evaluations of my progress might best be accomplished through watching videotapes of lesson segments that I teach. I can make notes of specific ways to improve my communications with the orchestra after I watch my videotapes of the rehearsal segments. I will also track extra words or 'filler' words by using a chart; I will note the frequency of 'fumbles' and hesitations. First, I need to understand when and why I get flustered with words while I'm teaching.

Justin's content knowledge goal included the following excerpt:

> This semester, I also want to gather materials, specifically exercises, that I could use with middle-school and high-school clarinet students in private

> lessons. I will compile a portfolio of exercises and activities that I find in pedagogical texts, articles, and clarinet methods books. I will also create a repertoire list of musical materials that are best suited for students at specific levels of playing achievement. I think these materials will be very useful to me in my future teaching.

By the conclusion of the semester, Justin had assembled a beautiful portfolio of goal achievement 'evidence'. His portfolio was reminiscent of school art portfolios and of professional artists' portfolios that highlight their skill, creativity, and productivity. Evidence for Justin's presentational goal included analysis matrices on which he charted his progress towards providing effective communication in the classroom. Criteria included asking divergent questions, using 'filler' words, using a variety of vocal inflection, and using effective eye contact. Justin also took excerpts from his teaching reflection essays and journal entries to indicate reflective practice in planning and implementing his teaching segments. He created a videotape of teaching excerpts that showed improvement in his ability to communicate comfortably with groups of students.

Evidence for Justin's content knowledge goal included a notebook of clarinet warm-ups, register studies, legato etudes, staccato etudes, and solo materials for students in middle- and high-school. Justin also compiled an annotated bibliography of books and research articles that he could use in middle- and high-school private clarinet lessons. Finally, Justin maintained a journal that included his reflections on using the material he had collected with his private clarinet students.

Portfolios might consist of drawings, original scripts, performance presentations, performance critiques, resource/materials collections, annotated bibliographies, actual artistic products (paintings, writings, videos and tapes of performances), lesson plans, practice and performance journals, and reflections of presentational style in front of an audience or in the classroom. Key to compiling a portfolio is reflective thinking. Pre-service arts educators might address the following questions: What did I achieve? What did I want to achieve that I did not? Why did this achievement happen/not happen? What are my next steps in continuing to investigate the same goals? What did I learn about myself and the artistic process? Which new avenues do I want to investigate? What is my plan for action? Written and/or conversational reflections with mentors serve to train pre-service arts educators to reflect-for action. They engage in the reflection-for-action cycle—problem identification, reflection, plan for action, execution of plan, reflection, and so on.

Writing portfolio goals and creating portfolios full of evidence from academic, pedagogical, and artistic explorations provide mentors and pre-service arts educators' opportunities to understand self and new paths of self-initiated discovery. Consequently pre-service arts educators become more aware of their own learning interests, processes, and progress toward achieving self-defined professional goals.

6. TOOL 4: VIDEOTAPED TEACHING REFLECTIONS

After my students teach a music lesson or rehearsal, they review their videotape and write a two- or three-page reflection. They submit teaching reflections prior to their next teaching experience (peer teaching or laboratory teaching segment), so that they have reflected, prescribed paths for change, and ultimately implemented those changes in their subsequent teaching.

In the opening paragraphs of the teaching reflection, students address two questions:

1. What details did you observe about your teaching, your presentation, your students' responses? Provide descriptions.
2. What about the lesson was especially effective? Why was it effective? What about the lesson needs improvement? Describe SPECIFIC strategies for improving that which you found needing improvement.

In the remainder of the reflection paper, students describe four 'Noteworthy Moments,' one from each of the following categories:

- pedagogy,
- classroom climate,
- active musical understanding/thinking/performing, and
- teacher and student behaviors.

For each notable moment, students rate the moment as being:

- a counterproductive act,
- a missed opportunity,
- an effective action, or
- a masterful action.

Then, they write an explanation for each rating and support it with specific observable evidence and specific prescriptions for improving upon the moments they selected.

As the students analyse their videotape and search for their 'Four Noteworthy Moments,' they also address the following questions:

1. How closely did you follow your lesson plan? Were you able to alter your plan to fit the needs of the children at the time of class?
2. How responsive was the class to your presentation? How responsive were you to their responses? Describe your personal interaction with the class during the rehearsal.
3. Did you ask questions? Did the class ask you questions? Describe the comfort level as you attempted to answer their questions. Describe the pace of the lesson. Did you know/feel when it was time to move on?
4. Did you speak too much? Were your instructions clear and concise? What kinds of directives did you give to the class? Was your voice harsh, soothing, too relaxed, definite? Did you speak loudly?
5. How did you feel in the role of a conductor, musician, educator? Did you command authority? Too much authority? Was there a mix of teacher-and student-directed instruction?
6. Describe any classroom management issues that might have been a concern. How did you handle the situation?

I provide no written feedback to the students until I receive their reflections. My goal is for the students to learn to develop and rely on their own observational, analytical, and reflective thinking skills, as well as their intuition and feelings, rather than on my comments. If, as I read the students' reflections, I find comments and analyses that significantly differ from my observations, I meet individually with the students; we review and discuss the videotaped teaching together. During the conference, the student and I point to specifics about their written reflection, discuss, and refine our understanding of each other's perspectives. The goal remains seeking ways to make teaching and learning more effective.

Videotaped teaching reflections can appear in a variety of formats, in addition to written and verbal commentary. Pre-service arts educators in artistic domains, including music education, might consider writing reflections in a free-style poetic manner, as a narrative story, as a drawing, sketch, or three-dimensional model, or as a drama script. The idea is for the mentor to guide pre-service arts educators to reflect in the most comfortable medium possible. Sometimes, words are ineffective representations for describing classroom occurrences, while other forms of representation get to the heart of the pre-service arts educators' reflective thinking. Non-verbal forms of reflection might also serve as springboards for students' subsequent reflective thinking and conversation that lead to action in the classroom.

7. CONCLUSION

So many arts educators truly love what they do—teaching others their artistic craft and teaching others how to teach. In order to maintain the excitement of teaching day after day and year after year, teachers need to think of each lesson as elaborating on lessons learned from previous classes. Literally, there are many types of lessons that can be learned in arts classrooms—technical (presentational and pedagogical), artistic, and social (interactions with students in the teaching-learning partnership). With practice, arts educators cultivate the ability to re-create themselves and their teaching situations, because they have artistic skills, humanitarian habits of mind, and feelingful instincts.

Arts educators who remain creative in their quest continue to develop themselves as reflective practitioners. In this chapter, I presented only four possible tools that lead pre-service arts educators closer to developing and refining their reflective thinking and teaching skills. River journeys, metaphor sculptures, portfolio goals, and videotaped teaching reflections are tools that can lead to questioning, dialogue, and revision in arts educators' classroom actions. Ultimately these 'teacher behaviors' lead to reflecting-on- and reflecting-for-action that positively affects classroom interactions and learning.

Parker Palmer (1998, p. 2) wrote that, as teachers, 'we must enter, not evade, the tangles of teaching so we can understand them better and negotiate them with more grace, not only to guard our own spirits but also to serve our students well.' And, so it goes with reflective thinking. At its crux is the journey to understand. As reflective practitioners, arts educators witness the evolutionary nature of their perceptions of self, students, and pedagogies that transform arts classes into inspirational venues of learning and interaction.

REFERENCES

Burnard, P. (2004). Using critical incident charting for reflecting on musical learning. *Mountain Lake Reader: Conversations on the Study and Practice of Music Teaching*. Spring, 7–21.

Dewey, J. (1933). *How We Think: A Restatement of the Relation of Reflective Thinking to the Educative Process*. Lexington, MA: Heath.

Kerchner, J. (2004). Portfolio assessment in music education methods courses: experiencing, modeling, teaching, assessing. In P. Shand (Ed.), *Music Education Entering the 21st Century*. Nedlands, Western Australia: International Society for Music Education.

Kerchner, J. (1997). Portfolio assessment: tracking development. *Journal of Music Teacher Education*, 6(2), 19–22.

King, P. and Kitchener, K. (1994). *Developing Reflective Judgment*. New York: John Wiley & Sons, Inc.

Norlander-Case, K., Reagan, T. and Case, C. (1999). *The Professional Teacher: The Preparation and Nurturance of the Reflective Practitioner*. San Francisco, CA: Jossey-Bass.

Palmer, P. (1998). *The Courage to Teach: Exploring the Inner Landscape of a Teacher's Life*. San Francisco, CA: Jossey-Bass Publishers.

SECTION 3

CASE STUDIES: REFLECTIONS IN AND ON ACTION

MORAG MORRISON, BRUCE BURTON
AND JOHN O'TOOLE

12. REENGAGEMENT THROUGH PEER TEACHING DRAMA

Insights into Reflective Practice

1. REFLECTIVE CONTEXTS: PEER TEACHING AND DRAMA

The power of educational drama to enhance learning; modify student behavior; and develop motivation, self esteem and skills of self presentation in adolescents has been widely documented over the past four decades [(Bruner (1986); Csikszentmihalyi (1990); Burton (1991); O'Toole (1992) Heathcote and Bolton (1995)]). Drama education has been particularly effective in dealing with the affective domain and motivating the learning of alienated students. In the countries where drama education is a school subject, current curriculum documents recognize and indeed specify learning outcomes related to self-esteem, communication, emotional intelligence, and social and self-awareness.

Similarly, peer and cross age mentoring have increasingly been shown to provide worthwhile opportunities for pupils to take an active role in their learning through teaching others, and the benefits to personal and social development have also been recognized. Formal peer teaching, where older students teach classes or groups of younger ones in specific subject areas has been relatively uncommon. However, contemporary research and practice (Goodlad and Hirst, 1998; Rubin and Herbert, 1998; Burton, O'Toole and Plunkett, 2005; Morrison, 2004) indicate that the self-reflective opportunities offered through formal peer teaching is a particularly potent learning strategy—especially for the peer teachers.

However, the use of drama and peer teaching as a combination of discipline and pedagogy which empowers students to be reflective practitioners is both very new and largely untested. The two projects discussed in this chapter are unique in harnessing drama and peer teaching with a view to offering reflective opportunities to address (a) the problem of negative leadership in UK schools and (b) conflict and bullying management in schools in Australia[1].

[1] Both the projects are part of much larger, on-going research programmes. The UK project, Risk and Responsibility, is part of major research into student empowerment funded by the Wallenberg Foundation. Research has considered the role student 'voice' might play in offering insight for more democratic approaches to teaching and learning in schools. The Australian research, Cooling Conflict, has been continuously funded by the Australian Research Council for eight years and was initially established as part of the International DRACON research exploring drama and conflict management in schools. DRACON projects in different parts of the world have considered a variety of dramatic approaches through which young people can learn about the nature of conflict and conflict management.

P. Burnard and S. Hennessy (eds.), *Reflective Practice in Arts Education*, 139–148.

Despite the differences in location, affiliation and intention, the two projects have produced strikingly similar outcomes in terms of their impact on the individual students engaged in them. In particular, two pairs of girls, one pair from an urban school in Cambridge, UK, and the other pair from a rural school in NSW, Australia, demonstrated transformational changes in their attitudes to school, their behavior as students, and in their self-images and self-esteem. For each of the four students, their active involvement in the peer teaching of drama to younger students and the variety of reflective opportunities this afforded appeared to be clearly responsible for these transformations.

1.1. *Reflection through Engagement in Drama*

It can be said that a central function of drama is to focus and intensify moments of life so that they can be comprehended on a stage or acting space. However, drama is actually more complex than real life in that it engages three quite distinct contexts simultaneously: the *real life context*, the fictional *dramatic context* and the *context of the performance*. The participants have three sets of roles offering three subtly different perspectives for reflection. The interaction and overlay of these roles on each other—the invocation and suspension of each of them—are what provide the learning potential.

1. The participants in *real life* are, say, thirteen years old. On a day-by-day basis their roles as children, family members and students are to some extent predetermined.
2. In the *fictional dramatic context* they become actors, representing characters whose behavior determines the nature and the narrative of the play. In this context their real life roles as students are at least partially suspended, to allow the dramatic narrative to unfold, and of course there are no consequences in the real context, because the context and the roles are fictional.
3. In the *context of performance*, which here is the drama lesson, they have another set of roles: as playwrights, directors, actors and audience of the play they are engaged in creating together. Here they experiment in earnest with the very notion of role. This includes:
   - techniques of role-reversal, of renegotiating aspects of the dramatic situation, of experimenting with different actions to improve or change the character and introducing new characters. These are all part of the *playwright*'s devices.
   - reshaping the audience point of view to provide more distance or more empathy, changing the physical parameters, accentuating the dramatic irony, or providing new internal insights as part of the *director*'s repertoire.
   - adopting a variety of postures, changing the energy level and responding in a range of ways, sometimes surprisingly, are all part of the *actor*'s box of tricks.
   - watching the action from inside or outside, deliberately changing one's point of view on the situation, sitting down in post-drama de-briefing, discussion and reflection, and even re-creating the experience in another art form—painting, poetry and song, or writing. These reflective responses are all part of the *audience*'s repertoire.

Thus, through the first—hand imaginative experience of drama, a student has the opportunity to consider an event (albeit fictional) from both within and without, and this unique approach adds depth to the reflective process.

1.2. *Finding a Voice through Reflecting on Peer Teaching*

Research by Goodlad and Hirst (1989, p. 73) suggests that peer teaching is an effective way of engaging students in their learning and that it can have strong educational benefits for both the peer tutors and their tutees. Most significant for these studies, however, is the claim that peer teaching can offer social and personal benefits for those involved, particularly the peer tutors. Studies frequently suggest that self-confidence and self-image are improved among pupils who have been peer tutors. Given that negative leaders often lack self-esteem and experience of constructive engagement in learning, peer tutoring seems a potentially worthwhile strategy to try out in frameworks designed to support positive change among young people. The benefits for difficult or at risk students are two-fold. First, at a simple level, teaching is an activity that requires listening and being listened to. Thus in a simple power relationship, negative leaders can expect to have a voice and for that voice to be heard. Second, there is the expectation that as teachers they will have something valuable to offer. Thus, peer teaching offers the opportunity for disaffected students to engage in activity which is meaningful and constructive.

2. CASE STUDY 1. THE UK PROJECT—RISK AND RESPONSIBILITY

2.1. *The Project*

The first phase of this project involved contact with the Drama co-ordinator of a local urban secondary school which had for some time been struggling to improve its overall profile locally. The Drama teacher had considerable experience of working with challenging adolescent pupils—her role was pivotal in selecting the students and in interpreting and monitoring the impact of the project on them.

The criteria for selection were straightforward: two pupils in Year 8 or 9 who seemed disengaged or uncommitted to school generally, but who were socially confident with their peers and popular. They also had to have strength in some aspect of Drama. Ashley and Kayleigh, both in Year 9, fitted the criteria. Both enjoyed Drama and were generally strong in performance components of the course. It was important to the project that the pupils selected recognised that they had some skill in the subject and both Ashley and Kayleigh thought that they were good at acting. They were also good friends which meant that they could work collaboratively as co-tutors.

The two girls were approached by their Drama teacher and asked if they would like to teach acting skills to a group of year six pupils. They were pleased and keen to help. It is worth noting that this very first step, asking the girls if they would share something that they were good at, seemed to have a very positive impact, seeming to make them feel competent and valued, clearly a rare experience, within the school context.

The project was designed to give the pupil teachers some sense of responsibility and power. For instance, the two students were directly involved in selecting the Year 6 pupils they would work with, in planning the material they would teach and then of course actually doing the teaching. The demands on them were considerable.

The students then devised a series of four Drama lessons for their Year 6 group. A fifth lesson was to be a performance of the play to the rest of the Year 6 class. In practice there were problems in getting a real flow to these lessons. Because there was generally only one Drama lesson a week the project spanned several weeks and some momentum was lost in between lessons. The idea of a culminating performance was probably too ambitious, but the year 6 pupils were very keen to perform in front of their peers and their 'teachers' did not want to disappoint them. The sense of responsibility the project engendered was a central factor in facilitating reflection and change.

2.2. *Ashley and Kayleigh: Reflective Practitioners*

Ashley, 14, was not achieving in most subjects other than Drama; thumbnail sketches provided by several of her teachers described her as volatile, disrespectful and disruptive. She was often in trouble at break-time, fought with other girls, and was described as bossy and aggressive if challenged. The respect that she had from others appeared to have been based on a combination of threat and fear. Ashley is the middle child in a family whose siblings had also exhibited behaviours that challenged school culture. Ashley had shown little interest in doing well at school and had low expectations of what she might achieve beyond school.

Kayleigh, also 14, did not have the same level of leadership among her peers. As Ashley's friend she no doubt commanded some respect by association, but was not as volatile. Her lack of engagement was manifest in more passive aggressive behaviors in the classroom and chronic non-attendance. Most teachers talked about her as having academic potential without motivation. Kayleigh had the easy confidence of someone who didn't appear to care and among her peers this made her look 'cool'.

When the project began both girls had a reputation as disaffected learners. Yet both enjoyed Drama and did have confidence in their ability in the form so approached the task of sharing their skills with some enthusiasm. At this point it is unlikely they envisaged the change that this opportunity would have on them. However, during the process of peer teaching Drama a variety of reflective opportunities emerged which offered the potential for personal and interpersonal change—changes which were observed and monitored by their teachers both formally and informally throughout. Regular meetings with Ashley and Kayleigh during the planning stages offered the opportunity for informal discussion. Spontaneous feedback followed each lesson, and the girls were keen to share their experiences with teachers when they returned to school following each teaching episode. More formal feedback was obtained through interviews at a number of points throughout the project with both Kayleigh and Ashleigh and a number of their teachers.

Some lessons went more smoothly than others and, unsurprisingly, it was at points when things did not work that the learning was most powerful. Reflecting, in the moment, the girls often had to think very quickly and make decisions based on immediate concerns. Both Ashley and Kayleigh were also able to reflect on classroom behaviour from a fresh angle—this time as teachers!

Ashley and Kayleigh's sense of themselves as responsible and reflective teachers was evident. Part-way through the project several of the year 6 drama group visited the high school for an orientation day. Ashley reflected on how pleased she felt when one of the year six pupils came up to her with some peers and introduced her as 'my Drama teacher'. This suggested that an authentic relationship based on mutual respect had been established.

Not all was smooth sailing but, as is often the case, it is at moments when most challenged that the richest learning can take place, and for Ashley this was during the third lesson when she had to take the drama group solo. Ill prepared for the lesson and on her own, several of the year 6 group picked up on Ashley's insecurity and began to 'test' her. The lesson did not go well; little was achieved and Ashley struggled to maintain the focus and commitment of the group.

In the conversation following this session Ashley's disappointment was obvious:

> I was all nervous and a bit frightened as well because I didn't want to muck up, but I did—so I felt gutted.

The lesson was however a turning point for Ashley. In the past she might well have made excuses, blamed someone else or just walked away and pretended that she didn't care. This time she actually admitted that she was frightened—she had actually allowed herself to engage with the project and it mattered to her.

The following lesson could have been a disaster, and it was feared Ashley would not return for more humiliation. However the incident had obviously forced Ashley to reflect at a very deep level on responsibility and commitment. She returned the next day well planned and with renewed determination. Ashley conducted a very successful lesson and later, tried to explain her feelings:

> I took control of them . . . I felt more confident, just bubbling . . . it made me really proud. Like the end of the session I thought to myself, 'you've done it, well done, you've proved everyone wrong.' I've even proved myself wrong, so it made me happy.

Ashley had managed to create the authentic connection that Brown and Gilligan (1992) had talked about: people were listening to her and she had overcome her self-doubt.

2.3. *Outcomes*

By coincidence the concluding day of the project coincided with the distribution of year 9 reports. Ashley and Kayleigh's Drama teacher was keen to share them with the girls and highlight the comments that had come from other teachers who were finding evidence of an improvement in their attitude and behaviour. This improvement seemed to coincide with their involvement in the peer teaching project and the personal reflection it had fostered.

It is clear that there is a connection to be made between emotional engagement, reflection and self-esteem. Teachers informally shared that Ashley seemed to be calmer and more focused in class. One teacher commented that she was also more willing to admit some of her own vulnerability through sharing her feelings and opinions more openly. The empathy and responsibility the project had engendered may have enabled Ashley to become more reflective in her schooling, and in her life more generally. She appeared to make closer connections with others, and had been encouraged to consider the effects of her behavior on herself and others.

Teachers also reported a visible improvement in Kayleigh's behavior; although attendance was still an issue, her reports indicated more engagement in school. Although Kayleigh had missed some crucial lessons in the middle of the project she had returned with commitment and determination. Kayleigh might well have seen picking up the threads as too difficult and given up—as she had with other things in the past. But she felt a responsibility to her year 6 pupils, and the project encouraged her to feel valued and respected.

3. CASE STUDY 2. THE AUSTRALIAN PROJECT: COOLING CONFLICT

3.1. The Project

This project involved nine annual cycles of action research centered on secondary school students in Queensland and New South Wales, and also incorporated primary school students. More than 30 schools have been formally involved, with a total of over three thousand students, and the research has developed in three phases:

- *DRACON* research (cycles 1–3, Brisbane);
- *Cooling Conflicts* (cycles 4–6, New South Wales);
- *Acting Against Bullying* (cycles 7–9 Brisbane and Queensland).

Throughout the research, the aim has been to use drama and peer teaching in an integrated way to assist young people in schools towards a cognitive understanding of the nature, causes and dynamics of conflict and bullying. The intention has been to give students the tools to take control of their own conflicts and conflict agendas, personally and in the context of the school community, rather than relying on externally imposed and hierarchical conflict management programs. The project throughout is embedded within the normal school curriculum, and the basic premise is that drama is not used with the aim of direct conflict or bullying resolution, but to provide 'conflict literacy' in the hope that the learners will be able to use this in dealing with their own conflicts.

Conflicts and bullying situations are explored through drama by a number of means, mainly through dramatic exercises, questionnaires and discussion, and sometimes from within curriculum. However, the great majority of areas and types of conflict studied have related directly to the students' conflicts and concerns.

The program begins in practice with a Year 11 Drama class learning about conflict theory and management, and using a range of drama techniques to explore conflict situations and develop their understanding on the causes and management of conflict.

This class then reinforces their own learning and starts the cycle of empowerment by teaching the concepts, again through drama, to younger classes in another curricular area, usually at Year 9 or Year 8 Level. These classes then reinforce their own understanding and are empowered to use the techniques to teach a third group of classes of younger students, either in the school or in local primary schools.

3.2 Alexia and Tracey: reflecting in action

Alexia was an Aboriginal Year 9 student in attending a secondary school in a country town in New South Wales. The school had achieved notoriety some time before when a race riot between aboriginal and white students in the school spread to the town. As a result, the staffing and culture of the school had been radically altered, and a major effort undertaken to restore cultural harmony. The Cooling conflict program was invited into the school as part of these initiatives.

When the Year 11 students came to her Aboriginal Studies class to do the peer teaching, Alexia, a slight, timid girl, sat totally silent throughout the session teaching, eyes downcast, reluctant to participate or even move. She was just as passive and silent during the planning and preparation for her own class's peer teaching, and was consigned to sit at the side and observe her bolder classmates.

On the day of the peer teaching, a transformation occurred in Alexia's behavior. The primary class visiting the school was too big (forty-six students), and very boisterous. Jim, a brash and rather overconfident classmate, made the mistake of over-exciting a group of ten very big and energetic Year 6 students who then ran out of control, becoming quite naughty. The teacher was about to rescue Jim when Alexia rose, walked over to the group, dispatched Jim unceremoniously to the sidelines with a toss of her head, quietened the rest of the room with another, and calmly took immediate charge of the younger children, who towered over her, but became like lambs in her hands as she quietly and surely got them back on task, taught them for fifteen minutes, and then handed them back to her astonished colleagues. Alexia's teachers who were present were astounded by her assertiveness and leadership.

After this experience, Alexia could really offer little explanation of why she had intervened other than:

> Well, I thought the day was pretty cool, how I handled it—I dunno—I just said it—it just came natural.

Assuming the role of peer teacher, and succeeding in it, clearly empowered Alexia. Perhaps her perception of the role of a teacher as an authority figure allowed her to assume that authority as a peer teacher in a way she would never have done as 'herself'.

The way she took control of the class, organised it and taught it demonstrated not only an impressive command of the role of teacher she was enacting, but also showed she was clearly aware of the mood and dynamics of the class and that she was modifying her teaching to suit these elements. This was clearly instinctive behavior on Alexia's part, but showing a strong intuitive understanding of that particular context of teaching.

Tracy was a thirteen year-old Caucasian student in Year 8 at the same school as Alexia at the time of the Cooling Conflict project. Like many others at the school, she was targeted for involvement in the Cooling Conflict project by her teachers due to her reputation as having severe behavior problems. Tracy's parents were no longer together and she lived in a low socio-economic area of the community—already known for its history of racial disharmony—where the residents also struggle with difficulties such as violence and alcoholism.

Tracy's early perceptions of the study were typical of many participants, in that she: 'thought it would be just so cool to get out of class and bludge for a period'. Tracy's decision not to take the program too seriously, to 'just hand [the consent form] in and see how it goes,' was born partly out of her belief that the project would be a waste of time, and partly through fear of drama. As for many of the other students, *Cooling Conflict* was Tracy's first real experience of drama. However her mother Eva was able to recognise positive changes in her behavior:

> Well she was in a terrible lot of trouble and she just needed a way out I think, and drama gave her that way out where she could express her feelings.

As Tracy began to overcome her feelings of shame and reluctance to participate, her attitude towards the program also started to change:

> . . . I never thought drama was my type, but now I think it's really useful and helpful . . . it turned out pretty cool . . . I like it actually.

Tracy started sharing her experiences with her mother:

> She used to come home and she'd say she's in this drama and that she liked it and you could see her face, just the change in her face when she'd talk about it.

Tracy's growing realisation that *Cooling Conflict* offered her new, constructive ways of dealing with conflict meant that her engagement and commitment to the project's success also grew.

Tracy's engagement in the study was coupled with an increasing awareness of self, not just as a leader, but in overall behavior. Such success was further tempered by a reflection on past approaches to conflict management being gradually replaced by new methods:

> I used to be really violent . . . Like, I'd fight a lot to solve all my problems, but that wasn't the best thing to do . . . it just makes it worse. Now I try and talk about it and if that doesn't work I just leave it.

This new approach to conflict management also opened the lines of communication between Tracy and her mother, who was kept informed about Tracy's progress by the principal and through written correspondence. After the project Tracy found she could:

> Always talk to mum, me and mum are really close. Like, we never used to be, we used to fight all the time and I used to lie to her but now . . . .

Eva confirmed that Tracy's approach to conflict management translated from school to home.

The project also enabled Tracy to transcend the limitations she placed on herself as well as her every-day anxieties:

> Drama takes away your feelings too . . . you forget about a lot of things and you have a lot of fun in there . . . the other day I came in depressed

> for some reason. And when I was doing my skits and that, I just forgot all about my depression and just let this other character take control inside of me.

3.3. Outcomes

Although there is no doubt to the impact the project had on both girls, their ability to verbally reflect on the experience differed. Alexia struggled to articulate the significance of the experience for her, but did intuitively understand that it had been part of a transformation in her attitudes and behavior:

> I thought it helped me because all last year me and my dad we fighted a lot and like we'd get into arguments and stuff, but after the Cooling Conflict I just realised that everything was—it was cool after that. It helped.

Later that term, she surprised her teachers again:

> Alexia auditioned for the musical! That's a huge outcome for her—she didn't even go to the musical we had the previous time, even though the main roles were for Aboriginal kids. She just turned up to audition. She was really confident, and I've never seen her present liken that before. She's usually totally quiet and shy. I think it's got a lot to do with the drama experience they had through Cooling Conflict.

Unlike Alexia, Tracey was able to reflect intensely and profoundly on the transformation that had occurred, and in the process to identify one of the key outcomes of the use of role in therapy. She even succeeded in articulating her awareness of self-transcendence—the ability to morph into a totally different person until in control of her emotions:

> Now if I am angry I just change into someone else and forget my old self until I am happy again.

These comments offer a remarkable insight into how Tracy now copes with her conflict situations, based on what she learned during the study. By copying appropriately positive behavior modelled by characters in the various forum theatre pieces she devised, enacted and intervened in, Tracy is able to transfer her learning in the drama classroom directly to the reality of her life and conflict situations.

4. INSIGHTS INTO REFLECTIVE PRACTICE: OPPORTUNITIES OFFERED BY PEER TEACHING DRAMA

The evidence from the two projects suggests that peer-teaching and reflection can have a positive impact on academic motivation and personal development. In both projects the process of reflection through peer teaching had an influence on the emotional development, of students and some very significant insights emerged from the research in this regard. As Goodlad and Hirst (1989) had noted, peer teachers particularly value the feeling of 'being needed'. However risky the situation, all four girls felt that their teaching mattered on some level. For education to be an enriching experience, meanings must become personal—only then will they be incorporated into experience and tried out in everyday living. For the students involved in these projects, the positive experiences of giving and of being accepted filtered back into their general sense of self-worth and their attitude to other areas of the curriculum.

The ability to reflect is a key component of drama, and the practice of peer teaching is by its very nature a reflective experience. The two case studies explored in this chapter demonstrate how the combination of drama and peer teaching operated to empower the students involved to become reflective practitioners in very different ways.

Ashleigh and Kayleigh were able to reflect on the transformation in their behavior as a result of their experience as peer teachers, and to recognize the increase in both self-esteem and self-awareness that occurred for them. Tracy's involvement in both drama and peer teaching assisted her to comprehend conflict situations and the individuals involved in them from a range of perspectives. The leadership she developed here also left her feeling needed, appreciated and useful, and her learning experiences were then able to become much more cooperative, collaborative and reciprocal.

The two projects, a world apart, offered powerful opportunities for reflective practice and common themes clearly emerged:

- Empathy and engagement are key to learning through peer teaching and reflection.
- Reflective opportunities can be personally empowering and emotionally developmental.
- Opportunities to reflect from another perspective, e.g. students as teachers, can foster more democratic relationships in the classroom.
- Personal insight offered through reflection can encourage disengaged students to redirect negative behavior into more positive behavior.
- Improved academic achievement as well as improved self-esteem is possible when students are motivated and engaged—practical opportunities for reflection are key.

REFERENCES

Bruner, J. (1986). *Actual Minds, Possible Worlds*. Cambridge, MA: Harvard University Press.

Burton, B. (1991). *The Act of Learning*. Melbourne: Longman.

Burton, B., O'Toole, J., and Plunkett, A. (2005). *Cooling Conflict: a new approach to managing bullying in schools*. Sydney: Pearson.

Brown, L. and Gilligan, C. (1992). *Meeting at the Crossroads–Women's Psychology and Girls Development*. Cambridge MA: Harvard.

Csikszentmihalyi, M. (1990). *Flow: The Psychology of Optimal Experience*. New York: Harper Perrennial.

Goodlad, S. and Hirst, B. (1989). *Peer Tutoring: A Guide to Learning by Teaching*. London: Kogan Page.

Goodlad, S. and Hirst, B. (Eds.). (1998). *Mentoring and Tutoring by Students*. London: Kogan Page.

Heathcote, D. and Bolton, G. (1995). *Drama for Learning*. Portsmouth, NH: Heinemann.

O'Toole, J. (1992). *The Process of Drama*. London: Heinemann.

Morrison, M. (2004). Risk and responsibility: the potential of peer teaching to address negative leadership. *Improving Schools*, 7(3), 217–226.

Rubin, J. and Herbert, M. (1998). Peer teaching-model for active learning. *College Teaching*, 48(1), 26–30.

DAWN JOSEPH

13. CROSS- AND INTERCULTURAL ENGAGEMENT

A Case Study in Self-reflection and Finding Meaning

1. CONTEXT

Before taking up my current post as lecturer in the Faculty of Education at Deakin University, Australia, I lived in South Africa for more than thirty-five years during the period of apartheid. Consequently I find myself placed between three worlds: Indian, Western and African, with a 'triple heritage' according to Mazrui's description (1986), and see myself as having a predominantly 'endogenous' rather than an indigenous perspective on my teaching. I align my musical identity and sense of being to Ntuli's (2001) notion of 'endogenous' which refers to the knowledge that is received from other sources outside the original. This 'received knowledge' has been assimilated and integrated into my indigenous perspective to the point that it has become part of what Ntuli refers to as a 'collective heritage'. The values, beliefs, and cultural and educational systems of 'the rainbow nation' of South Africa, a term coined by Archbishop Desmond Tutu, have continued to affect my sense of belonging. Hence I am challenged in my own understanding of African music and culture, and in transmitting it to my Australian students.

Since 2001, I have taught undergraduate and postgraduate units in music and education studies courses. This includes the Bachelor of Education (Primary) degree where I teach generalist teachers who undertake *Primary Arts Education 1* in the third year of their course. This five-week unit on Primary Arts Education focuses on musical understanding, skills and pedagogy principally through the so-called creative music approach, developed by such educators as Self, Paynter and Schafer. Bachelor of Education (Primary) students wishing to continue music as an elective unit in their fourth year undertake *Primary Arts Education 2* for an entire semester. Here they are introduced to the pedagogies of Orff, Kodály and Dalcroze through the teaching of recorder and classroom instruments.

As a new lecturer, it was evident then that my predominantly Anglo-Celtic students were exposed almost exclusively to Western music and, in the main, to Western curricular knowledge systems. After my first year, I questioned why students were only exposed to Western music even though Australia is a multicultural society and students were being prepared to teach in multicultural settings. It was also evident that at that time on the campus where I teach, no Aboriginal music or musics of other cultures were taught as part of the *Primary Arts Education 2* music course. I questioned how this might change and how I could introduce students to other types of music. Part of the challenge in my teaching then was to restructure the existing music course. To achieve this I focused on the *Primary Arts Education 2* course that aimed

P. Burnard and S. Hennessy (eds.), *Reflective Practice in Arts Education,* 149–158.

to prepare students as non-specialist teachers of classroom music. The course content not only included European music education approaches (Dalcroze, Orff and Kodály) but also African music methods of teaching and repertoire, together with a study of recorder and djembe drumming. I planned to introduce students to Indigenous Knowledge Systems (IKS[1]), specifically African Indigenous Knowledge (AIK[2]).

I believe that teaching the music and culture of my own country is a good starting point for my students to experience and learn about 'other' musics. Although I am a trained western classical music educator, I felt that students' knowledge base and experience would expand if they learned through a new genre. I started with songs from the Zulu, Sotho and Xhosa people of South Africa, working from a repertoire with which I am familiar. Another challenge that I, together with other tutors, faced was to reclaim 'quality and diversity' in pursuit of an international education agenda in terms of teaching, research and service. I started my 'journey of change' by aiming to make a difference within the culture of my institution.

2. THEORETICAL PERSPECTIVES

It is within a conceptualisation of cross- and intercultural dialogue between African, Western and Indian musical traditions that I situate my research and teaching. My teaching of African music to Australian teacher education students was intended to encompass both content and pedagogy, as well as promoting cross-cultural understanding. With demographic changes in our classrooms, catering for and taking advantage of individual and cultural differences in learning is crucial in the development of effective pedagogies. Part of the challenge of rethinking my teaching and curriculum structures was not only to prepare students for a specific and well-defined profession (primary teaching), but also to prepare them for active participation and adaptability in a world where change is inevitable—a world where knowledge is globally linked no matter how locally specific its uses. Preparing students to see change as a positive experience and to manage it effectively should be a central aim not only in internationalising the curriculum but part of ongoing reflective practice.

---

[1] The notion of Indigenous Knowledge Systems (IKS) is concerned with knowledge that belongs to and is transmitted by a specific ethnic group and is also concerned with common practices that are indigenous to a specific area in which a designated population lives. IKS may even be interpreted as traditional knowledge that is based on cultural identity. As IKS is a multi-faceted concept it can be referred to as traditional or local knowledge on the internet.

[2] Africa, as a large continent, populated by people from different ethnic origins represents a diversity of cultures and traditions and poses many challenges for those who seek to identify a uniform approach to issues confronting the continent based on a uniquely African perspective. One of the major issues confronting African philosophers, historians, anthropologists and educators is the proposal that African Indigenous Knowledge Systems (AIKS) should become more prominent, particularly in a society such as South African which has only recently become emancipated from a Western-imposed apartheid system and wishes to reclaim its indigenous heritage and traditions.

2.1. *Change in Action*

Change is a multifaceted phenomenon and a prerequisite to improvement (Guskey, 2002). Fullan (1982) contends that:

> one of the most fundamental problems in education today is that people do not have a clear, coherent sense of meaning about what educational change is for, what it is, and how it proceeds. . . . What we need is a more coherent picture so that people who are involved in or affected by education can use it [change] to make sense of what they and others are doing (p. 4).

He believes that teachers need to be considered in the role of 'teacher as learner' within four aspects: technical skills, reflective practices, collaboration, and teacher as enquirer.

The notion of 'change as progress' aptly describes my journey as an academic within the tertiary learning community. As a 'change agent' I have to pay attention not only to the musical content of my teaching but also to enabling my students to be proactive in performing, creating, analysing and debating social issues, hence making meaning in cross- and intercultural dialogue. Since learning and change are interconnected, the use of African music gave my students the opportunity to reflect and discuss wider social issues. Such an innovation was a 'change in action', and different to what students normally experienced. Williams (1992) aptly describes such a strategy for deeper analysis of and critical reflection upon issues as 'peeling the onion'. As there are many facets of teacher change and teachers' practice, it may be argued that teachers who want to change are teachers who want to grow and challenge the current *status quo*. They are teachers who are reflective and who are continually trying to do what is best for their students. Schubert and Ayers (1992) argue, that it is only reflective teachers (not those who teach by recipe, technique, or doctrine) who are able to grow continuously. It seems that a pervasive factor of teacher change is ongoing reflection.

2.2. *Reflective Practice*

As teachers are viewed as 'agents of change' and knowledgeable professionals, I locate myself as an 'agent of change' (both as teacher and as researcher) recognising and documenting my own activity of teaching African music and culture as a 'new' and 'different' experience through the perspectives of my students (Joseph, 2002, 2003a/b, 2004a/b).

Reflection is a voyage of on-going self-discovery and change, and is very challenging. In terms of my own teaching, reflection on *what, how* and *why* I taught African music at Deakin University took place not only during and immediately after each workshop session but also from one year to the next. The immediacy of reflecting during and after workshop sessions offered me the opportunity to both question my own teaching practice and reflect on students' experiences and reactions. During the intervening semester I was able to engage in a different form of reflection that allowed for comprehensive review, enabling a synthesis of all of my more immediate reflections on the workshops. Accordingly, what I taught on the first occasion was slightly different to the activities and approaches I used the second time round.

Based on the experience of what students enjoyed and were able to cope with, I changed some of the African songs that I included in my teaching repertoire. The new songs were simpler and more repetitive in their melodic and rhythmic structure that helped students to sing better in the African language. I also found that students preferred to move and play rather than to sing. Reflecting on this, it became clearer to me why my students were reticent to sing in front of their peers—singing is part of everyday life in Africa, but not so in Australia. Even though students did not feel comfortable singing initially in front of their peers, more emphasis was placed on drumming in the second year. I encouraged students to be part of the group music making process at every workshop; this helped them to feel more confident and competent in singing with their peers. For students, emphasising the value of participation and understanding the cultural/narrative meaning of the songs became more important than just performing the songs. They found it much easier to play and to peer teach the drumming than any of the other music activities included in the unit. During the intervening semester, my own skills in drumming had increased through professional development and this meant that I spent more time teaching something that I found personally enjoyable and in which I was now more highly skilled. I also spent more time teaching about wider cultural and social issues associated with African 'ways of knowing and doing' during the second year of offering this unit. This allowed both students and myself to reflect, particularly from a cross-cultural perspective, in personal journals.

Over the two years, it became increasingly apparent to me that students also needed to reflect on their experiences and so they were encouraged to keep a journal as a useful means of either recording their reactions for inclusion in their assignment task or for referring to during class or group discussions. The increased use of video and audio-tape recordings of African music, dance and culture during the second year of offering this unit also proved to be a most worthwhile. Through the use of these as teaching resources, students were exposed to more African music and culture than the previous class whose experience was mainly through me. It was rewarding to see how a new musical genre motivated students to learn not only about the music, but also the wider cultures of which it is a part.

3. AFRICAN MUSIC AND CULTURE

As educators in a changing world preparing students for teaching in a global 'village', the constant challenge we face is being inclusive of 'the other' when we are surrounded by a diversity of people. What is this 'other' and why should we as educators provide such an experience of 'the other' for our students? Thompson (2002, p. 16) raises the point that 'the other' is often constructed as a homogenised category, which she refers to as that which is 'static to geographical spaces'. In relation to this 'other' is the notion of music being understood as an aspect of the culture of which it is part. This point is further highlighted by Nettl (1992, p. 4) who affirms, 'understanding music in turn can help us to understand the world's cultures and their diversity'. It is only when we move out of our own context and into 'the other' that we begin to make the cross-cultural connections that may be invisible in the music of our own culture. By opening up the mind's eye and ear to 'the other' one engages and interacts with a new and different culture: 'you find yourself in someone else's music' (Ray Phiri, the famous black artist, quoted in Massingham, 1998, p. 426).

Miller (1989) affirms that understanding the differences between cultures not only opens the way to a deeper appreciation of the people who create and use that music, but it also brings a new perspective to the world of Western music. By exposing students to other cultures and musics, we explore cross-cultural possibilities more fully, richly and critically than previously: 'a growing awareness of other cultures is not only more possible but also necessary to achieve' (Oehrle, 1991, p. 26). I saw the use of African music in my teaching as a means of developing students' abilities in improvisation and creativity and, by extension, their learning, understanding and skills.

Incorporating music, or indeed, any art form of another culture or finding oneself in someone else's music or arts practice may assist in assimilating new elements and experiences, thereby establishing new understandings of musical style and the broader culture (Nketia, 1988). Nketia also maintains that 'practical experiences of a simple aspect of the music process that we can manage, such as singing a simple song, clapping or stamping where this is part of the music or some simple movement, helps in our efforts to get to know and understand the music' (p. 103). He further contends that what appears to be different cross-culturally may operate in similar contexts, hence the discovery of common principles, usages and behavioural patterns (Nketia, 1988, p. 98). I agree with Nketia who argues that it is not just the music we hear, but a knowledge of the culture of music makers, their lives, what they do, and the occasions when they make music that puts us in a frame of mind to explore their music (p. 101). A similar view is shared by Gibson (2003) who claims the 'work of music' cannot be divorced from the social networks of people who make and promote it, and the sites they occupy in order to do so.

4. DEAKIN UNIVERSITY AFRICAN MUSIC PROJECT

The focus of the research was a case study of thirty-one students in 2002 and thirty-five in 2003 who undertook a music education unit for a single semester. My research focused on the extent to which African music can improve students' skills, confidence, competence and motivation. It further identified attitudinal changes and cross-cultural connections in the teaching of classroom music. One of the problems I faced with teaching African music was diluting traditional knowledge and practices in order to make them accessible. The teaching of African traditional music and practices (for example Zulu, Sotho, Xhosa music, dance and language) cannot be mastered in just one semester.

As part of recording the 'change process', I kept a reflective journal and engaged in participant observation. In addition, an anonymous questionnaire to all students and interviews with self-selecting members of the student cohort at the end of the 2002 and 2003 semesters, together with triangulation of observation and journaling, informed the results of my study. Analysis of the data involved identifying relevant themes and issues, and engaging in reflection informed my teaching.

5. FINDING MEANING

Finding meaning in the 'other' for both students and myself draws on what Brookfield (1995, p. 2) calls different 'lenses'—my own reflection as well as student questionnaire and interview data. My contention for including African music in my teaching was that it could enhance students' understanding of music concepts, increase levels of motivation, confidence and competence; and engage students in cross- and intercultural connections. Each week during and after the music workshops, I took notes and reflected on how students engaged with the learning activities with each other and with me. In the main, my pedagogy was based on three action words 'hear', 'do' and 'see' which are in no particular order, resonating with the African way of oral and aural teaching. For example, I performed the songs which students rote learned, they then copied my movement and finally saw how singing, actions and instrumental playing can be combined. Initially they found this difficult, inhibiting and challenging. However as the semester progressed students became less self conscious and actively participated in the music activities and discussions about African life and culture; and students began to comment on the benefit of learning about other music and culture.

Through their engagement in a number of activities (singing, moving, playing instruments, dancing and dramatizing the content of the songs and story telling), students contrasted the African understandings and learning styles with the Western tradition. The music workshops provided a context for students to discuss, deliberate and debate the marginalisation and patronising attitudes towards the music of particular ethnic groups.

Bearing in mind that these students only had five weeks of music in their third year of study, I began by teaching simple South African children's action songs (Zulu, Xhosa, Sotho and Pedi). These were initially studied as oral repertoire hence the subject matter and context allowed for contrasts, variations, and similarities to be discussed. Such a multidisciplinary approach incorporated AIK, which encompassed local knowledge that is culture and context specific. Moreover the pedagogy that I employed focussed on non-formal knowledge that is orally transmitted, which correlates to traditional African ways of transmitting knowledge. I did not have to significantly adjust my pedagogy; rather I adopted a slower pace in the first two weeks in order to make students feel comfortable with my teaching style and the activities. The drum was the highlight and main attraction of the unit. I often started each workshop with drum activities as students thoroughly enjoyed this. When teaching rhythm, I began with simple body percussion patterns and counting before transferring them to the drum. It was challenging for students to play poly-rhythms on the drum and to sing at the same time; however it was most rewarding to see how their concentration developed and they became more confident and competent to combine singing and playing.

Students in both interview and questionnaire data reported that they gained greater musical skills and knowledge about African music as it was 'new', 'different', 'exciting', 'rhythmic' and 'real'. The fact that I am African seemed to authenticate the learning experience and this was evident in comments such as 'it was more real otherwise it would be just technical . . . it was relevant and it is who you are and so you were able to teach it . . . it's part of your culture'. Another student added: having you teach it made a difference, it means more coming from someone who knows the things they are talking about. I could read all I ever wanted about Africa but I could not teach it with that same passion I guess that you showed us'. Week-by-week I noticed how students' eyes literally lit up when I spoke about the context of the songs they learnt, or my own personal experiences in South Africa as a non-white person 'making music' with other people rather than just 'playing for someone'. This notion of 'making music' with others in the class I consciously built into the course. They had the opportunity to play, move, sing or improvise during the sessions and generally work at their own pace. By rote teaching drum patterns, songs and movement, students in my opinion felt more confident to play together without the pressure of having to read western staff notation. I noticed they felt much more confident and competent to improvise when using djembes: 'we learnt about timbre, beat accent and meter most effectively through drumming. Although the learning of poly-rhythms was challenging for many students, one reported 'listening, is an important aspect when learning about rhythms . . . you can get lost in it if you don't concentrate on your [own] part and repeatedly play other parts'.

Such vibrant 'hands on' engagement like singing, moving and playing in African music was seen by both students and myself as an effective way to teach about music elements (Joseph, 2003a/b, 2004a/b). Through such music making they began to understand how simple repeated rhythmic and melodic patterns could be effectively experienced, understood and enjoyed. All students in the questionnaire reported that their level of confidence and competence in drumming improved over the semester. They were also highly motivated to learn through a new type of music and the drumming experience especially provided a 'space' where group camaraderie and bonding were fostered. The music workshops created an opportunity for students to 'bounce off teaching ideas', peer teach, and assess each other's work without feeling inhibited. As stated earlier it was most rewarding for me to see how they participated in this 'music making' process during the semester as most students entered the course with little or no musical background. The smiles on their faces illustrated they were not only enjoying themselves but also feeling confident and competent enough to make music with each other. Students invariably would say as the semester progressed 'is it time to go already?' which was a good indicator for me that they enjoyed the workshops.

When designing the music course I also considered that my students were non-music specialists and could use music as an effective medium to integrate with other primary school subjects. Most students felt that the teaching and learning area of Social and Environmental Studies (SOSE), Language and Mathematics were most relevant for children at school to learn about another culture. SOSE in particular lends itself to thinking about issues of difference, diversity and culture, thus challenging both teacher and student to embrace the multifaceted concept of 'change'. One student succinctly commented: 'part of SOSE is to explore one's own and other culture and therefore African music and culture can be integrated into this learning area very well'. Another added 'African music is a great way to explore culture, you learn about people, their lives, their history, language, food . . . kids would be experiencing and learning about another culture'.

The experience of 'seeing', 'doing' and 'talking' about African music for my students was not just another enriching experience but rather an opportunity for 'windows to be opened' and for them to gain the musical skills, knowledge and understanding necessary to promote an inclusive curriculum. It was most rewarding for me to observe how students' music skills and knowledge increased from week to week. It was also contentious at times when they questioned the current curriculum and its relevance in multicultural Australia. In the main I was touched by comments like 'you made a difference to my learning . . . I can teach some of it . . . your method is easy to follow and I can apply it when I teach in a real class' and ' I have a better understanding of African music now and the people who make it'. Another student said 'we came into the course with little music background and we have learnt so much over the weeks . . . I want to try it out, I have the confidence and would like to motivate my students like you have motivated us . . . I can see how I really can make a difference in the classroom through music'. Such positive comments made me realise just how valuable this course is for future offering. As part of my ongoing reflections, I will continue to change current repertoire and teaching strategies and will invite a South Africa 'artist-in-residence' to team-teach with me.

6. WHAT WERE THE CROSS- AND INTERCULTURAL MEANINGS RESULTING FROM REFLECTION?

Having situated this chapter in my reflective practice in the teaching and learning of African music, I have also considered the wider context. The use of African music served as a 'springboard for action' in terms of students' music learning, creativity, improvisation and cross- and intercultural dialogue. Workshops were seen as an invaluable arena to model my teaching as well as encourage students' peer teaching. The workshops represented openness, learning and trust for both students and me. This environment improved instruction, increased collaboration and promoted success for a diverse population of students in the music course. It can be argued that both students and I found that workshops were highly engaging and catered for a broad range of abilities, which provided a 'level playing field' for everyone.

The teaching of African music was seen as successful in that students and I found meaning in this 'different' experience—it incorporated new insights, linking information and approaches not for their own sake but to improve cross- and intercultural understanding as well as instructional practice. As Brookfield (1995) and Thiel (1999) suggest, the reflective process helped me engage in self-observation and in the evaluation of my own actions and the reactions of my teaching on my students' learning. Although reflection took time and effort, it gave me the opportunity to question what, why and how I was teaching and the effect of this on my students. My reflection occurred in many different forms, giving me the opportunity to intentionally examine, analyse and synthesise my teaching through active engagement. This is part of an ongoing process that considers how changes are made in the classroom (Farrel, 1998) and supports the idea that any small change can have an impact on teaching and learning (Gebhard, 1996). The power and rhythm of the African drum in this instance provided a useful platform for 'connecting the disconnected' in terms of pedagogy, cross- and intercultural dialogue, and finding meaning for my students and myself. African music at Deakin University is a step in my personal odyssey to transmit 'the other' in Australia.

REFERENCES

Brookfield, S. (1995). *Becoming a Critically Reflective Teacher*. San Francisco, CA: Jossey-Bass.

Farrel, T. (1998). Reflective teaching: the principles and practices. *Forum*, 36(4), 10–17.

Fullan, M. (1982). *The Meaning of Educational Change*. New York: Teachers College Press.

Gebhard, J.G. (1996). *Teaching English as a Foreign or Second Language*. Ann Arbor, MI: University of Michigan Press.

Gibson, C. (2003). Cultures at work: why 'culture' matters in research on the 'cultural' industries. *Social and Cultural Geography*, 4(2), 201–215.

Guskey, T. (2002). Professional development and teacher change. *Teachers and Teaching: Theory and Practice*, 8(3/4), 381–391.

Joseph, D.Y. (2002), 'Umoja: teaching African music to generalist teacher education students', Research matters: linking outcomes with practice. In J Rosevear (Ed.), *Proceedings of the Exit Annual Conference of the Australian Association for Research in Music Education* (pp. 86–98). Adelaide: AARME.

Joseph, D.Y. (2003a). An African music odyssey: introducing a cross-cultural curriculum to Australian primary teacher education students. *Music Education International*, 2, 98–111.

Joseph, D.Y. (2003b). 'Cross cultural engagement: teaching African music to Australian students', Curriculum innovation in Music. In *Proceedings of the Fourth (Biennial) Asia-Pacific Symposium on Music Education Research* (pp. 142–147). Hong Kong: Hong Kong Institute of Education.

Joseph, D.Y. (2004a). The African difference: results and implications of using African music in teacher education. In *Proceedings of the XXVth Annual Conference of the Australian Association for Research in Music Education*. Brisbane.

Joseph, D.Y. (2004b). Communicating new sounds of Africa to Australian teacher education. In *Proceedings of the 26th Conference of the International Society for Music Education*, International Society for Music Education.

Massingham, A. (1998). Working in the third world: Evangelist or rip-off artists? In C. van Niekerk (Ed.), *Ubuntu—Music Education for a Humane Society: Proceedings of the 23rd World Conference of the International Society for Music Education* (pp. 411–426). Pretoria: International Society for Music Education.

Mazrui, A.A. (1986). *The Africans: A Triple Heritage*. London: BBC Publications.

Miller, A. (1989). Music Making: Survival and Celebration, *Music Making: Survival and Celebration*. Retrieved 12 December 2002, from http://www.mcc.org?respub.occasional/26survival.html.

Nketia, J.H.K. (1988). Exploring intercultural dimensions of music education: a world view of music education. In J. Dobbs (Ed.), *Proceedings of the 18th World Conference of the International Society for Music Education, Canberra* (pp. 96–106). Australia: International Society for Music Education.

Nettl, B. (1992). Ethnomusicology and the teaching of world music. In H. Lees (Ed.), *Music Education: Sharing Musics of the World: Proceedings of the 20th World Conference of the International Society for Music* (pp. 3–8). Christchurch: International Society for Music Education.

Ntuli, P. (2001). Cultural Hegemony and the Re-Investigation of the Indigenous Knowledge Systems, A paper presented at the *Apex Art Conference*, July 2001, Rio de Janeiro, Brazil. Retrieved 10 December 2003, from http://www.apexart.org/conference/Ntuli.htm.

Oehrle, E. (1991). Emerging music education trends in Africa. *International Journal of Music Education*, 18, 23–29.

Schubert, W.H. and Ayers, W.C. (Eds.). (1992). *Teacher Lore: Learning from Our Own Experience*. White Plains, New York: Macmillan.

Thompson, K. (2002). A Critical discourse analysis of World Music as the 'Other' in Education. *Research Studies in Music Education*, 19, 14–21.

Thiel, T. (1999). Reflections on critical incidents. *Prospect*, 14(1), 44–52.

Williams, R.L. (1992). Social advocates and action learning: the discontent dancing with hope. In L.A. Cavaliere and A. Sgroi (Eds.), *Learning for Personal Development, New Directions for Adult and Continuing Education* 53 (pp. 37–50). San Francisco, CA: Jossey-Bass.

BETTY ANNE YOUNKER

14. REFLECTIVE PRACTICE THROUGH THE LENS OF A FIFTH GRADE COMPOSITION-BASED MUSIC CLASS

1. INTRODUCTION

This chapter examines the role that critical reflection plays in practice through the lens of a case study of one fifth-grade composition-based music class, as conceived and implemented over the last eight years by a music educator in a public school located in the Midwest, U.S.A. The theoretical framework for examination is built on the writings of those who have offered insights about critical thinking and the role of such thinking in reflective practice and artistic experiences (e.g. Dewey, 1933/1991; Jorgensen, 2001, 2003; Bowman, 2002, 2005; Reimer, 2003; Woodford, 2005), theories of and justifications for reflective practice (e.g. Schön, 1987; Elliott, 1995), and the value of constructing meaning at individual and group levels (e.g. Bruner, 1960, 1996; Vygotsky, 1978; Engestrom, 1996; Wiggins, 2001).

The first part of the chapter will provide a brief overview of critical thinking and how such thinking is an integral part of reflective practice (for in-depth discussions, see earlier chapters). The second part will reveal the role that critical reflection can play, in and on practice, within a case study setting. Thick descriptions supported by vignettes provide an inside view of one music educator's view of pedagogy, and the interactions and strategies that occurred within this setting. The various examples are representative of data collected, analyzed, and reported over a three year-period (see Younker, 2003a/b, 2004, 2005a/b).

2. THE ROLE OF CRITICAL THINKING IN REFLECTIVE PRACTICE

2.1. *Critical Thinking Defined*

Dewey (1933/1991) discussed critical thinking (referred to as reflective thinking by Dewey) as a process that occurs before an action or belief is adopted and as conclusions are reached. More recent writers (see Ennis, 1980, 1987; McPeck, 1981, 1984, 1990; and Paul, 1987, 1993) concur with Dewey's thinking and expand upon his initial definitions within the frameworks of dispositions and abilities (see Younker, 2002, for expansions of these definitions and applications to music). The process, as articulated by Dewey (1933/1991, 1938) involves responding to an experienced dissonance by examining and re-examining held assumptions, identifying relevant facts, formulas, and theories, and generating solutions to bring closure to situations that are

P. Burnard and S. Hennessy (eds.), *Reflective Practice in Arts Education*, 159–168.

uncertain, are controversial, and involve doubt. This active and persistence inquiry is mindful, uses what is understood, and constructs new meanings.

2.2 *Critical Thinking in Reflective Practice*

Integral to reflective practice is thinking critically as knowledge is used and constructed within 'experience-based' environments (Vygotsky, 1978; Schön, 1987; King and Kitchener, 1994; Bruner, 1996; Wiggins, 2001). In such environments, experiences can produce sensitivity and responsiveness, connect with past and future, provide challenges that are accessible and yet evoke reflection, and require critical reflection (Vygotsky, 1978; Bruner, 1996; Bransford, et al., 2000; Noddings, 2004).

A significant aspect of reflective practice is possessing a habit of mind that thinks beyond prescribed methodologies and approaches to planning and improvising in the practice, and involves students in the practice as active participants; and in this context, as active artists (Bowman, 2002, 2005; Galbraith, 2002; Jorgensen, 2003; Woodford, 2005). Reflective practice is critical in pedagogy because of the need for situated judgments, i.e., not fixed or rigid, when making choices about approaches, materials, and students' involvement (Jorgensen, 2003). In arguments for exercising reason in teaching, Jorgensen (2001) suggests that practitioners are better served when ambivalence, vulnerability, surprise, and joy are embraced as challenges before choices are made.

2.3. *Critical Thinking in Reflective Practice in Arts*

Another significant aspect is recognizing the role of all stakeholders in the community of learning, and connecting students to each other and the practice through active engagement. Experiencing a community of learners in arts education requires the practitioner to think critically about when to guide and facilitate as students question and construct understanding in collaboration with others. The focus becomes learning in and through the arts rather than teaching in and through the arts, and the examination of pedagogic practices focuses on intra- and inter-engagement and activity that is organic (see Jaffurs, 2004).

3. THE CASE: REFLECTIVE PRACTICE IN A FIFTH-GRADE COMPOSITION-BASED MUSIC CLASSROOM

Through employing the case-study approach, the role that critical reflection plays in a fifth-grade composition-based public school music class is revealed. This particular composition-based setting involved a music practitioner who makes thoughtful choices about her practice, and students who are empowered to think critically and musically in composition. Within the setting students were engaged in composing music as problem finders and solvers, i.e., defining many constraints and freedoms (Burnard and Younker, 2002), where constructions of musical meaning occur at individual and group levels. It should be noted that I have been a participant observer researcher in this music classroom for a three-year period, and will continue to use this particular site as a setting for a research program.

Laura (a pseudonym) has taught for twenty-five years and has been the music teacher at this particular school for twelve years. After informal conversations, initiated by me through my interest in school-based composition curricula, Laura invited me to observe and work with her students as they engaged in composition. From that, formal permission was obtained for three consecutive years during which time I was a participant observer. During this heuristic inquiry (Patton, 2002) I have observed; interacted with the students; dialogued with Laura face-to-face, via phone and email; engaged her in three semi-formal interviews; analyzed and reported on students' written answers to questions given by Laura at the end of the year; and analyzed and reported on data, collected via a digital camera, of students' collaborative experiences in composition (Younker, 2003a/b, 2004, 2003a/b).

Laura's belief is that school-based music programs should provide opportunities for all students to be active music makers. She organized a composition curriculum that involves students in collaborative composition and culminates in students performing their original works. This ensures that every fifth-grade student has a critical role in the development and implementation of the final concert.

From October to March, the curriculum, consists of students (1) being introduced to a variety of composing techniques and musical concepts, and (2) collaboratively composing and performing the compositions to show conceptual and musical understanding. This time period also includes involvement with a variety of activities, such as assemblies, outings, assessments of knowledge and skills, and interactions with guest artists. From the end of March to the middle of May (six to eight sixty-minute sessions), groups of students create compositions and perform them in two separate concerts.

3.1. *Critical Reflection in Practice*

Vignette 1

Students entered the room. It was October and they had been introduced to ostinati patterns the week before during music class. Laura introduced the concept through questioning, listening, and guiding the class through the creation of a variety of ostinati patterns; and when necessary, giving explanations. The students' assignment in this lesson was to form groups (or in some cases groups chosen by the teacher), go to the designated space, compose ostinati patterns, and return to the class after 30–35 minutes to perform that which was created for their classmates. After each group finished the piece, the following questions were asked: (1) 'Did they do the composition' or 'Did they finish the assignment?' (2) 'If they did, what worked, what was good about it?' (3) 'If they didn't, what could they change in order to make it work?' After each question was posed, students were given time to respond, and if answers weren't forthcoming, Laura initiated responses, which often became rich explanations.

Vignette 2

It is April and students have been working on their final compositions that are to be performed in the final concert.The students, three girls and two boys, performed what had been created thus far but before they begin, one student described the piece and asked specific instruments to be played as the desired sound was described. The first part consisted of music for a variety of pitched and unpitched classroom instruments, while the second half included parts of a rap piece (recorded by an artist) to which one of the students danced. After the performance was complete, Laura started with, 'Let's discuss. You have my attention— you created this piece that makes one pay attention—that's a very good sign. Tell me please what is the form of your piece?' Students answered simultaneously (ABAC, C being the 'rap' section) and were required to be more specific when Laura asked, 'The go down, is that a variation or a new thing?' to which students replied, 'Totally new thing,' thus the 'C'. The conversation became quite specific about a student's reasons for certain pitches that did not provide a 'do' for the ending of a melody, as student's solution for getting more sound from her instrument, and a student's differing endings that caused some concern for another student because it meant that a part of the composition ended differently each time. In response to the concern, Laura asked, 'Does it still fit?' and in response to the student's 'Yes' suggested that 'the free form can be fine if it feels like it fits each time,' thus allowing the student to follow his 'muse'. Another student described how she varied the end of the second 'A': 'The other thing is that when we do the last A it is kind of a variation because when the first one I do 'dun dun dun' [while playing] and then it goes like down but on the other one I do it a little scale and I do it at the end.' This generated comments about what needed to be the ocus to know when the A section finished. The conversation ended with a student playing a possible ending: We were actually kind of thinking of having these at the end and going really fast' to which Laura responded, 'That is for you guys to figure out.' She reminded them that the composition allowed each student to reveal and display his or her strengths, and left, complimenting them on the work done thus far.

Vignette 3

After students played what had been created thus far, Laura described what she heard and then, through questioning strategies, provided conceptual knowledge to further their understanding, and used the content of what they had composed to extend their thinking about possibilities and changes. Students' responded by discussing amongst themselves and as a result, identified problems and generated possible solutions. As they talked, Laura asked questions to clarify what was being offered and to uncover motivations for the solutions. Students had created an A and a B section but were in disagreement about what constituted each section (which affected the length of each section) and whose part was played in each section (which affected the aesthetics of the piece). The influence of their interaction and Laura's input resulted in extending one section of the composition. Specifically, the issues, as identified by the students and Laura during their interactions, included: (1) the length of the A section, (2) a lack of completion of the A section, (3) the desire for a tonal center, and (4) the balance of repetition and contrast.

The role reflection played during Laura's interaction was evident in the strategies used when approaching students and their music. Describing what had been heard, asking questions for clarification and further insight, and providing and constructing knowledge to extend students' understanding represented reflecting on the action (Schön, 1987; Dewey, 1933/1991; Bruner, 1996; Wiggins, 2001). Asking questions to guide students' reasoning required them to think critically about what they had created and evaluated, and to offer reasoned judgments for choices made (Bransford et al., 2000; Bowman, 2002). Laura reflected with the students as she encouraged and prompted them to identify and solve problems, and to think and act like composers. In these instances, her reflection was on the action as she engaged with the students in the process.

3.2. The Extended Community

While creating the final compositions, students were given continuous feedback from two sources, Laura and me, and, during the final few sessions, also from a graduate composer. Laura values the multiple feedback because it provides students with other perspectives and allows her to have more time with single groups, knowing that there are two other people around to provide feedback and spend time with each group. The immediate feedback allowed for conversations to take place between students, and between the teacher, participant observer, composer and students, for clarification and justifications to be revealed, and for further possibilities to be generated for the composition. The experiences involved reflecting during interactions and critical reflection on processes and products with input from all involved. The events embodied the notion of a community of learners in which learning is constructed in conjunction with multiple sources of knowledge Bruner, 1996).

3.3. The Composer-in-residence

Laura's idea of 'hiring' a graduate composer for the final few weeks before the composition concert, stemmed from her belief that students would learn about how composers think and act, and how they practice their art form.

Vignette 4

The students entered and began to collect their instruments chosen for their compositions. Laura encouraged students to move quickly, as time was of essence, while the composer sat and observed the students organize each other and themselves. The students were introduced to the composer and asked to volunteer to go first and play what had been created thus far. There was always one group that would volunteer, either to get it done or out of eagerness to receive feedback from the composer. The students played their composition and the composer began a question and answer strategy that uncovered more information about intentions. She then provided constructive feedback in response to what was heard.

The first visit was structured around students playing what had been created thus far and receiving constructive feedback from someone who does what they are doing. This space allowed students to hear a composer 'talk aloud' in response to what was heard and experience the composer thinking critically about *their* music. Laura ensured that there was time at the end of the class for a question and answer session with the composer about the composer's work.

3.4. The Participant Observer Researcher

As Laura responded to a question about possible relationships between theory and her practice, reflections on having 'another' observer researcher in the environment evolved: 'I love you being part of it, because it's nice to have the camaraderie as well as help and another person to bounce thoughts off of. The help is very helpful.'

In addition, there were thoughts about having other people in the room working with her students as she worked amongst the groups. Dialogue between researcher partners, in this case, Laura and me, allowed for insight into each other's perspectives, and recognition of flaws or weaknesses in our thinking. Such insight is achieved with empathy, open-mindedness and generosity of spirit whilst learning from and sharing with each other (Jorgensen, 2001). Through such dialogue, shared understandings emerge which can become means for action (Freire, 1990). These exchanges also revealed appreciation for support received from those in the academic world who research and write about composition in classrooms, and a space in which questions can be asked, clarifications can be aired, confirmation and affirmation can be obtained, and successes can be shared, thus a space in which reflection on practice can occur.

3.5. Laura's Reflection on Her Practice

Insight about Laura's reflections on her practice was gained through analysis of data that were collected during three separate semi-structured interviews. Many questions were asked about a variety of issues, including (1) her original intent and how that played out, (2) characteristics of her role in such a context, and (3) thoughts about what students learned and experienced. Analysis of data revealed construction of new understandings through insights from her context that developed over the years and throughout the interviews. There was evidence of Laura using her own experiences as references for investigation and evaluation of what teaching and learning was

Vignette 5

During my first semi-structured interview with Laura, she reminisced about that first composition concert, and her value for designing such a curriculum: '. . . I care more to make musicians who enjoy music than "good little choir members" '. Her conversation continued and included her amazement about the amount of learning that took place, learning that included analysis and that went beyond her expectations.

occurring, all of which reflected the situatedness of the experiences (Lave and Wenger, 1991).

Laura began with an idea that evolved from strong thoughts on how students can and should be engaged in music making experiences. The interview provided opportunities for her to reflect on what had occurred over the previous years and time for thoughts that had guided her decisions to become explicit to her and to me, the interviewer:

> The assessment of composition is very strongly right on the spot . . . and no matter what it is [whether or not the answer is 'yes' or 'no', or if they are confused], we talk about it right away . . . if it worked beautifully . . . we identify . . . what could they have done to make it work . . . it's a very strong teaching tool for the other students in the group.

This thinking about what her role and the students' role when assessing what had been created was prevalent in much of her talk and action. She clearly viewed her role as someone who moved between advising, coaching, mentoring, and teaching, and involved students in active learning. The movement was engendered in response to the needs of the students and the situation encountered with each visit to each group. This value was made explicit during her reflections on what students can gain through such experiences: '. . . and that feels so right. That feels like, "This is now your work; this is your creation." '

A consistent theme was how a space had become an organic environment in which students and the process flourished:

> [T]he first year . . . I was so surprised . . . should I stop that one? but I didn't because it was so organic . . . kids are learning to work with other kids that they don't generally work with, find value in it . . . I never know what's going to come out with final compositions. I never know.

Laura often expressed wonder at how composing unleashed music making for those who had not experienced success in previous musical and other educational experiences. This realization strengthened her belief in the process that unfolded

> Vignette 6
>
> Laura passed out a questionnaire after the composition concerts and the viewing of the concert video were completed. She reminded the students of her interest in what they learned and what they thought about their composition experiences. She gave each student a questionnaire and a pencil and requested that they answer honestly and thoughtfully. Laura was curious about what students thought of it all, this experience of composing, one that is espoused by so many thinkers in the arts world. In this spirit, one question she included was, 'Tell me how I could have helped you better throughout the year'?

each year in her music classroom and provided fuel for her philosophical and pedagogical thinking about music making.

3.6. *The Questionnaire: Students' Time to Reflect*

As an example of reflection in practice, Laura presented a questionnaire to each of the students after the concert was completed. On the questionnaire, questions were posed about the processes and students were invited to respond.

Laura didn't ask what their thoughts were about how she helped them, but asked *how she could have been more effective*. This is significant in that, true to one process of critical reflection on one's practice, Laura took the risk to examine her effectiveness in something she values by asking for input from one group of the stakeholders. This question allowed Laura to reflect on her practice and guide her when making decisions about composing in the classroom *and her practice.*

3.7. *Reflecting on the Relationship of Researcher to the Community*

Another question was directed at my presence and interactions. I, as one member of the community, was open to other stakeholders' opinions in terms of my effectiveness. The question that was asked to unearth their thoughts and opinions was as follows: 'For those of you who had Betty Anne Younker come to your class, how did you like her being around and helping? Give me a couple of examples of how she helped you?'

The question about my input was not about how I could have improved but how I helped and whether or not they liked having me around. This was a much different question from the one Laura constructed for her evaluations. She was more objective with the question concerning me and less open to suggestions for my possible improvement. I found this curious and have yet to follow-up or reach any conclusions about reasons for her choice of questions.

What is created and experienced, in this case, is a practicum in which students, a music educator, and I serve as learners and mentors with the added expertise of a composer (Schön, 1987). Students' understanding about music making through composition is constructed collaboratively (Dewey, 1933/1991, 1938; Bruner, 1996) in groups that are situated socially and culturally (Vygotsky, 1978; Wiggins, 2001), all of which is mediated through artifacts and tools (Engestrom, 1996). In this community of music making, voices are heard and negotiated as meaning is shared through construction (Jorgensen, 2001, 2003; Allsup, 2003; Jaffurs, 2004; Woodford, 2005).

4. INSIGHTS INTO THE ROLE OF REFLECTION IN GOOD PRACTICE

As students and teachers, think critically—they generate possible solutions for a problem that has been either identified or formulated, and then evaluate the viability of those solutions (Dewey, 1933/1991, 1938). During such processes, they are active agents in their learning and have a voice as problems are identified and solved. During these constructive, educative experiences, perceptions and understandings are brought to the learning context as new understandings are grasped (Donovan, et al., 1999). As knowledge and skills are acquired, an explicit awareness of relationships between what is already known and can be done, and what is being required, takes place. Through such active engagement the acquired knowledge is active and not inert (Dewey, 1938; North Whitehead, 1967), and understanding is transformed, solidified, and continues to grow.

What has been offered here is one case study in which the students, teacher, participant observer researcher, and composer were engaged in a reflective practicum, and in which the music educator reflected on her practice through her and her students' experiences. The call to the field of arts education is to build opportunities in which students are engaged in arts practices that involve, not just the practitioners in the field and the students, but also those in the practice and academy. Music as a discipline has more challenges to this call, particularly in North America, because of the strong product-based affirmations that infiltrate and guide school-based music programs. These affirmations support programs in which students have a minimal voice in the process and the music teacher's mission is to cover the curriculum as set forth through methods, approaches, theories, and repertoire; and result in products that can be assessed and standardized.

While one can debate about the need for such programs, the profession is required to investigate other experiences such as those described in this chapter. There is a need for experiences that necessitate reflective engagement by all those involved. If one of the goals of education is to empower future citizens to think critically about what is experienced, then the process needs to begin in school-based and community-based environments.

REFERENCES

Allsup, R. (2003). Mutual learning and democratic action in instrumental music education. *Journal of Research in Music Education*, 51(1), 24–37.

Bowman, W. (2002). Educating musically. In R. Colwell and C.P. Richardson (Eds.). (2nd ed.). *The Handbook of Research for Music Teaching and Learning* (pp. 63–84). New York: Oxford University Press.

Bowman, W. (2002). *More Cogent Questions, More Provisional Answers: The Need to Theorize Music Education*. Keynote address at Fourth International Research in Musica Education Conference, April 2005. University of Exeter, School of Education and Life Long Learning, Exeter, England.

Bransford, J.D., Brown, A.L., and Cocking, R.R. (Eds.). (2000). *How People Learn: Brain, Mind, Experience, and School*. Washington, DC: Committee on Developments in the Science of Learning and Committee on Learning Research and Educational Practice, National Research Council, National Academy Press.

Bruner, J. (1960). *The Process of Education*. Cambridge, MA: Harvard University Press.

Bruner, J. (1996). *The Culture of Education*. Cambridge, MA: Harvard University Press.

Burnard, P. and Younker, B.A. (2002). Mapping pathways: fostering creativity in composition. *Music Education Research*, 4(2), 245–261.

Dewey, J. (1933/1991). *How We Think*. Buffalo, NY: Prometheus Books.

Dewey, J. (1938). *Experience and Education*. New York: Collier Books, Macmillan Publishing Company.

Donovan, M.S., Bransford, J.D., and Pellegrino, J.W. (Eds.). (1999). *How People Learn: Bridging Research and Practice*. Washington, DC: National Academy Press.

Elliott, D.J. (1995). *Music Matters*. New York: Oxford University Press.

Ennis, R.H. (1980). A conception of rational thinking. In J.R. Coombs (Ed.), *Philosophy of Education* 1979 (pp. 3–30). Normal, IL: Philosophy of Education Society.

Ennis, R.H. (1987). A taxonomy of critical thinking dispositions and abilities. In J.B. Baron and R.J. Sternberg (Eds.), *Teaching Thinking Skills: Theory and Practice* (pp. 9–26). New York: Freeman.

Freire, P. (1990). *Pedagogy of the Oppressed*. New York: Continuum Press.

Galbraith, L. (2002). Research in visual art education: implications for music. In R. Colwell and C.P. Richardson (Eds.), *The Handbook of Research for Music Teaching and Learning* (2nd ed.) (pp. 962–976). New York: Oxford University Press.

Jaffurs, S.E. (2004). The impact of informal music learning practices in the classroom, or how I learned how to teach from a garage band. *International Journal of Music Education*, 22(3), 189–200.

Jorgensen, E. (2001). A dialectical view of theory and practice. *Journal of Research in Music Education*, 49(4), 343–359.

Jorgensen, E. (2003). *Transforming Music Education*. Bloomington, IN: Indiana University.

King, P.M. and Kitchener, K.S. (1994). *Developing Reflective Judgment*. San Francisco, CA: Jossey-Bass.

Lave, J. and Wenger. E. (1991). *Situated Learning: Legitimate Peripheral Participation*. Cambridge: Cambridge University Press.

McPeck, J.E. (1981). *Critical Thinking and Education*. New York: St. Martin's Press.

McPeck, J.E. (1984). Stalking beasts but swatting flies: the teaching of critical thinking. *Canadian Journal of Education*, 9(1), 28–44.

McPeck, J.E. (1990). *Teaching Critical Thinking*. New York: Routledge and Kegan Paul.

Noddings, N. (2004). War, critical thinking, and self-understanding. *Phi Delta Kappan*, 85(7), 489–495.

North Whitehead, A. (1967). *Aims of Education*. New York: Free Press.

Patton, M.Q. (2002). *Qualitative Research and Evaluation Method*. (3rd ed.). Thousand Oaks, CA: Sage.

Paul, R.W. (1987). Dialogical thinking: critical thought essential to the acquisition of rational knowledge and passions. In J.B. Baron and R.J. Sternberg (Eds.), *Teaching Thinking Skills: Theory and Practice* (pp. 127–148). New York: Freeman.

Paul, R.W. (1993). *Critical Thinking: How to Prepare Students for a Rapidly Changing World*. Santa Rosa, CA: Foundations for Critical Thinking.

Reimer, B. (2003). *A Philosophy of Music Education: Advancing the Vision*. (3rd ed.). Englewood Cliffs, NJ: Prentice Hall.

Schön, D. (1987). *Educating the Reflective Practitioner*. San Francisco, CA: Jossey-Bass.

Vygotsky, L.S. (1978). *Mind in Society: the Development of Higher Psychological Processes*. Cambridge, MA: Harvard University Press.

Wiggins, J. (2001). *Teaching for Musical Understanding*. New York: McGraw-Hill.

Woodford, P.G. (2005). *Democracy and Music Education*. Bloomington, IN: Indiana University Press.

Younker, B.A. (2002). Critical thinking. In R. Colwell and C.P. Richardson (Eds.). *The Handbook of Research for Music Teaching and Learning* (2nd ed.). (pp. 162–170). New York: Oxford University Press.

Younker, B.A. (2003a). *Inside the Practitioner's Mind: Reflections on Experiences with Fifth-Grade Composers*. Paper presented at the Third International Research in Music Education Conference, April 2005. University of Exeter, School of Education and Life Long Learning, Exeter.

Younker, B.A. (2003b). Inside the practitioner's mind: intentionality of involving fifth-grade students in composition. *Music Education International*, 2, 23–36.

Younker, B.A. (2004). *Relationships between Research and Practice*. Paper presented at the Annual Meeting of the American Educational Research Association (AERA), April 2005. San Diego, CA.

Younker, B.A. (2005a). *Fifth-graders' Constructive Musical Understanding through Composition: Reflections from a University- and School-based Music Educator*. Paper presented at the Biennial General Music Colloquium, May, 2005. Mountain Lake VI.

Younker, B.A. (2005b). *Investigating the Role of Revision in Collaborative Group Composition*. Paper presented at the Fourth International Research in Music Education Conference, April 2005. University of Exeter, School of Education and Life Long Learning, Exeter, England.

Yrjö Engeström, Y., Miettinen, R., and Punamäki, R.J. (Eds.). (1999). *Perspectives on Activity Theory*. Cambridge: Cambridge University Press.

ANNA LEDGARD

15. FAIR EXCHANGE

Shared Professional Development and Reflective Action

1. PREFACE

> The greatest social impacts of participation in the arts arise from their ability to help people think critically about and question their experiences and those of others, not in a discussion group but with all the excitement, danger, magic, colour, symbolism, feeling, metaphor and creativity that the arts offer. It is in the act of creativity that empowerment lies, and through sharing creativity that understanding and social inclusiveness are promoted (Matassaro, 1997, p. 84).

This chapter explores the roles of teachers and professional artists in participatory arts activities with schools and communities in London through the work of the London International Festival of Theatre (LIFT)[1].

Over two decades LIFT has been a powerful force for change in London and elsewhere pioneering an approach to producing and showcasing international experimental theatre. The biennial festival was launched in 1979 at a time when international theatre was programmed in London sporadically, and often without a sense of context or connection to the city. In the early 1990s LIFT began to rethink both how artists were commissioned and how London communities might engage with the festival, transforming itself radically in response to the changing context of the late 20th century. In an increasingly interconnected world international festivals became the sites for debate about the role and purpose of the arts and LIFT sought to operate actively on the shifting boundary between the arts and education. From 1991–2001 LIFT pioneered a distinct Learning Programme that has since built a resource in the city for wider participation for young and old in international performance-making with artists playing a crucial role in assisting communities to express their culture and values in meaningful ways[2].

This account will look briefly at the main principles of the LIFT Learning programme and in detail at three associated research programmes: the LIFT Teacher

---

[1] In two decades LIFT brought 4500 artists from 62 countries to perform in locations across London and the UK.

[2] LIFT has provided a context for training and professional development schemes such as the LIFT Teacher Forum (1999–2004, LIFT Business Arts Forum (1996–2004), Project Phakama (1996–2005), Animarts Action Research Programme (2003).

P. Burnard and S. Hennessy (eds.), *Reflective Practice in Arts Education*, 169–182.

Forum (a part-time professional development programme for teachers in London schools in association with the Institute of Education, University of London); the *Animarts Action Research* programme (an investigation into the skills and insights required of artists to work effectively in schools and communities); and the Teacher Artist Partnership initiative (TAP), which has attracted major funding to explore the same themes and validate the robustness and transferability of their models of practice.

The assumption behind all three projects is that the best way for artists and teachers to learn how to work effectively in schools is for them to do their learning in partnership and through their own direct engagement with inter-disciplinary arts processes in the belief that: ‘it is in the act of creativity itself that empowerment lies’ (Matassaro, 1997, p. 84). A further assumption is that teaching is a subtle and complex art and that successful teachers, like artists, view their work as a continuing process of reflection and learning. Structured reflection—whether shared, in programmes of seminars; individual, in video or reflective journals; or in pairs, whilst planning and undertaking practical research in schools—is central to all three programmes.

This approach is explored over a period (1995–2005) in which UK arts education has undergone substantial change, shifting from a tendency towards short-term arts projects designed to deliver specific curriculum objectives, to a more strategic and integrated approach aimed at sustaining dialogue between schools and arts organisations and legitimised by recent reviews of the arts in the curriculum (Ofsted, 2003a/b). Throughout these profound shifts, LIFT personnel (myself and Tony Fegan—Director of Learning, LIFT), have adhered to a philosophy and set of principles, rooted in democratic models of comprehensive education from the 70s and 80s. Originally both teachers, we have evolved a hybrid professional role for ourselves combining the roles of tutor, creative learning producers and arts practitioner and have sought to engage increasingly with theoretical frameworks and methodologies.

In all three programmes research methods include all participants in practice-based action research over a period of a year looking at the possibilities and problems of artists and teachers working in partnership. As the projects have evolved so too has the rigour of our approach to research. The research methodology is rooted in principles expounded by Lawrence Stenhouse (1975) with pedagogy and values being scrutinised and tested in the classroom. The current TAP programme involves research specialists in a thorough qualitative and interpretive based evaluation methodology with extensive use of video, interviews, protocol and document analysis. Since TAP is a collaborative venture tutors, organisers and participants are all action-researchers engaged in recording interpretations and judgements. TAP is following the action research model developed by Stephen Kemmis and Robin McTaggart in the *Action Research Planner* (Carr and Kemmis, 1986) with additional reference to Donald Schön’s elaboration of the reflective practitioner (Schön, 1983).

2. INTRODUCTION

2.1. *LIFT Learning: Evolving a Model of Participatory Practice*

Much of the work of LIFT from 1990 on was dedicated to investigating relationships with the city through participatory projects such as Factory of Dreams (1997)[3], Cellarworks (1999)[4], Style of Our Lives (2000)[5], in order to find a methodology that enabled artists and schools to work collaboratively over sustained periods within an emancipatory pedagogy without compromising their respective principles and priorities. LIFT began to evolve a set of principles of procedure for its democratic and collaborative arts learning programme, as follows:

2.2. *LIFT Learning Principles*

2.2.1. Participant-centred[6] Tony Fegan, LIFT Learning Director, reflected:

> The aim is to create as many entry points . . . which let in as many participants as possible, each bringing their own skills, life experience, curiosity, passion—and also a readiness to put themselves at risk[7].

This democratic arts process with its collectively generated ideas provides a context for encountering the real in a metaphorical space, allowing for the exploration of ambiguity and uncertainty, and simultaneously achieving immediacy and distance.

2.2.2. Reflective Reflection is central to the work of any artist or teacher and is impossible to detach from the creative process. As ideas are shared, they are selectively woven into the creative process. Given time and trusting relationships different perspectives can be exchanged and, through negotiation, participants arrive at the possibility of shared visions and values.

2.2.3. Involving collaborative art forms Arts based investigations which build on collectively generated ideas, tend to do so irrespective of particular arts disciplines. This demands that both artist and teacher collaborators remain responsive, spontaneous and open to the unpredictable. For artists this can mean putting aside any fixed relationship to a product. For teachers this may involve them in abandoning the set plan in order to pursue unanticipated opportunities.

---

[3] Factory of Dreams was a collaboration between LIFT, international and London based artists and Stockwell Park School in 1997.

[4] Cellarworks—presented at LIFT 99 by Theatre rites in collaboration with William Patten Primary School, London.

[5] Style of Our Lives—January–July 2000 in collaboration with William Patten Primary School, Stoke Newington Secondary School, London.

[6] The methodology drew inspiration in part from the principles of person-centred learning (Rogers, 1961) and models of drama in education (Bolton, 1984; Heathcote and Johnson, 1991).

[7] Tony Fegan, Recorded in an Animarts Seminar at LIFT, September 2000.

2.2.4. Cross-cultural and cross-sectoral LIFT Learning projects sought to reflect the social and cultural diversity of London. In schools projects brought together international artists with UK based artists from a range of experience and cultural backgrounds with teachers and students, adult helpers and parents where possible.

2.2.5. Site-specific Many commissions were rooted in investigating spaces beyond the physical boundaries of institutions such as bus garages, warehouses, abandoned cellars, and derelict hotels. LIFT Learning promoted and explored this approach both as a challenge to the status quo of conventional theatre practice and through a thematic interest in the multiple histories and meanings of place.

These principles of procedure were common to LIFT Learning activities whether in South Africa, Bombay or London and underpinned the curriculum for their professional development programmes from 1999.

2.3. A Shifting Context

By 1997/8 the situation *vis a vis* the marginalisation of the arts in the national nurriculum for England was reaching a crisis point. LIFT struggled to balance an approach that valued the place of the imagination in schooling with the demands of an increasingly instrumental curriculum.

Over the years LIFT's experimental programme has attracted artists of the finest calibre: ground-breaking, independent, risk-takers and inventors, open to collaboration and experiment. Such artists deal with ambiguities and uncertainties: they experiment, test ideas, are open to unknown outcomes. Reflective teachers engaged in scrutiny of their own practice might also be seen to share some of these qualities. However the 1990s preoccupation in schools with a means/ends outcome driven model of curriculum design geared to instructional teaching mitigated against such investigative approaches and the more open-ended learning outcomes which were associated with them.

Although through the 1990s growing numbers of artists were working in schools there was evidence that schools were finding it difficult adequately to manage such relationships. Teachers often felt demoralised and frustrated by their lack of autonomy and tended to be understandably wary in this climate of exploring radical ideas with artists. This was due as much to the climate and the low status of arts activity within the curriculum as to inadequate quality control measures and a lack of clarity from arts organisations about their roles (Ross, 2003). Driven in part by funding directives, many arts organisations were approaching schools with one-off 'workshops' designed to 'deliver' specific national curriculum objectives, thus often bypassing the opportunity for sustained dialogue that was necessary if projects were to have any long-term impact. A further inhibiting factor was that a new generation of teachers was emerging whose training in a predominantly results-oriented assessment culture had undervalued the reflective and experiential models that might better have prepared them for participation in arts-based programmes (Rogers, 2003). There was a real danger that artists would be reduced to the status of occasional visiting specialists thus losing a rich opportunity for them both to nurture their own practice and act as a resource for teachers as well as pupils. It was at this point that

LIFT began conversations with other arts organisations and head teachers to discuss a strategic response.

2.4. *The LIFT Teacher Forum 1999–2004: A Resource for Teacher Development*

What follows is a description of the LIFT Teacher Forum which set out to explore how artists could become a resource for the professional development of teachers. The account also explores how the mechanisms of shared learning, mixed learning communities, and reflective practice and enquiry-based learning worked.

The Teacher Forum was organised from 1999 as a cycle of practice-based reflective learning over a period of a year. Each involved a residential weekend induction, a group exploration of teacher and artist's own learning, motivation and values, paired observations of teachers and artists in the work place and reflection on the shared experience of theatre (via their own participation in performance workshops or attendance at LIFT shows/debates). Within the Forum process artists and teachers in pairs undertook a five day arts-based investigation in school, and teachers each completed a research report. By 2001/2 the Forum had received accreditation from the Institute of Education, University of London.

The case study below describes the outcome of one research partnership between a teacher, Lawrence Gallio, at Tuke Special Secondary School (London), and performance artist Mark Storor. Their enquiry looked at the relationship between student autonomy and adult intervention when working creatively with students with specific learning difficulties.

2.5. *Re-defining Public Space in Peckham: A Case Study*

On a dull grey morning in Peckham, South London something extraordinary is unfolding in a run-down tenement block. A table is set for a tea party, festooned with bunches of violets and anemones and generous mounds of brightly coloured cup cakes. Beside the tenement block is a busy main road and beyond it can be seen a group of twenty people in white disposable paper suits chattering loudly as they approach a crossing. The white clad figures enter the courtyard, whoop in delight at the vibrant scene, and start to play on swings, roundabouts, and a playground horse. Music and laughter float in the air. Curtains twitch at the windows of the run-down flats, other residents appear at their doorways: ‘Come on down’, a white-suited man calls as he pours tea for everyone, making sure that no one is left out. It is difficult to know who is a parent, a child, a teacher, a performer, or ‘audience’; or indeed how much is accidental, and how much planned. In spite of these dissolved distinctions, we know that for a brief moment some sort of ‘performance’ has taken ownership of a public space, forcing all those caught up in its magic to reconsider the familiar iconography of everyday life.

2.6. *Testimony*

A year later at the LIFT Enquiry 2004, the same white suited man is applauded on completing his testimony as one of the 100 enquirers invited to respond to the question

What is theatre to you?[8] He is the teacher, Lawrence Gallio, whose retrospective performance took the form of a dialogue between the single performer and a disembodied voice, his alter ego, presented against a wall of evocative video images. The footage showed the journey of a group of eight young people with severe learning difficulties in creating the public performance piece described above. The same piece, in the form of a play script, had been successfully presented as a research assignment to the Institute of Education a year earlier.

2.7. *Shared Learning*

The Teacher Forum adopted the same core principles as the LIFT Learning programmes, giving equal value to the contribution of both teacher and artist and drawing as much on the experiences and insights of participating teachers and artists as on external stimuli:

> Teachers and head teachers do not enter into CPD (Continuing Professional Development) as empty vessels. . . . They usually enter CPD courses brimful of thoughts and feelings; with implicit or explicit beliefs about education and their work with children. They come with differences, disagreements, preconceptions, uncertainties, missions. These are all very useful resources which can be drawn upon and studied in CPD processes. (Dadds, 2001, p. 51).

The premise was that the most valuable learning would occur through reflection on their own experiences of learning and the arts in partnership with artists. This mirrors the principles of person-centred psychology expounded by Rogers (1989): 'the only learning which significantly influences behaviour is self-discovered, self-appropriated learning' (1989, p. 302), and explored in Gale's work on teachers and post-compulsory education (Gale, 2001). This approach was in stark contrast to the systematic undervaluing of teachers' own insights that had been prevalent in much of the formulaic style CPD of the 90's in England.

2.8. *Mixed Community of Learners*

Each Forum recruited a mixed community of learners and the shared learning framework was enriched by the diversity of the learning group. Teachers were recruited from nursery, primary, secondary, FE post-16 colleges and special schools, and artists from a diverse range of cultures and art forms, each bringing differing but equally valuable insights to the collaborative enquiry.

2.9. *Reflective Practice and Enquiry-based Learning*

Teacher/artist partnerships worked most effectively when underpinned by some reflection on those insights and qualities which, when shared, tended to be revealing

---

[8] In 2001 LIFT transformed the biennial festival into a five-year Enquiry examining the purpose and nature of theatre in today's world. In June 2004 one hundred Londoners aged 4–96 offered personal testimonies twice daily on the place of theatre in their lives.

of values or differences in common. The case study performance described above offers a provocative and insightful view of the complexity of the notion of partnership. It honestly depicts the struggle of artist and teacher to achieve consensus, to challenge the familiar in their practice and to find a holding form for their work with these youngsters which was truly democratic and student centred as well as promoting valuable learning. To achieve this required openness, flexibility and extensive dialogue.

The Forum structure provided a foundation for building strong relationships with its agreed ground rules governing respect and mutual support, strong pastoral framework, accessible tutors, regular one-to-one tutorials, a peer support system, and an e-mail network.

> Only within a strong ethical framework in which trust between partners is established—which may be implicit, tacit and embedded in practice, as well as written and codified, can collaboration and partnership operate effectively (Jeffery, 2005, p. 35).

The implication is that the Forums were engaged as reflective practitioners in enquiry-based rather than discovery-based learning, exploring the feasibility and practicability of the LIFT value consensus in classrooms. This is in keeping with how Lawrence Stenhouse famously redefined '*the curriculum problem*' with values and pedagogical hypotheses open to scrutiny and testing in classrooms (Stenhouse, 1975). LIFT was increasingly exhibiting an action research approach following the model developed by Stephen Kemmis and Robin MacTaggart in the Action Research Planner (Carr and Kemmis, 1986).

3. LIFT TEACHER FORUM: THE LEGACY

In examining the impact of the Forum from 1999–2004 some common features were emerging.

- Enhanced teacher understanding of the value of making relationships with artists from other cultures and communities: 'The Forum inspires me to look out from the sides of my "teacher-ness" to remember what else is outside.'[9]
- Increased confidence to experiment with new approaches to teaching: '. . . it helped me to understand the importance of giving time for reflection [and] stimulated the ongoing debate about structure and freedom in everybody's learning.'[10]
- Enhanced confidence to disseminate teacher learning within schools: 'it gave me confidence to plan an inset for staff on creativity which I could never have imagined doing before.'[11]
- Changed perceptions of the role of artists and the potential for the arts within the curriculum: 'It alerted me to the reality of other intelligences in that I had to make

---

[9] D. Coates (personal communication, March 2002).

[10] I. Dove (personal communication, March, 2002).

[11] I. Dove (personal communication, March 2002).

a mental leap to perceive things as an artist might. This was tough for me at times! But I realised that there were approaches other than those I favoured that could yield truly effective results.'[12]

- Altered perceptions about the role of the arts in shifting cultural values and understanding: '. . . the arts, done well, go beyond just self-expression. . . . There is the opportunity to develop self-discipline and a sense of place in the world . . . the arts enable children to see themselves as (cultural) producers whilst all around they are being groomed as customers.'[13]

As teachers reflected on the impact of the Forum for them as individuals, we had questions to ask about the relationships of participating teachers to their school settings and their impact on the sustainability of good arts partnership practice.

4. SCHOOLS AS CREATIVE COMMUNITIES

Where institutions were already demonstrating an institutional commitment to the arts, the Forum became a complementary element in a series of strategies to support creativity across the school community. In one particularly successful case, this has included: sustained funding;[14] the participating teacher given delegated responsibility for the arts and allocated non-contact time to support this role; a whole school commitment to the arts enshrined in staffing and curriculum policies; a whole school in-service training day for all staff each year facilitated by experienced arts educationalists; and continuity of CPD with another staff member taking part in the most recent TAP Programme (successor to the Teacher Forum).

Where a teacher was more isolated and the school did not demonstrate an institutional commitment to the arts or creativity, more tensions were apparent as one teacher reflected:

> The education world and the arts world do not always communicate effectively . . . this leads to a lot of frustration and wasted opportunities. I'm much more convinced of this potential since the forum and, I think, more aware of the pitfalls. The main pitfall for me is short-term thinking. Yes, schools are under ridiculous pressures for results but they still can afford (cannot afford not to) to step back and consider how to integrate learning about and through the arts into daily school life. This requires consultation, negotiation and this equals time and money.[15]

Some teachers expressed fears that their schools would not be able to accommodate their renewed determination and passion to make changes:

> Once you have been witness to this, all things look slightly different. Questions remain unanswered. I want to speak with colleagues who are

[12] D. Chetty (personal communication, May 2003).

[13] D. Chetty (personal communication, May 2003).

[14] Millennium School, Greenwich was in the London South Creative Partnership region and used its regular funding to promote a whole school arts approach.

[15] D. Chetty (personal communication, May 2003).

> excited by this adventure and look them in the eye and say: What shall we do? Once awareness had been raised it is impossible to go back.[16]

Such tensions are well known to be a consequence of reflecting closely on practice in whatever professional arena, and have been described before notably in the work of Donald Schön:

> When a member of a bureaucracy embarks on a course of reflective practice, allowing himself to experience confusion and uncertainty, subjecting his frames and theories to conscious criticism and change, he may increase his capacity to contribute to significant organisational learning, but he also becomes, by the same token, a danger to the stable system of rules and procedures within which he is expected to deliver his technical expertise (Schön, 1983, p. 328).

A closer analysis is needed of the long-term impact of the Forum on teacher development. It has to be recognised that changes in professional practice are rarely solely the product of one intervention, and are closely related to the factors that have motivated teachers to engage in the process in the first place. If change happens it is likely to be as a result of a combination of factors, of which the Forum may only be one.

The numbers of teachers who made career changes on completing the Forum would however suggest a shift towards a more dynamic stance in relation to their own and others creativity. Whether this was directed back into the school or beyond, was largely dependent of the extent to which the schools were prepared to embrace a teacher's enhanced commitment to creativity. In general the Forum had engendered a heightened sensitivity to the complexity of this work, and given teachers some tools to advocate for the arts with colleagues in school and to take a more proactive part in managing partnerships with artists, and seeking out artists in response to identified priorities.

By the time we had completed two cycles of the Forum, the experiences of the teachers were well-documented. However, less attention had been paid to the impact of the Forum process on the practice of the artist (this after all had not been the intention of the first Forums where artists were present to facilitate the learning of the teacher). Yet Forum artists suggested that their engagement with the teachers in the shared reflective process provided them also with invaluable professional development that did not seem to be available to them elsewhere.

Despite a growing recognition of the critical importance of the arts leader in sustaining inclusive arts education practice, there was still little theoretical or pedagogical underpinning for collaborative arts practice (Ross, 2003) and limited recognition for professional development opportunities for artists and arts leaders (Robinson, 1999). A shared concern about this state of affairs brought LIFT together with The Guildhall

[16] D. Gallio (personal communication, March 2004).

School of Music and Drama (GSMD) and Animarts[17] in a practical research initiative—The Animarts Action Research Programme.

This continued to further LIFT's general shift in the direction of action research, with a concomitant desire to explore and test the robustness of the LIFT model in a variety of settings in which artists and teachers were working together.

5. THE ANIMARTS ACTION RESEARCH PROGRAMME

The proposed programme was to look at issues surrounding the 'growth' of the profession of artist in education or 'animateur'[18] in a climate of increased cultural interaction with diverse communities. A year-long practice based research investigation was set up to examine the relative roles and abilities of artists and teachers, and to explore the wider implications for training and professional development. The resulting report suggested:

> That the skills and interests of artists and teachers are different, though complementary; that shared professional development is an important way of promoting diversity of achievement in students and of enriching the professional experience and connections of artists and teachers alike (Animarts, 2003, p. 14).

The Animarts research, based on the model of the LIFT Teacher Forum, was rooted in practice based research. This confirmed what the Teacher Forum findings had indicated, that success comes when the teacher/artist partnership is based on mutual understanding of the distinct and equally valuable contribution of both teacher and artist to the partnership. The research showed the importance of both artist and teacher participating in creative endeavour, taking risks and daring to experiment together. This is corroborated by a longitudinal Canadian research study (Upitis and Smithrin, 1997) which also concluded that:

> profound changes to teachers' practices and beliefs arose when teachers worked directly with artists and experienced the artistic process while making their own art (Upitis and Smithrin, 1997, p. 6).

The Animarts research engaged teachers and artists in reflection about how the practice of the artist can enrich the classroom and how in turn the classroom can

---

[17] Animarts first appeared in 1999 as a proposal drawn up by Christopher Lucas (formerly Director of the RSA, 1977–94).

Animarts' long-term mission is to enhance the professional standing of the artist in education and the community. It is Animarts' premise that this can only happen when there are adequate, appropriate, recognised training opportunities for the growing numbers of artists working in this field.

[18] Animateur-defined in the Animarts report as: 'a practising artist, in any art form, who uses her/his skills, talents and personality to enable others to compose, design, devise, create, perform or engage with works of art of any kind'. *Art of the Animateur*, 2003.

enrich the practice of the artist. Firm generalisations began to emerge from the experience:

> The combination of teacher and artist can only work where there has already been established a framework of trust, friendliness and mutual respect.[19]

One of the artists commented perceptively on the terms of engagement:

> For the animateur to be able to explore and take risks, the teacher almost 'holds' the whole structure steady. . . . For this to occur, the teacher needs to trust the animateur, and believe in the project. This trust has to be earned, and should not be assumed (Animarts, 2003, p. 48).

The 'earning of trust' in this case came through a shared experience and interrogation of a creative process. As artist and teacher put themselves equally 'at risk' the shared serendipity became a point of contact between them.

The Animarts research findings suggest particular implications for the professional development of artists and teachers. Collaboration of this kind must be underpinned by a framework of shared values; it requires deep reflection, sharing knowledge, expertise and experience warts and all. This is risky, demanding, challenging and rewarding. As with the LIFT Teacher Forum strategies such as mentoring, peer support and supportive pastoral and academic tutor support are critical to the success of this model.

The findings provided a detailed analysis of the tacit knowledge used by the artist/animateur in practice (Animarts, 2003, pp. 38–44), highlighting the difficulties for arts and education organisations alike of managing the evaluation and assessment of implicit skills and knowledge and the need for more flexible models of continuing professional development within higher education. Gale's analysis of four theoretical models for post-compulsory teacher education (Gale, 2001) provides a useful theoretical framework against which to consider the emerging model being developed though the LIFT Teacher Forum and Animarts Action Research.

6. TAP (TEACHER ARTIST PARTNERSHIP)

The 2003/4 Teacher Forum graduation and review coincided with the publication of the Animarts Report. In a climate of increased resourcing for the arts in schools,[20] both served to accentuate the urgent need to increase the pool of artist and teacher practitioners equipped to work in effective partnerships in arts education. However both models,

---

[19] Tim Crouch and Gill Foster—Animarts Action Research Team—(personal communication, January 2002).

[20] Creative Partnerships is a government initiative which between 2002–2005 has invested £112 million in 36 areas of the UK to support the positive development of young people through cultural practice and creative learning.

described by one funding body as the 'Rolls Royce end of the spectrum' needed greater scrutiny and robust evaluation in order to prove the need for a transferable CPD model that could demonstrate the effectiveness of jointly training artists and teachers.

To this end, a consortium of eight organisations joined forces in the TAP (Teacher Artist Partnership) professional development research initiative.[21] The TAP Consortium has devised the structure and curriculum for an initial two-year Continuing Professional Development initiative for 30 artists and 30 teachers in London which commenced in April 2005. 'TAP is funded by: The Paul Hamlyn Foundation, Creative Partnerships, Esmee Fairbairn Foundation, Department for Education and Skills Innovation, Arts Council, England'.

In recognition that forms of evaluation for such professional development had to be sensitive to the nuances and complexities of this work, David Jenkins has initiated an arts-sensitive evaluation strategy for TAP. The main research methods are qualitative and interpretive, and fieldwork based, using participant and non-participant observation, interviews, protocol and document analysis. Video documentation is an important tool, both for the collection of process data and for dissemination. Since the TAP project is a collaborative venture, all members of the consortium are action researchers, keeping reflective journals and recording interpretations and judgements, together with cameos, vignettes and anecdotes.

Initial findings from the research team are encouraging, a particular strength being the balance within the curriculum of reflection and playfulness, and the space for participants to construct their own intuitive and analytical enquiries with artists and teachers. Teachers welcome the individualised learning approach and the opportunities for non-judgemental peer observations, concretising experiences by relating them to theory, and being part of a community of learners from other professional settings. TAP is also experimenting with WebCT and other on-line learning resources as flexible discussion tools.

There is recognition that there is a need for subtle management of the implicit paradox at the heart of the action research paradigm, that is, a willingness to explore with openness of hearts and minds the practicality of ideas to which individuals are also at some level deeply committed. Related to this is the need to look closely at the range of facilitation and learning processes employed by TAP. Gale's (2001) analysis of Heron's (1989) work on creative approaches to the facilitation of learning is an important reference point. Heron describes four interdependent learning forms: experiential learning, imaginal learning, conceptual learning and practical learning in a model which places the experiences of the learners at the centre of the development of their own learning process. This requires a framework of facilitation in which 'the facilitator enters into a relationship with the group in which there is an attempt to reach all group members through a variety of facilitative strategies' (Gale, 2001, p. 107).

---

21 The TAP Consortium comprises: Animarts, CAPEUK (Creative Partnerships in Education), Guildhall School of Music and Drama (GSMD), LEAParts (formerly London Education Arts Partnership), LIFT, NewVIc (Newham Sixth Form College), LONSAS (London Schools Arts Service) and PLEY (Proactive Learning from Early Years).

Malcolm Ross's work on arts organisation education programmes points to the lack of 'disciplined consideration of the structure of concepts integral to the realm of creative arts education as a whole' and the need to draw up 'an evaluation matrix that reflects the particular role of arts organisations within it' (Ross, 2003, p. 75). It is hoped that the TAP research process will go some way towards defining some key principles for collaborative arts education practice as well as establishing an evaluation matrix which acknowledges the complexity of the role of the artist in education and its potential as a resource for teachers.

It will also be necessary for TAP to ensure that the form of validation is sufficiently flexible to accommodate a group which is all the richer for its widely varying experiences and academic starting points, as well as finding a form of assessment which is suited to the programme content and methods.

7. CONCLUSION

In action research, increased understanding is always in the service of better practice; it is research that seeks to make a difference. Reflection is central to such an approach, and the ability to reflect systematically is a skill that must be learned. The LIFT, Animarts, TAP initiatives are all experiments in the organisation of systematic opportunities for reflection over time. Teachers and artists reflect individually, in pairs, in groups, with peers, with colleagues from other sectors, professional and cultural backgrounds. They collaborate, moving in and out of practice and reflection as communities of learners, looking for commonalities and differences, testing assumptions, exploring other models of practice or theory against which to link experiences, adjusting and modifying their practice. At the heart of these experiments is the engagement of reflective learners in a collective creative process.

The future of this work is in the hands of artists, teachers, managers and facilitators. Alongside the need for an overarching theoretical framework is the need for a professional framework that describes and values the role of the arts leader in a changed and changing world. Only then will we find ways to establish a recognised pedagogy for the arts in education, and value those who are essential in delivering this. Only then will the series of innovations involving LIFT and many others have secured their lasting legacy, contributing to a curriculum capable of empowering artists and teachers as agents of change to the benefit of a civil society that gives proper value to the power of the imagination.

ACKNOWLEDGEMENTS

The central players in this narrative are the teachers, artists and students who have participated in LIFT, Animarts and TAP projects. My thanks are also due to David Jenkins, Lucy Neal and above all to my co-collaborator Tony Fegan.

REFERENCES

Animarts. (2003). *The Art of the Animateur—An Investigation into the Skills and Insights Required of Artists to Work Effectively in Schools and Communities*. London: Animarts.

Carr, W. and Kemmis, S. (1986). *Becoming Critical*. London and Philadelphia: Falmer Press.

Dadds, M. (2001). Continuing professional development: nurturing the expert within. In J. Soler, A. Craft, and H. Burgess (Eds.), *Teacher Development, Exploring Our Own Practice* (pp. 50–57). London: Open University.

Gale, K. (2001). Teacher education within post-compulsory education and training: a call for a creative approach. In A. Craft, B. Jeffrey, and M. Leibling (Eds.), *Creativity in Education* (pp. 103–115). London: Continuum.

Heron, J. (1989). The Facilitators Handbook London, Kogan page, referred to on page 107 of K. Gale's Chapter: Teacher education within post-compulsory education and training: a call for a creative approach, already cited in the references to my chapter.

Jeffery, G. (2005). *The Creative College: Building a Successful Learning Culture in the Arts*. Stoke on Trent: Trentham Books.

Kemmis, S. and McTaggart, R. (1988). *The Action Research Planner*. Geelong, Victoria: Deakin University Press.

Matarasso, F. (1997). *Use or Ornament? The Social Impact of Participation in the Arts*. London: Comedia.

Ofsted. (2003a). *Improving City Schools: How the Arts Can Help* (HMI 1709). London: HMSO.

Ofsted. (2003b). *Expecting the Unexpected: Developing Creativity in Primary and Secondary Schools* (HMI 1612). London: HMSO.

Robinson, K. (1999). *All Our Futures: Creativity, Culture and Education*. London: Department for Education and Employment, Department for Culture, Media and Sport, National Advisory Committee on Creative and Cultural Education.

Rogers, C. (1961). *On Becoming a Person*. London: Constable.

Rogers, C. (1989). *The Carl Rogers Reader*. London: Constable.

Rogers, R. (2003). *Time for the Arts? The Arts in the Initial Training of Primary Teachers: A Survey of Training Providers in England*. Wednesbury: Wednesbury Education Action Zone.

Ross, M. (2003). Evaluating education programmes in arts organizations. *Music Education Research*, 5(1), 69–79.

Schön, D.A. (1983). *The Reflective Practitioner: How Professionals Think in Action*. London: Avebury.

Stenhouse, L. (1975). *An Introduction to Curriculum Research and Development*. London: Heinemann.

Upitis, R. and Smithrin, K. (1997). *Teacher Development and Elementary Arts Education*. Presented at National Symposium on Arts Education, August. 1997. Cape Breton, Nova Scotia.

SARAH HENNESSY

16. THE CONDITIONS AND CONSEQUENCES OF REFLECTIVE PRACTICES IN ARTS EDUCATION

> 'The business of reflection in determining the true good cannot be done once and for all . . . It needs to be done over and over again, in terms of the conditions of concrete situations as they arise' John Dewey (1932, p. 212).

This chapter attempts to draw together some of the issues and themes which emerge from the individual contributions to this book. Our invitation to authors in Section 1 was to contribute their perspectives and insights into an aspect of professional reflection. In Section 2 authors were asked to describe and discuss particular applications of tools to facilitate a reflective process in a specific context, and in Section 3 more detailed explorations of the place of reflective activity and its effects in a variety of settings are presented. The context for all these perspectives is arts education and three principle sites for activity recur: school classrooms, teacher education programmes, and partnership projects involving artists, teachers and other professionals working with young people in and out of school.

The experiences described and discussed do not cover all possible sites and aspects of practice, but do offer a diverse range of purposes and contexts for reflection. I have attempted to identify some key elements and features which have emerged from my reading of this collection. These seem to me to be significant in understanding what characteristics of the reflective process are, the conditions which support it and its consequences.

The fundamental act of reflection, the arguments for its value and the purposes it serves are reiterated throughout these stories and descriptions. What is distinctive is the variety of contexts and applications which might resonate with the conditions and practices of readers' own circumstances. In education and arts practices it is the specifics of context which demand constant review, reappraisal, refinement, rehearsal, redefining—all activities in which critical reflection is implicit. On every occasion when people come together to play, improvise, devise, invent, share ideas and new understandings in art making; the medium/s, the place, the timescale, the levels of ability, dispositions, expectations and ambitions of participants; and the socio-cultural affordances or constraints all have a bearing on how the experience will take shape and evolve. Every factor interacts with every other creating a unique condition to which arts practitioners must not only be especially sensitive but also be able to exploit or ameliorate in creative and appropriate ways.

P. Burnard and S. Hennessy (eds.), *Reflective Practice in Arts Education*, 183–192.

Reflection in professional practice is a catalyst for change (Ghaye, 2005). The motivation for change may arise from the conditions of failure and its avoidance, or of success and the desire to capture and recreate or build on it. Both encourage us to be more critical of our practices, however it is self evident that we are more likely to engage in reflection as a result of things going wrong. We celebrate success but are less inclined to want to analyse what made it successful—the very term 'critical' we associate with a negative, judgmental stance rather than one that is celebratory and constructive. There is a case to be made for trying to identify the conditions which appear to underpin successful teaching or projects, but the danger is when these are presented as contributing mechanistically to a model of 'best'—or 'good'—practice, the implication being that the model can be applied elsewhere to the same effect. This is fraught with difficulties, not least because so much of what contributes to the success of a project or a lesson is the coming together of, and interactions amongst many variables, some of which are in themselves unstable and ephemeral. It may be easier to learn from omissions and weaknesses than to try to clone the factors which appear to lead to success.

In the context of the arts the notion that we reflect to solve a problem or capture the ingredients of success so that they can be reapplied is rather limited and mechanistic. Artists thrive on obstacles and problems—one can apply Bowman's discussion on research (2005), to practice in the arts: 'problems are not things to be done away with . . . they are valuable assets. Inquiry doesn't so much 'solve' problems as it transforms them into other problems . . .'(p. 162). Art making demands risk taking, questioning, challenging the status quo, bending if not breaking the rules, speculation, disturbance, conflict, discomfort and shock.

As argued by several authors in this book art making *is* a reflective process. Grushka (2005) claims that 'for artists reflective orientations are essential between the affective self, engagement with their medium and their socially discursive constructed ways of knowing' (p. 354). In the context of the visual arts she goes on to suggest that 'Image creation is a process of stabilizing an idea (as image) . . . which allows one to critically reflect, edit and refine—to be communicated as reflection—in—action' (p. 355). Thus teaching the arts should engender reflection as a habitual trait. The fact that it doesn't always do this points to the possibility that much arts teaching may not result in authentic artistic learning (see Swanwick's 'Teaching Music Musically', 2000). Reflection is also a 'value—laden' enterprise which demands the right conditions of place, time, processes, people, dispositions, cultures and ethics. In formal educational contexts—as in schools or teacher training settings it may be that reflective activity is somewhat compromised by the constraints inherent in institutional cultures.

The argument that real change in values and attitudes leading to more effective practice in teaching can only take place through professional reflection is strongly supported by evaluations and observations of initiatives and projects presented here (Upitis, Ledgard, Kerchner, Harris) and elsewhere. The rhetoric of the UK government (through the Teaching Development Agency) makes many references to the importance of reflective practice in teaching. Yet, there is clearly a hypothetical (at least!)

tension in adopting a continuously critical stance which, if successful would generate a state of permanent revolution within the educational and perhaps wider community. If reflection results in change there are clearly risks attached for those engaged in the process; for the organisation; and for those it serves. The reflective process in professional contexts is inclined also to have a democratising and decentralising effect (Ghaye, ibid.)—whether it be amongst teachers, amongst learners or (and especially) between teachers and learners. I am not convinced that that is what governments or most parents and teachers actually want. Teachers are often characterised as an inherently conservative group within society despite the obvious truth that they are engaged in potentially transformative and liberating endeavour. Perhaps this innate conservatism is the only thing keeping the lid on things!

It is also borne out again and again in working, in particular with experienced teachers who return to post graduate research studies in higher education or undertake significant action research in their own classrooms, that reflecting in a systematic, sustained and supported way often leads to radical and sometimes traumatic upheavals in the student's sense of professional identity, confidence, and philosophy which can spill over into their personal lives. The consequences of professional reflection can be life changing and thus carry a degree of risk:

> The effects of encouraging students to pursue a line of thinking . . . may cause them to question or challenge the values and practices of their own workplaces . . . .. Reflection may lead to revolution or alienation from the very profession for which the reflective activity is designed. (Hunt, 2001, p. 276)

Those who stimulate and/or support the process carry, therefore, a great responsibility not only for the individual but for the professional community of which they are a part.

Different arts disciplines have, historically, developed their pedagogies and curricula in very diverse and distinct ways—only consider the huge difference between the discourses in practice and research of music and drama education. In England, music in the formal education sector occupies the high ground of scholarly and cultural respectability but is outstripped by Art and Drama in terms of levels of participation amongst young people beyond primary school. One wonders whether a collective failure on the part of music educators to reflect *critically* on what, why and how they teach may have been a contributing factor. Recent developments in research and practice (discussed in the Upitis, Ledgard and Glover/Hoskyns chapters) have encouraged teachers and arts professionals to consider new ways of working in partnership which in some cases may undermine the role of school based teachers and challenge their pedagogical certainties. A good example of a project attempting not only to offer a radically different approach to teaching music but also to engage the profession in debate and critical thinking is Musical Futures (www.musicalfutures.org.uk). Teachers and community musicians are working in partnership to respond to and give structure to the musical interests and aspirations of 11-to-14 year old students in school music lessons. At the time of writing the two-year project is at the midway point. Through downloadable publications and their website forum, teachers and artists are invited to reflect on their own practices in the light of the project's emerging findings (Price, 2005). This is probably the first time since the consultations surrounding the writing and subsequent revisions of the national curriculum during the 1990s in England that a genuine attempt has been made to engage the professional community as a whole in reflecting on their pedagogical practice.

1. CONTEXTUAL INFLUENCES

What emerges from the content of this book is that despite the shared focus there are inevitably strong contextual influences on how reflective experiences and practices are framed and what they are used for. These contexts can be described in terms of their locality and scope: national, local, institutional; their domain: sociocultural, artistic or pedagogical; and their scale: time, range of activities and numbers of participants.

Different art forms have evolved their educational principles and practices in quite distinct and different ways. As a result of the particular pedagogical theories and discourses attached to each art form specialist teachers and artists embrace critical thinking rather differently. It is also an obvious point but one worth remembering, that the temporal and ephemeral nature of performing arts often makes for very different solutions to capturing and making sense of experience compared to the visual or digital arts. Where different artforms and practitioners are brought together much can be gained through the quality of collaborative thought and action which acknowledges such distinctions in practice and seeks to complement and find new ways of working. The articulation of this process contributes to new understanding. This is also true of the discourses between teachers and artists who may share artistic knowledge and understanding but express and apply it in very different settings and which might lead to *mis*understandings and difficulties in working in partnership (see the Glover/ Hoskyns' chapter). There is perhaps, also, an interesting dichotomy between the teachers' tendency to want to find the 'middle way', tidy solutions and to avoid confrontations—and the artists' need to embrace messiness, uncertainty, and risk. As suggested earlier these tensions and possible paradoxes are not necessarily obstacles but may well lead to fresh discoveries.

2. PURPOSES OF REFLECTION

From the case studies and tools explored emerge three main purposes for reflection:

1. To develop, transform and improve one's own teaching whether as beginning teacher, as experienced practitioner in the formal sectors of schools or higher education, or as artist educator.

In this category it is usual to find that the protagonist has identified a problem in their practice either through something going wrong or a realisation that in order to move into new territory a heightened level of self awareness and critical evaluation is needed. Dawn Joseph chooses to introduce a music unfamiliar to her students and, as an innovation (within the teaching programme) needs to monitor and analyse its effectiveness. At the same time she is aware that this unfamiliarity will cause her students to be challenged to engage with the newness (otherness) of the music making, jolting them out of their long held perceptions of themselves as musical (or not). The opportunity for students to reflect on their own attitudes and where these have come from—to be challenged to reflect with their peers in a safe and supportive environment may lead to new understanding and new confidence in themselves as music makers. Jody Kerchner and Linda Rolfe describe and discuss reflective exercises which support learner teachers in their developing practice and professional identity. It should be noted that the pace and intensity of the training programme in England puts a severe strain on the concept of 'breathing space' or a 'still point' considered necessary for reflection to take place (Hunt, 2001). In contrast Kerchner's students, in a less pressurised environment, are able to engage with a variety of modes of reflective experience. Visual mapping, sculpting in clay, alongside journals and semi structured conversations may enable individual students to find their favoured approach to expressing, interpreting and communicating their experience in order to learn from it. It may also be the case that there is a double disadvantage in the UK example for performing arts teachers where, not only is the course as a whole very short, but the nature of teaching dance (or music or drama) makes the ability to reflect in action on their teaching, during practical lessons, problematic. Betty Ann Younker records the reflective conversations and exchanges between a teacher, her pupils and a visiting composer. Her role as participant observer enables her to gain access to the teacher's and children's thinking over a significant period of time (months rather than hours), and enables her to engage in sustained reflection as researcher.

2. *To evaluate practitioners' work and specific programmes or projects encompassing the informal or non-formal arts education sectors.*

Evaluation is the most formal, public and structured purpose for reflection in educative contexts. For the purposes of accountability, 'standards' and various degrees of control (some benign others less so), teachers, are expected to evaluate their teaching in ways that can be scrutinised by managers and inspectors. Arts projects funded through private or charitable sponsorship, or public funds, are also required to be monitored and evaluated. Jo Glover and Janet Hoskyns' analysis and discussion of evaluating arts projects with young people out of school and Anna Ledgard's chapter on the work of LIFT both point to the multifaceted, cross-cultural nature of such work. Where teachers, artists, youth workers and young people (often, in such projects, disenfranchised in some way) negotiate shared values and meanings for the work, and make judgements about its effectiveness, they make highly visible the skills which often become submerged and blurred in the more controlled or predictable (and perhaps mundane) conditions of the classroom. Although partnership projects are increasingly common in arts education there is always a sense that each new project must be a new creation—that knowledge of what works is buried in the minds and bodies of charismatic practitioners; that to discuss what works and why will kill the quality and 'magic' stone dead. Unfortunately in much of the practice I have observed this inability to learn from previous work through sharing of failures as well as attempting to identify the factors which contribute to success, results in much frustration and one fears much mediocre activity. Time spent in purposeful reflection during and post project is not a luxury but, as both these chapters testify, a powerful contributor to success. As Glover and Hoskyns point out, the nature of the funding culture often mitigates against planning time for this kind of activity; but where it does happen the quality of the experiences and outcomes (for everybody) are invariably better (Hennessy et al., 2003; Ofsted, 2004; Harland et al., 2005).

Another outstanding value of collaborative activity is that through the necessary dialogic relationships which develop, teachers and artists can gain valuable professional development. The report on a two-year arts intervention programme for schools carried out in England, identified enhancement to teachers' artistic knowledge and skills, their classroom practice and school wide effects. Two of the three factors cited as giving rise to these effects were 'the nature and extent of planning' and 'the artist-teacher relationship' (Harland et al., 2005), both imply reflective interactions, and it is unlikely that either were achieved through unfunded time.

3. To nurture in oneself or others the ability to make sense of learning in and through the arts.

Research and, in particular, action research, is a systematic form of reflective activity. Charlotte Peel describes her approach to making sense of her own and then children's art making through inventing a variety of recording tools which in themselves become kinds of art work. At the same time these tools reveal new understandings about the experiences recorded and nurture in others the ability to reflect, whether they be children, teachers in training or one's peers.

Lave and Wenger (1991) characterise learning as a socially situated phenomenon which takes place in 'communities of practice'. Within such communities experienced practitioners act as mentors to the novices who gradually become immersed in the knowledge and practices of that community. The role of mentor is formally promoted in teacher education but is not usually the term used to describe the relationship of educator to pupil in the formal school setting. The projects described in Morrison, Burton, and O'Toole's chapter offer convincing evidence of the power of peer teaching to transform individual learners' sense of self, confidence and attitudes to school and learning. Within a framework of mentored action and reflection, pupils who were considered disaffected and disruptive (see Kushner's remarks on this) were able to be successful in teaching drama and participating constructively in drama making. There were high levels of personal and professional risk involved (the girls in both projects risked failure and loss of status—and perhaps also the researchers and teachers were pushing the boundaries of safety and trust). Certainly in the UK project the relationship between pupils and researcher enabled and supported a safe environment in which to take reflect.

The children in Charlotte Peel's project and the participants in the Hoskyns/Glover projects are given the means and the space to contribute ideas, influence and negotiate the shape of the activities and share in a democratic community of practitioners. The invitation to (and the expectation that they are able to) reflect on their experience is in itself educative: creating a virtuous circle (perhaps spiral) of inclusion, respect, self esteem, self knowledge, confidence, competence, and increased independence.

3. CATALYSTS OF REFLECTION

'Reflection is both catalyst and response to learning' (Ghaye, 2005).

1. Critical events and disruptions

Several of the chapters make reference to and discuss the idea of 'critical events' or crises which can stimulate action, a change of direction, identification of a problem, a solution, or a revelation. Such moments or events have been identified in the context of attempts to understand creative teaching (Woods, 1995); and the creative process (Burnard), as well as a means of generating professional reflection within groups or for individuals. In contrast, one might characterise the trigger or motive not so much as an event but more as an essential ingredient in the framing or condition of a learning experience which causes a disruption or dissonance in expectations. Dawn Joseph refers to the 'otherness' of African music for her students; Morrison et al. invite students to become teachers; partnership projects place participants in unfamiliar settings and engage them in unfamiliar modes of working; student teachers apply their training and knowledge in the classroom for the first time. It is in such circumstances that we can become most aware of the water we are swimming in (Kenny, 1984) and thus are more able to express and articulate our responses; and engage in thoughtful conversations with peers and knowledgeable others about what we understand and what we may now need to do next.

2. Reflective task design

The 'tools' for reflection discussed in Section 2, in themselves, generate and shape the nature and quality of the thinking they are designed to support. It is perhaps self evident that engaging in thinking and being asked to communicate that thinking is most likely to be a linguistic exercise (this is certainly true of schooling and formal assessments). This may in itself present a problem if participants lack confidence in speaking or writing—or have, for whatever reason, limited vocabulary. The strength (and beauty) of the arts is that they communicate through media other than verbal language: we can gain access to the artist's thinking through their work—we don't usually have to interrogate the artist about what their work means (and when we do we discover that not all artists are particularly articulate!). The dilemma in arts education is that in some circumstances learners (especially perhaps with young learners or novices) may not only be limited in their ability to express themselves artistically but also in their ability to talk about their learning. Finding imaginative, sociable, non-threatening and alternative modes for the latter can help.

3. Playfulness and enjoyment

Making the process engaging and enjoyable will also stimulate thinking, as in Charlotte Peel's 'memory table', for instance, and Jody Kerchner's use of metaphor sculptures (see also Dolloff's use of drawings in work on teacher identity, 1999). Drama techniques such as in role work, hot seating, and freeze frame (Neelands, 1990) offer a means of 'distancing' which facilitates the sharing of personal experience and ideas which might otherwise lie buried. The social interactions and imaginative 'as if' world of drama in education (as described by Morrison et al.) generate and nurture just the kinds of reflective behaviours that we may seek.

This social dimension is present also in the more apparently individual modes of reflection promoted by the use of diaries and learning journals (Kerchner and Rolfe). Here, although the writing process is a solo act, the journal becomes the basis of conversations with peers, tutors or mentors which can help to tease out and structure meanings and understandings from the writing. Discovering that others have experienced similar or indeed quite different responses to the same activity or context can help to make sense of and legitimate one's own responses.

The use of elearning forums, described in Jane Cheung and Eton Kung's chapter, also enables the individual response to be 'published' in a fairly informal but structured and accountable way.

4. CONSEQUENCES OF REFLECTION

1. Recognising meaningful learning

To access and appraise the value of an arts experience there is no doubt that engaging in reflective conversations and other carefully designed activities with the participants, will yield relevant evidence. The multiple perspectives and responses which inevitably emerge reflect the messiness of the realities of learning in and through the arts.

The evaluator, however formally this role is inhabited, needs then to reflect on these differences and attempt to explain and interpret their significance—how they reflect the aims of the project or course of study; what is the 'value' for the participants (and perhaps the community they are part of); and what have been the features and qualities of the whole endeavour which can inform future work.

One of the difficulties for evaluators is how to gain evidence which shows measurable value—something dear to the hearts of sponsors, managers and politicians who want proof that money is well spent, serves their agenda, and can provide the justification for asking for more. Impact measures are at best very limited and at worst elusive and contestable. If the only hard data emerging from a project is that school attendance improved slightly for participants, does this weaken or strengthen our case? Interestingly, in a drumming project I evaluated (Hennessy, 2003), one of the 'at risk' boy's school attendance rate dropped during the project- this turned out to be because he would miss registration so that he could help unload the drums for sessions! His own view, in reflecting on the whole 6 month project, was that apart from wholeheartedly enjoying the project, he had become calmer, and generally more focused in school. The musician who led the project considered that the boy had also learned to play taiko with some competence, confidence and style; and at the same time become more cooperative and socialised within the group. As the project could not be funded to continue there was no real possibility of the boy continuing to play taiko; and without following up 6 months or a year later it would be difficult to gauge how lasting the behavioural changes were—and in fact how much was directly attributable to project. Qualitative approaches are entirely appropriate for the evaluation of arts education activity but still cause problems for our 'masters'.

Through arts experiences mediated by teachers, artists and their peers, in the settings reported on here, young people learn about themselves in relation to others.

If this learning is real and lasting it must, perforce, have engendered changes in perceptions, attitudes and beliefs. We hope they also gain artistic knowledge and skills which might contribute to their confidence and fluency of expression within and perhaps beyond the particular media involved. We hope that they will learn to be intellectually and emotionally flexible and robust. Evidence of this is wrapped up and sometimes obscured in layers of cultural values, attitudes and imperatives. The cases described in this book suggest that in order for arts education to have such meaningful and lasting effects those who are responsible for framing and guiding it need to develop in themselves the skills and attributes of critical reflective practice in order to foster them in learners. They need to operate in a spirit of openness, respect and mutuality.

2. *Professional confidence*

The preparation of new recruits to the teaching profession and support for their ongoing development should and can include serious attention to their ability to think and act flexibly, with empathy and openness towards their students and other professionals. A confident and critical teacher should be more able to resist and challenge policies and practices which undermine, as well as advocate and, if necessary, defend what they value. Artists who work in the formal and/or informal education sectors also need the opportunities to acquire the habits of reflecting not only, as they are bound to do, on their own art making, but also on their role as co-workers, mentors, teachers and facilitators.

3. *Towards autonomy*

Learning in the arts must be seen as meaningful, authentic and worthwhile in order to engender emotional engagement, commitment and mutual trust. Participants need to feel that they are in a reciprocal relationship with those who manage and support the activity—and never more so than when it is aimed at vulnerable, unconfident young people or novice professionals. There are many references in chapters in this book to the democratising role of reflective experience towards greater self-awareness, self—worth and confidence, autonomy and responsibility.

If this is to be realised, not only for young people but also for teachers and other professionals then, as I and others have alluded to, there are bound to be some problems ahead when centralised control of education becomes an unbearable strait jacket. We have a great responsibility to not shy away from such problems and to work energetically to resolve them. The theoretical perspectives presented and the practices described, analysed and celebrated in this book offer valuable support for this endeavour.

REFERENCES

Bowman, W. (2005). More enquiring minds, more cogent questions, more provisional answers: the need to theorize music education, and its research. *Music Education Research*, 7(2), 153–168.

Dewey, J. (1932). Ethics. In J.A. Boydson (Ed.), *The Later Works of John Dewey* (Vol 7, 1925–1853). Carbondale and Edwardsville: South Illinois University Press.

Dolloff, L.A. (1999). Imagining ourselves as teachers: the development of teacher identity in music teacher education. *Music Education Research*, 1(2), 191–207.

Ghaye, T. (2005). Reflection as a catalyst for change. *Reflective Practice*, 6(2), 177–188.

Grushka, K. (2005). Artists as reflective self-learners and cultural communicators: and exploration of the qualitative aesthetic dimension of knowing self through refelective practice in art-making. *Reflective Practice*, 6(3), 353–366.

Harland, J., Lord, P., Stott, A., Kinder, K., Lamont, E., and Ashworth, K. (2005). *The Arts-Education Interface: A Mutual Learning Triangle?* Slough: National Foundation for Educational Research (NFER).

Hennessy, S. (2003) Different drummers—learning taiko against the odds, *National Association of Music Educators Journal*, 11, 40–46.

Hennessy, S., Haynes, G., and Wragg, C. (2003). *Singing Challenge 3 Evaluation Report*. London: Youth Music.

Hunt, C. (2001). Shifting shadows: metaphors and maps for facilitating reflective practice. *Reflective Practice*, 2(3), 275–285.

Kenny, M. (1984). Seeing the water. *2D Journal for Drama/Dance Education*, 4(1), 14–24.

Lave, J. and Wenger, E. (1991). *Situated Learning: Legitimate Peripheral Participation*. Cambridge: Cambridge University Press.

Neelands, J. (1990). *Structuring Drama: A Handbook of Available Forms in Theatre and Drama*. Cambridge: Cambridge University Press.

Ofsted (2004). *Tuning In: Wider Opportunities in Specialist Instrumental Tuition for Pupils in Key Stage 2*. London: Office for Standards in Education.

Price, D. (2005). *Transforming Musical Leadership: Shaping Music Education—An Emerging Vision*. London: Musical Futures/Paul Hamlyn Foundation.

Swanwick, K. (2000). *Teaching Music Musically*. London: Routledge.

Woods, P. (1995). *Creative Teachers in Primary Schools*. Milton Keynes: Open University Press.

NAME INDEX

SUBJECT INDEX

CPSIA information can be obtained at www.ICGtesting.com
Printed in the USA
LVOW070442130312

272805LV00002B/75/P

9 781402 095658